Citizen now

MANCHESTER
1824

Manchester University Press

Citizen now

Engaging in politics and democracy

Elizabeth C. Matto

Sean,

Thank you so
much for the
Support!

Best wishes,

[signature]

Manchester University Press

Copyright © Elizabeth C. Matto 2017

The right of Elizabeth C. Matto to be identified as the author of this work has been
asserted by her in accordance with the Copyright, Designs and Patents Act 1988.

Published by Manchester University Press
Altrincham Street, Manchester M1 7JA
www.manchesteruniversitypress.co.uk

British Library Cataloguing-in-Publication Data
A catalogue record for this book is available from the British Library

ISBN   978 1 5261 0567 7 hardback
ISBN   978 1 5261 0568 4 paperback

First published 2017

The publisher has no responsibility for the persistence or accuracy
of URLs for any external or third-party internet websites referred to in this book,
and does not guarantee that any content on such websites is, or will remain,
accurate or appropriate.

Typeset by Out of House Publishing
Printed in Great Britain
by CPI Group (UK) Ltd, Croydon, CR0 4YY

For Jane and Eddie,
with love and great admiration

Contents

Figures

Tables

Acknowledgments

It seems only fitting that I begin my acknowledgments by thanking some young adults. I first want to acknowledge and express my gratitude to the three groups that agreed to serve as case studies for this text and the people who bring these groups to life. Thank you to Ryan Schoenike of The Can Kicks Back; Jorge Heredia, David Ngo, Miriam Nieto, Marven Norman, Michael Segura, Richard Tejada, and Fabian Torres of San Bernardino Generation Now; and Jen Mishory and Rory O'Sullivan and the rest of the team at Young Invincibles. Your participation in this research not only enhances our understanding of youth political participation but also offers a meaningful model for young adults who are finding their way into the political process. Your willingness to participate in this project says a great deal about your dedication to advancing the interests and well-being of your generation.

Next, I want to offer my thanks to my students – those who worked closely with me on this text and the many who offered inspiration over the years. In the early stages of this process, I was fortunate to have the assistance of Steven Mercadante, Kunal Papaiya, and Yagmur Soybakisli as a database of newspaper articles was being built and content was beginning to be analyzed. I also want to acknowledge Zachary Eisenberg and Amanda Hannah for creating a few of the prototypes of the tables and graphs that ultimately were designed. Thank you to Hillary Cohen, who spent some of her summer break from the University of California, Berkeley proofreading this manuscript and offering valuable suggestions. A special acknowledgment to Analee Patwell for her time working on another project I administer entitled RU Ready, for which she created a number of engaging and educational political learning activities including the social media activity featured at the end of the second chapter.

Two students in particular deserve specific recognition and have earned my utmost gratitude. Aaron Jaslove began working with me as a Research Assistant from Rutgers University's Aresty Research Center and then stuck with the project for a few more months. In addition to offering a "Millennial" take on the research questions and text, Aaron dedicated much time to compiling and presenting the data offered in the second chapter. He also offered valuable support in the content analysis of the case studies' web and social media content. Aaron, your intelligence is matched by your dedication and passion for making a difference. Thank you for your work on this project – I look forward to following your success.

Like Aaron, Ashley Choy began her work with me as an intern but remained with the project until its completion. A graphic design student from Rutgers University's Mason Gross School of the Arts, Ashley has worked on a number of projects for the program I direct and is responsible for the design of this text's tables, graphs, and figures. Ashley, you showed great commitment, creativity, and patience as this project moved forward. You're a talented young woman and are destined for great things.

In no small way, this text was inspired by my work with students – both inside and outside the classroom. It was our discussions, voter registration drives, debate watches, conferences, and civic engagement workshops that underscored the need for such a text but also formed its contours. Thank you for your insights, hard work, and probing questions (both those I could answer and those I couldn't). Like much of the work I do, this text is fueled by young adults as they begin to engage the political process. I am grateful for their work on *Citizen now* and value their participation. Although I can't take credit for all of it, I do take complete and total responsibility for the text and data presented in this book.

I want to offer my heartfelt thanks to my colleagues at the Eagleton Institute of Politics at Rutgers University – my professional home for over ten years. Thank you to Eagleton's Director Ruth B. Mandel who planted the seed for writing this text and has offered boundless support throughout this effort and throughout my time at Eagleton. I also thank Eagleton's Associate Director John Weingart, who shows, in word and deed, that politics is all about relationships, mutual interest, and respect. Together, Ruth and John have established a professional culture that is supportive and collegial but that sets a high standard for excellence and brings the Institute's mission to life – to link the theory of politics with its practice. I also thank my colleagues at Eagleton. I'm frequently reminded how lucky I am to genuinely like the people with whom I work. I offer my thanks and admiration.

This text began in Bloomsbury Academic. I want to thank Matthew Kopel for reaching out to me a few years ago about writing it, shepherding the proposal through the review process, and starting me off on the right foot. Thank you to his successor Ally Jane Grossan and also to Michelle Chen of Bloomsbury Academic for her assistance. I'm pleased to be working now with Manchester University Press – many thanks to Tony Mason and Rob Byron for their good-natured support and guidance.

Throughout the process of writing this book, and all the time that's preceded it, I've been grateful to my family for their unwavering support and enthusiasm. Thank you to the Matto and Gass families for their encouragement – an extra special thank you to my in-laws Mike and Rachel. I'm grateful to my father and stepmother Ann for their excitement about this and other recent adventures – a special thank you to Ann for her California hospitality. My grandmother Jeannie, my aunt Amy and my uncle Luke always have been my champions. Whether we're living in the same city or only connected virtually, your support has been constant and appreciated. Much love to the Thomas family and a special thank you to Frederic, Olivia, Rose, the dearly departed Sugar and Joy for our Spanish study breaks.

My sister Sarah has been my companion, sounding board, and inspiration. Throughout this process, her notes and talismans of encouragement have come just at the right time and have been displayed around my computer to keep me on task. Many thanks and much love to you. My mother has served as a model of dedication, intellect, and hard work – it's no wonder that both of her children have made careers centered on education and service. Thank you for the life's worth of love you've provided and the constant support you offer.

Finally, I want to thank the four mammals closest to me who keep me going and without whom life wouldn't be the same. A special thank you to my darling Brandy – our daily walks pried me away from my computer and allowed me to clear my mind and return to work rejuvenated and refreshed. My husband Rich has been my steadfast companion and unwavering supporter from graduate school to today. I'm immensely fortunate and terribly grateful for all that you do for me and our family. Finally, I want to acknowledge Jane and Eddie. As I've told you before, you're the best people I know – interesting, thoughtful, and destined for greatness in unique and meaningful ways. From Jane's boundless enthusiasm to Eddie's well-timed "how's your book going Mom?," your support has meant the world to me. I hope, by completing this book, you'll see what people can accomplish with enough passion, determination, and love from the people closest to them. This book is for you and thanks to you.

Introduction

"Will they turn out to vote this year?" With every election, it seems that this is the question most commonly asked about young adults. Unfortunately, the answer isn't always clear. After years of steady decline, the 2008 election marked an uptick in youth voter turnout rates and, seemingly, in political interest and enthusiasm as well. Then came a 6 percent decline in rates in 2012, followed by record low rates of registration and turnout in 2014. As the 2016 election loomed on the horizon, yet again, there were signs of hope. Youth voter turnout rates throughout the primaries and caucuses broke records.[1] In classrooms and around campus, students were talking about the election, turning out in record numbers to debate watches, and rushing to register to vote. Still, we found ourselves wondering, "will this enthusiasm last?"

The Millennial Generation, those born between about 1980 and 2000, is an age cohort that is demographically unique and brimming with democratic promise, and yet it's a body filled with contrasts and contradictions that challenge our understanding of them as citizens. These dichotomies permeate not only their voting behavior but also media coverage of Millennials, scholarship on youth engagement, and even the attitudes of young adults themselves. As the oldest members of the Millennial Generation approach 40 years of age, the time is right to take stock of what we know about this body of citizens; to address these contrasts and contradictions and, hopefully, make some sense of them; and to chart a course for future study and better understanding of this sizable portion of the citizenry.

To be sure, fluctuations in turnout rates make it difficult to get a handle on young adults as voters. The media frame through which the Millennial Generation is covered also offers a muddled picture – one that emphasizes the impact of the generation on the workplace, the economy, and culture and yet depicts Millennials as having a negligible effect on politics. Contrasting academic conclusions about the democratic health of young adults confuse the matter even more. At one end of the spectrum, low turnout rates among young adults spark alarm, even prompting one scholar to wonder if they'd been "exposed to some anti-civic X-ray that permanently and increasingly rendered them less likely to connect with the community" (Putnam 2000, 255). Others, who are less alarmed about rates of turnout, are heartened by young adults' sense of citizenship – characterizing it as one that "includes an ethical and moral responsibility to others in the polity, and beyond" (Dalton 2009, 23) and manifests itself in "non-electoral activities such as buying products for political reasons and being active in civil society groups" (Dalton 2009, 29).

These contrasts are seen in the attitudes of young adults themselves. Survey research suggests that Millennials possess healthy levels of political confidence and believe their vote can make a difference, and yet indicate little willingness to make use of the political process to solve public problems. Educators even see these dichotomies in the classroom – some students are critical of their generation and its sense of citizenship and others laud its promise.

For the past 20 or so years, Millennials have been a generation in progress and that's made it difficult to make definitive pronouncements about the quality of its citizenship. Instead, much of our effort has been directed towards comparing Millennials to generations of the past and declaring them either "engaged," "disengaged," or somewhere in between. Moreover, scholars have broached the topic of youth engagement from a fairly common approach and using a fairly common methodology. This text offers a contrast – an examination of how "citizen now" is engaging in the political process and connecting with democracy, the issues prompting their actions, and what they hope to accomplish with their activities. The qualitative methodology employed, case studies of three youth-led organizations, offers a fresh take on the subject of youth political participation that promises to inform future study.

The text's overarching argument is that the Millennial Generation is a generation worth understanding, given the impact it stands to have on democracy's future. Our somewhat myopic approach to studying youth engagement has limited our understanding, though. Conceptually, debates have centered on the appropriate rendering of engagement – one focused on traditional definitions of political participation versus a more enlarged sense of engagement. This conceptual debate has filtered into the theoretical frameworks used to study youth engagement and, thereby, have informed scholars' varying pronouncements about the health (or lack thereof) of youth participation. Throughout, scholars have focused nearly exclusively on the actions of young adults in the aggregate (often as they compare to other generations) rather than other meaningful facets of participation.

By looking at youth engagement from another angle, the viewpoint of youth-led groups formed around an issue important to young adults, there's much to be learned about the nature of engagement among "citizen now." Most importantly, this approach suggests that youth-led organizations offer a promising route (albeit with some limitations) for reaching and representing young adults and even teaching the skills of citizenship. Moreover, such efforts manifest a mixture of youth sensibility and savvy with quite traditional elements of politics – elements that often are discounted by those motivated by a traditional understanding of engagement and overlooked by those who view engagement broadly.

The book's origins and purpose

Citizen now was conceived where many books are conceived – in the classroom. A political scientist by training, I find myself in a growing field of teacher-scholars within the discipline dedicated not only to educating my students about the science of politics but preparing them to be informed and engaged citizens. In my teaching and work with students, then, my purpose is twofold – to lay a theoretical framework of young people's engagement in the civic and political community and to compare and contrast it to the realities of youth engagement. Often this is done in conjunction with political learning opportunities such as conducting voter registration drives around campus or administering workshops in local high school classrooms.

In preparing to teach the topic of the Millennial Generation and its role in the political process, it became clear that, although the volume of both the academic and popular discussion was quite high, the voices were far from in unison when it came to the political engagement of young people. The texts available offered starkly different conclusions. More meaningful perhaps, and another source of motivation for writing this text, was the approach and tone of these works – either terribly dismal and critical of young adults for not matching the behavior of previous generations or utterly hopeful, offering boundless enthusiasm for the engagement of the generation but providing little evidence of its effects. As students are being introduced to the fundamentals of American political thought, elections, and research methods, there also seems to be a need to consider these topics from their perspective – through the viewpoint of young adults.

Citizen now is meant to be a resource to which students of politics, as well as educators and practitioners, can turn for both theoretical understanding and practical advice regarding the Millennial Generation. In short, it offers a synthesis and critique of both popular and academic consideration of the political engagement of young people that highlights how we have studied youth political participation, what we've learned, and where we've fallen short. This effort is then complemented with an example of how we might look at the subject matter differently and what we can learn from this new approach. The text's central assertion is that our understanding of the political engagement of the Millennial Generation, an age cohort that stands to significantly impact democracy's future, is confused and limited due not only to contradictions within the generation but also to our scholarly approach. By changing our perspective, we stand to deepen our understanding.

To underscore the importance of better understanding the causes and consequences of the civic engagement of this sizable portion of the citizenry, the text begins with a detailed description of the demographics of the generation and their political participation. Utilizing publicly available secondary data, including data from the US Census Bureau and the American National Election Studies, a detailed description of the demographics of the nation's youngest cohort is offered as well as the historical context in which this generation was raised. In addition, the nature and intensity of political participation among young adults is described. Over the years, widely disseminated survey research, working papers, and special reports regarding youth engagement by such institutions as the Center for Information and Research on Civic Learning and Engagement (CIRCLE), Harvard University's Institute of Politics, and the Pew Research Center have provided timely and useful data, but of a localized and time-bound nature. *Citizen now* pulls together this piecemeal information and offers readers a fully sketched portrait of the generation and their involvement in the political process.

Nearly as important as the demographics and activities of Millennials is how they are perceived. This book explores the media frame through which this generation has been viewed by systematically examining news coverage of Millennials that has appeared in leading national newspapers as this age cohort has matured. We know that the media play a critical function through "gatekeeping" and that the manner in which the press presents or "frames" the news affects the public's perception of politics. Through content analysis of this collection of news articles, conclusions are drawn about how this generation has been perceived over time and why these perceptions matter as we consider their lives as citizens.

The heart of the text is a critical review of the scholarly literature that addresses the state of youth political engagement. The conceptual frameworks utilized to understand the phenomena of engagement have evolved throughout the history of the discipline of political science. Earlier conceptions, those of Milbrath (1965) and Verba and Nie (1972), conceived of "engagement" as political in the strict sense of the word – activities designed to influence the make-up and action of government, with a heavy emphasis on voting. Over the years, this conceptualization has broadened considerably and engagement has come to be understood as multi-faceted in nature, including such activities as contributing to a political blog, "buycotting" or consumer activism, and even verbally challenging someone who states something offensive (Levine 2007; Macedo 2005).

Much of the scholarly literature regarding the Millennial Generation extends this trend – broadly envisioning the notion of engagement (Dalton 2009; Rimmerman 2005). Early on, Verba and Nie pronounced that one's evaluation of a group's democratic health tends to be a function of how democratic participation is defined (1972, 29). The notion certainly rings true when we explore the body of literature addressing youth participation. For those who maintain a fairly traditional definition (Putnam 2000; Wattenberg 2012), the state of youth engagement (characterized by low voter turnout) is considered to be quite poor. For those with a broader definition, the quality of youth engagement today, with less emphasis on traditional engagement but notable rates of activism (especially via social media), signifies a new and possibly even more robust iteration of democracy.

This text argues that this exercise has given us an incomplete understanding of youth political participation. What gets lost in debates regarding the definition of engagement and the health of youth political participation is a clear and complete appreciation of *how* youth are engaging in the world of politics, *why* they are taking the actions they're taking, and *what* they're accomplishing. This is due mainly to our tendency as political scientists to study youth engagement in a limited manner – nearly exclusively utilizing the "political actions" approach. As Brady (1999, 742–744) lays out in his assessment of the discipline's study of political participation, there are three approaches to studying political behavior. The "political actions" approach, heavily reliant on survey research, focuses on describing the political acts an individual or group of individuals pursues. The "institutions" approach focuses attention on the context in which political activities can occur – institutions such as organizations, workplaces, churches, and families. The "problems" approach aims to identify the issues or problems that might prompt actions and then examine the activities the problem prompts.

For the most part, we've looked at the subject of youth political participation in one way and our arguments have swirled around the same subjects. For various reasons, restricting ourselves not only to one approach but nearly exclusively to one methodology (survey research) has drawbacks. Given stark inter-generational differences, there are limits to looking at youth engagement through a generational lens or ascribing the quality and intensity of youth political participation to features unique to their generation and the times in which they've come of age. Moreover, although highly valuable, the use of survey research (especially longitudinal) is far from ideal in the study of Millennials' political participation – the utility of common measurements of participations between generations is debatable, as is the representativeness of samples of youth populations.

Analysis both of the demographics of the Millennial Generation and the manner in which we've studied their political behavior suggests that there is value in approaching the subject matter not only from a different starting point but with a different methodology. A culminating argument advanced in this text is that the discipline would benefit by considering youth engagement from the perspective of the problems or issues prompting behavior as well as the groups concerned with these problems. Moreover, utilizing a qualitative methodology would allow researchers to view political participation from the vantage point of the objects of study – young people themselves.

In an effort then to chart a different course of study, case studies of youth organizations that have engaged the political process are offered. In addition to a fresh approach, these case studies suggest possible themes or categories that might inform future theoretical frameworks and research designs. Specifically, the three groups that are highlighted organized in response to the top issue overshadowing the Millennial Generation – their economic health. Although their missions and structures differ, San Bernardino Generation Now, The Can Kicks Back, and Young Invincibles provide a glimpse into the motivations, strategies, and end goals of young adults engaging the political process in an effort to advance the interests of other young adults. These case studies add to our understanding of how young adults today go about such work and suggest a path as we further develop our theoretical understanding of youth political participation and the methods for studying it. Specifically, the activities of these youth-led groups, although multi-faceted and supported by contemporary tools, are consistent with traditional conceptions of political action – conceptions that aren't always given full consideration in our current research on Millennials as political actors.

The potential benefits of these case studies extend beyond research and theory, though, and into practical politics and democracy. Although the Millennial Generation is large in size and scope, its connection to the political process, voting in particular, is tenuous. By highlighting and examining prominent youth-led efforts to address a problem confounding young adults, this effort also offers a model to students of ways in which their peers are engaging in politics and democracy.

Plan of the book

Over the next six chapters, *Citizen now* will offer a comprehensive depiction of Millennials' demographics and behavior, a synthesis and critique of our study of youth political participation, and case studies of three youth-led and youth-focused groups that allow us to rethink how we study young adults as citizens. Given that this text was in many ways inspired by and written for students, each chapter offers exercises to deepen understanding of the subject matter. "Think It Out" offers prompts either for written reflection or class discussion and "Act It Out" includes hands-on political learning opportunities that, hopefully, link our thinking about politics with the doing of it.

Chapter 1 provides the context necessary for our consideration of the political engagement of young adults. In this chapter, the Millennial Generation is situated in the succession of generations preceding it and the milestones of the time period in which this group has matured are highlighted. Using multiple sources of secondary data, the key demographic features of the Millennial Generation are outlined, including current and projected size, ethnic diversity, educational attainment, and social media habits. Finally, through content analysis of a database of over 300 news articles, conclusions are drawn about perceptions of the generation – including our perceptions of them as political animals.

With the demographics of the generation firmly established, Chapter 2 provides a picture of the political participation of young adults, including the current voting behavior of young adults, longitudinal data on Millennial voting, and inter- and intra-generational comparisons in voting rates. Extra-electoral activities also are considered, including participating in campaigns, following the news, and the use of social media or "hashtag activism." This portrait is juxtaposed with the history of the passage of the 26th Amendment lowering the voting age and the expectations surrounding this milestone.

The critical synthesis of the study of the political participation of young adults can be found in Chapters 3 and 4. Chapter 3 charts how the concept of engagement has evolved from a "bullseye" approach focused on direct forms of political action, to one that differentiates these modes into quadrants or a "box-like" approach, to a broader "umbrella-like" depiction in which a number of activities, both political and non-political, fall under the category of engagement. This background leads to a discussion of the study of youth political participation and conclusions that have been drawn about its quality, which are then plotted along a continuum ranging from "disengaged," to "engaged differently," to "better engaged."

Chapter 4 outlines the theoretical frameworks that scholars have used when seeking to explain, predict, and understand youth political participation as well as the methodologies commonly utilized. The most common theoretical approach in studying youth engagement has been generational with a reliance on survey research nearly always focused upon the political actions of individuals rather than issues prompting action or the institutional context in which actions take place. The review of the literature highlights key aspects of participation that aren't being considered, as well as the benefits of broadening our approach and changing our perspective.

The case studies of efforts led by and for the benefit of young adults can be found in Chapters 5 and 6. Chapter 5 reviews the survey research indicating that the economy has been an issue of top concern not only for the public at large but also for young adults. Also offered is a description of the origins, missions, and structures of three groups focused upon the effects of the economy on young adults that emerged in analysis of news coverage of Millennials: Young Invincibles, The Can Kicks Back, San Bernardino Generation Now.

Chapter 6 addresses the research questions explored via the case studies – the activities of these groups, the targets of their actions, the context out of which these actions arise, and the effects of these efforts. This research suggests that the groups engage in a variety of actions meant to raise awareness, serve the public, and influence the political process. Although they make use of the technological tools of their generation, their actions are in line with traditional conceptions of political action with attention to their outcomes and impact.

The final chapter weaves these threads together by identifying what these case studies suggest not only about youth-oriented groups but also young adults in general. Consideration also is given to the normative implications of current and potential research addressing youth political participation, focusing upon the extent to which our current conceptualizations match the ideals of American democracy. Lastly, practical suggestions are offered, rooted in research, of actions parents, educators, policymakers, and even young adults themselves can take in order to encourage and equip them to be active citizens. Ultimately, it's not enough to compare today's youth to previous generations, throw up our hands, and declare them "disengaged." At the same time, it's not enough to idealize today's young adults and offer them as the democratic wave of the future or "better engaged" without demonstrating that their efforts serve the interests of their generation or instructing them how to make use of this enlarged version of democracy. At the very least, we can take the steps we know will work to ensure that today's young adult – citizen now – is a full participant in the political process.

Note

1 "Youth Voting in the 2016 Primaries," Center for Information and Research on Civic Learning and Engagement (CIRCLE): http://civicyouth.org/youth-voting-in-the-2016-primaries/?cat_id=6.

## 1

America's emerging citizens: realities and perceptions

Depending upon where you draw the generational line of demarcation, the oldest members of the nation's youngest generation have surpassed the age of 30 and are nearing their forties. As researchers, the media, and the public at large have taken notice of this age group over the years, a good deal of data have been gathered, analyses conducted, and opinions drawn about their character and the impact they're exerting and will continue to exert on the nation. This chapter begins to take stock of this body of information and the generation that has come to be known as the "Millennial Generation."

A central premise of this text is that, given the significant impact this age group stands to have on American democracy, it's critical that we approach our study of young adults in a way that will produce a full understanding of them as citizens. An important first step is appreciating the generation's composition and outlook. This effort allows us to more easily appreciate not only the nature of youth engagement today but also our study of it. For example, the growing numbers of non–college-bound youth discussed in this chapter highlight the methodological problems associated with using survey data solely from college campuses. Additionally, the widespread use of new media tools across the generation links to scholarly conversations regarding broadening the conceptualization of engagement as well as the significance of online or "hashtag activism."

Children of the late 1970s and 1980s, Millennials' entry into adulthood has paralleled our collective entry into the twenty-first century and a new millennium. Like generations that preceded them, this age group shares a unique set of experiences that undoubtedly shape their outlook and behavior. This chapter synthesizes what we know about the demographics of the Millennial Generation, the context in which Millennials have been born and raised, and this age group's outlook on their lives and their future. What this exercise makes clear is that the political process impacts the Millennial Generation on numerous fronts – from immigration policy to student loan debt relief to online privacy. At the same time, this generation possesses the size and character to influence politics significantly and in ways that previous generations have not.

Additionally, this chapter considers the media frame through which this generation has been viewed through a systematic examination of news coverage of Millennials that has appeared in leading national newspapers as this group has matured. Content analysis of this collection of news articles suggests a media depiction of Millennials as elusive and even negligible politically – a depiction reflected in scholarly study of youth political participation that focuses on what Millennials are doing but pays little attention to the strategies influencing these actions or their effects.

The generational perspective

When it comes to studying and appreciating the engagement of young adults today, a good deal of scholars' time has been spent comparing them to the young adults of the past, from their turnout rates to their sense of civic duty. Much of the discussion of who Millennials are has tended to revolve around who Millennials aren't. Beginning with the publication of Robert Putnam's seminal *Bowling Alone* (2000) and culminating recently with Paul Taylor's *The Next America: Boomers, Millennials, and the Looming Generational Showdown* (2014), considerations since the turn of the century of the nation's youngest generation have consisted, to a large extent, of a comparison to those who have preceded it. More specifically, much of the recent attention paid to Millennials has come from a generational perspective. Understanding who the key players are in this generational discussion is an important starting point.

Utilizing a generational framework or, to use Taylor's term in *The Next America*, a "generational lens" to examine the causes and consequences of an age group's outlook and behavior assumes that a shared set of historical, cultural, and political milestones make a mark on those raised in the shadow of these milestones. A generational perspective also assumes that the mark made on that age group will persist – members of that group won't "grow out of it." As Jean Twenge writes, "The society that molds you when you are young stays with you the rest of your life" (2006, 2).

The effect of a historical time period on a group of people is distinguishable, then, from the effects of a person's stage in life. As Putnam summarizes, "Life cycle effects mean that individuals change, but society as a whole does not. Generational effects mean that society changes, even though individuals do not" (2000, 248). For example, speculations regarding young adults' current propensity to vote or to attend local meetings must take into account whether the nature and intensity of their activities are attributable to some unique generational qualities or merely to the fact that they are young, leading busy lives, preoccupied by building a career and personal relationships, etc. It may be that, once this group is more mature and settled, their voting and civic behavior will change. Determining whether a group's attitudes or activities are ingrained or are simply a function of their stage in life is, then, a critical (and not altogether easy) consideration when employing a generational perspective.[1]

Exploring a group of individuals' attitudes and behavior as a product of their generation poses challenges, as does drawing lines between age groups. As Zukin *et al*. point out, the process "is a risky activity, one informed as much by a general sense of how the social and political environment has differed across time as by empirical data about individual differences among age groups" (2006, 13–14). The names used to identify the dominant generations of the twentieth and twenty-first centuries have varied, as have the dates utilized to mark the inception of each age cohort. Figure 1.1 outlines the names and dates utilized by a selection of scholars, all of whom are considered in this text, to characterize the succession of generations that have led to today's youngest group of citizens. For the most part, these terms have become a part of the common parlance but often are used imprecisely. Again, generational scholars hold that the context in which these groups have lived has made an indelible mark on those raised during the period, and as a result, these generations possess a collection of qualities and traits. Although they may not be ingrained in each individual raised in that period, they tend to pervade the generation as a whole. Awareness of these traits not only allows us to track the progression of generations that have led us to Millennials, but, as content analysis of news coverage will show later in this chapter, awareness of contrasting generational traits also helps to explain current perceptions of today's youngest citizens.

Those born and raised in the shadow of the Great Depression and World War II have been referred to by such names as "the Greatest Generation," "Dutifuls," and even the "Silent Generation."[2] Given the gravity of the historical context, those born and raised during this time period often have been recognized for their sense of duty and sacrifice and their strong work ethic. As Zukin *et al*. write, they were a group "who paid their dues by working hard for a better life and upholding the responsibilities and privileges of citizenship" (2006, 14). Putnam referred to this age group as "exceptionally civic – voting more, joining more, reading more, trusting more, giving more" (2000, 254).

The so-called "Greatest Generation" produced the "Baby Boom" generation – a term, interestingly enough, that has been commonly utilized to characterize this age group. Thanks to the sheer size of the generation (76 million), Baby Boomers were an influential presence in the twentieth century. The group matured during a period of post-war prosperity and significant social and political change, including the civil rights movement, the women's movement, and the Vietnam War. According to Putnam, the combination of these forces led Boomers to be "distrusting of institutions, alienated from politics, and … distinctively less involved in civic life" (2000, 257).

Delineating the lines of post-Baby Boom generations and naming these age groups has been a messier business. "Generation X" has been used most frequently, but as Figure 1.1 indicates, Putnam utilizes the terms "Generation X" and "Millennial Generation" interchangeably while Twenge hung the rather potent label of "Generation Me" on those born and raised in the late 1960s and early 1970s. Getting a handle on the attributes of this age cohort has been less messy. For the most part, this age group has been commonly understood as self-absorbed and concerned about little

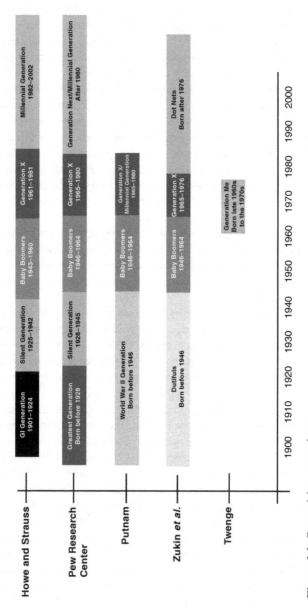

Figure 1.1 Categorizing generations

more than themselves. Dubbed the "poster child for poor citizen-ship" (Zukin *et al.* 2006, 15), Generation Xers came of age during a period of financial unease, social and cultural change due to such social phenomena as increased divorce rates and the spread of the HIV/AIDS virus, and foreign policy crises such as the Iran–Contra affair that alienated them from the political process.[3] According to Generation Xer Twenge, her generation wasn't so much "spoiled" but raised to believe in the importance of self-esteem: "We simply take it for granted that we should all feel good about ourselves, we are all special, and we all deserve to follow our dreams" (2006, 49).

Fast-forward to the present, and various monikers have been tossed around to characterize the youngest age cohort, from "Dot Nets" to "Generation Next" to "Generation Y." The name that seems to have stuck, though, is the "Millennial Generation." According to journalist Bruce Horovitz, the term "Generation Y" was created by *Advertising Age* in a 1993 editorial but later abandoned and replaced by "Millennial Generation" (*USA Today*, May 3, 2012). Howe and Strauss are generally credited for coining the term, and its grandeur reflects the authors' views about the promise of the generation itself: "the Millennial Generation will entirely recast the image of youth from downbeat and alienated to upbeat and engaged – with potentially seismic consequences for America" (2000, 4). Although the Millennial Generation is still a work in progress (further along for some than others), speculation has begun on how Millennials' successors, the newest youngest generation, will be termed. Names in the running include "Generation Z," the "Homeland Generation," and even "Generation Wii."[4]

It's also worth noting how broadly defined the Millennial Generation is compared to others – spanning nearly 40 years. This reality must be taken into account when considering, for example, the number of people composing the generation. Moreover, it also may explain differences in behavior among younger and older Millennials that are beginning to emerge in survey research. Again, drawing these generational lines of demarcation is a combination of art and science – there is no rulebook on how or where to draw calendar distinctions between groups of citizens. Instead, it may be history that tells us how well (or poorly) we've done at grouping these bodies of individuals together.

Putting a generation into context

Millennials' generational milestones (such as reaching the voting age, becoming a legal adult, and turning 30) are a function, then, of the generational lines of division drawn by scholars. In Table 1.1, the generational boundaries set by scholars are contrasted with a selection of these "coming of age" milestones. For example, if we use the generational parameters set by Zukin *et al.*, Millennials are within striking distance of their fortieth birthday and are nearing the point where they no longer can or should be considered our "newest" or "youngest" citizens. In contrast, according to the generational parameters set by Howe and Strauss, Millennials won't turn forty until 2022.

Table 1.1 also contrasts these dates and milestones in the history of the Millennial Generation with the corresponding top news event that year.[5] This is not necessarily a unique exercise. For example, Zukin *et al.* present a timeline contrasting the age range of the succession of generations (from "Dutifuls" to "Dot Nets") with a selection of historical, political, economic, and cultural events that took place at the same time (2006, ch. 2). Howe and Strauss (2000) conduct a similar exercise – placing the formative years of Baby Boomers, Generation Xers, and Millennials into historical, cultural, and even technological context.[6] In line with this text's purpose, the focus here is just on Millennials' coming of age years.

The information focuses on the years that constitute the heart of Millennials' growth as a generation and allows us to identify the issues that dominated this period and, at least according to generational theory, have marked them. For example, surveying the information presented for this selection of Millennial milestones, we see that partisanship and international terrorism have played a prominent role in these pivotal early adult years. Appendix A documents the top three news events that dominated the national agenda in each year since 1983 as Millennials have come of age and shows that relations between the United States and the Soviet Union featured prominently in the news for the first years of the Millennial Generation, whereas terrorism has been a fixture throughout much of the period but most especially in recent years. Economic and environmental concerns also have marked the national agenda as Millennials have matured.

Table 1.1 Millennial timeline

Year	Millennials' age	#1 news story	#2 news story	#3 news story
1976 (Zukin *et al.*)				
1977	1			
1978	2			
1979	3			
1980 (Pew Research Center)	4			
1981	5			
1982 (Howe and Strauss; Winograd and Hais)	6			
1983	7	Soviet Union condemned for shooting down South Korean airline they claimed had been on a spy mission	United States assigns finding cause of AIDS as top priority	Soviet leader Andropov consolidates his power as relations with US flounder

(*cont.*)

Table 1.1 (*cont.*)

Year	Millennials' age	#1 news story	#2 news story	#3 news story
1984	8	Suicide terrorist blows up Marine headquarters at Beirut International Airport	US invades Grenada at request of Organization of East Caribbean States	Walter Mondale selects a woman, Geraldine Ferraro, as vice-presidential nominee
1985	9	Shiite Muslim extremists hold hostages taken from TWA airliner for 17 days – one American killed	President Reagan orders partial sanctions of South African government in response to apartheid	Mikhail Gorbachev succeeds Chernenko as leader of USSR
1986	10	Space Shuttle *Challenger* explodes moments after lift-off	Soviet authorities wait 3 days to announce major accident at the Chernobyl nuclear power plant	Ferdinand Marcos flees the Philippines and Corazon Aquino named new president
1987	11	Iran–Contra becomes the most serious crisis of the Reagan Administration	Oil tankers in Persian Gulf become targets of Iranian and Iraqi missiles and warplanes	Spread of AIDS one of the many issues considered regarding deadly disease

1988	12	George Bush elected as 41st President while Democrats retain substantial majority in both House and Senate	Host of environmental concerns including drought, closed beaches due to waste management, "Greenhouse Effect," ozone depletion, acid rain, radon contamination	Negotiations result in signing of the INF Treaty by President Reagan and Soviet leader Gorbachev
1989	13	Student demonstrations in China crushed by military forces, resulting in many deaths and arrests	Alaska's Prince William Sound site of one of largest oil spills after Exxon Valdez struck a reef	In Poland, rise to power of Solidarity and formation of new government under Lech Walesa
1990	14	Reunification of Germany after 45-year division into Communist and non-Communist states	Saddam Hussein's forces overrun and annex Kuwait – leads to UN-backed economic sanctions against Iraq and US military intervention	President Gorbachev attempts to move USSR from Communist authority rule to democracy and capitalism

(cont.)

Table 1.1 (*cont.*)

Year	Millennials' age	#1 news story	#2 news story	#3 news story
1991	15	Republics of USSR prepare to sign union agreement and mark demise of Communist Party and reorganization of Soviet Union	US-led coalition defeats Iraqi forces in Persian Gulf, liberates Kuwait but leaves Saddam Hussein in power	Unstable economy due to savings and loan failures, recession, unemployment, health care costs, budget deficits
1992	16	Bill Clinton elected 42nd President of the US, Democrats retain control of House and Senate	Economy heads list of issues in 1992 presidential campaign – recession, unemployment, taxes, budget deficit	Rioting and racial tension in South Central Los Angeles after 4 police officers charged with assault and excessive force against Rodney King are acquitted
1993	17	Bill Clinton inaugurated as the 42nd president	Clinton proposes to Congress plan to provide health insurance to all Americans and hold down health care costs – plan controversial and complex	Clinton wins passage of a bill to reduce federal budget deficits by $496 billion over 5 years

1994	Millennials turn 18 (Zukin model)	Republicans win resounding victory on Election Day 1994 – taking control of both houses of Congress for first time in 40 years and winning 3/5 of nation's governorships	Haiti's President Jean-Bertrand Aristide, in exile since being overthrown by Haitian military, restored to power with aid of US troops
			First Republican-controlled Congress in 40 years convened
1995	19	In worst terrorist act on US soil, Federal Building in Oklahoma City target of car bomb, killing 169 people	Middle East peace process continues – results in limited Palestinian autonomy in Gaza Strip and West Bank
			O.J. Simpson tried for murders of wife Nicole Simpson and friend Ronald Goldman and acquitted
1996	20	Bill Clinton re-elected President of the US	TWA flight 800 traveling from NYC to Paris explodes and crashes into the Atlantic Ocean off the coast of Long Island
			Boris Yeltsin re-elected president of Russia
1997	Millennials turn 21 (Zukin model)	Billions mourn death of Princess Diana	After more than 150 years as British colony, Hong Kong, restored to Chinese rule
			Timothy McVeigh convicted and sentenced to death for bombing of Murrah Federal Building in Oklahoma City

(cont.)

Table 1.1 (*cont.*)

Year	Millennials' age	#1 news story	#2 news story	#3 news story
1998	Millennials turn 18 (Pew model)	US House votes along party lines to authorize House committee to consider impeachment of President Bill Clinton	In off-year elections, Republicans fail to make any gains in Congress	Representatives of Catholic and Protestant groups in Northern Ireland sign major peace accord
1999		Bill Clinton second President in US history to be impeached by House and tried in the Senate	NATO begins airstrikes against Yugoslavia to force Serbian retreat	2 teenagers fatally shoot 12 students and a teacher at Columbine High School before killing themselves
2000	Millennials turn 18 (Howe and Strauss)	In dramatic election night, George Bush and Al Gore battle for electoral votes with neither gaining a majority	In major scientific triumph, scientists discern structure of genome	Yugoslav President Slobodan Milosevic concedes defeat
2001	Millennials turn 21 (Pew model)	In worst ever terrorist attack on the US, hijackers commandeer 4 commercial airliners, crash 2 into the World Trade Center and 1 into the Pentagon	Violent clashes between Israeli and Palestinian forces	George W. Bush sworn in as 43rd President

2002		United States and allies continue war on terrorism	Congress passes mandate giving president broad powers to use military force	Violence between Israelis and Palestinians continues
2003	Millennials turn 21 (Howe and Strauss)	Saddam Hussein deposed in Iraq	Space Shuttle *Columbia* disintegrates during re-entry	US economy continues to grow at a steady pace but number of jobs continues to decline
2004		15 months after invasion, US transfers authority to Iraqi government War in Iraq continues	George Bush in tight race against John Kerry	Fighting terrorism – 9/11 report issued
2005			Hurricane Katrina hits United States	Pope John Paul II dies, Cardinal Ratzinger of Germany elected
2006	Millennials turn 30 (Zukin model)	Sectarian violence in Iraq – continued opposition to US presence undermines elections	US midterm congressional elections to decide if both houses remain under Republican control as they have since 1995	US and allies continue to fight global war against fundamentalist Islamic terrorists

(cont.)

Table 1.1 (*cont.*)

Year	Millennials' age	#1 news story	#2 news story	#3 news story
2007		In Iraq, Bush outlines new war strategy featuring "surge" of some 30,000 troops	Housing market starts to crumble as foreclosure rates spike	Democratic majorities pass increase in minimum wage and new ethics rules
2008		Global economy in turmoil	Financial crisis raises fears of US recession	Obama triumphs in Democratic sweep
2009		Obama presidency begins	Recession in US ends but jobless rate rises	US pull-out from Iraq takes place but build-up in Afghanistan
2010	Millennials turn 30 (Pew model)	Republicans take House of Representatives and win big in state races	Economic recovery stalls	US winds down conflict in Iraq but conflict surges in Afghanistan
2011	Millennials turn 35 (Zukin model)	Arab Spring uprisings sweep North Africa and Middle East	Japanese earthquake and tsunami cause nuclear disaster	Commando raid in Pakistan kills Osama Bin Laden
2012	Millennials turn 30 (Howe and Strauss)	Barack Obama wins re-election	Supreme Court upholds "Obamacare"	Middle East news dominated by terrorism, turmoil, and transition

2013	
2014	
2015	Millennials turn 35 (Pew model)
2016	Millennials turn 40 (Zukin model)
2017	Millennials turn 35 (Howe and Strauss)
2018	
2019	
2020	Millennials turn 40 (Pew model)
2021	
2022	Millennials turn 40 (Howe and Strauss)

Millennials: what we know

The preceding section was meant to provide a sense of where
Millennials fall on the generational timeline and the environment in
which they've been raised. Attention turns now to *who* Millennials
are or a thumbnail sketch of the group's key features. Such quick
or abbreviated renderings are risky – there is always the danger of
omitting critical information or depicting a phenomenon according
to one's own biases. When it comes to depicting Millennials, a complete picture of the vital statistics of this generation as well as an
account of the full range of their attitudes and habits is beyond the
scope of this project. This work has been done elsewhere, and a rich
body of information has emerged regarding the composition, habits,
and attitudes of this generation.[7]

The focus of this text, though, is on how these young adults engage
in politics and democracy. In this section, then, I make use of these
secondary data to highlight those features that distinguish Millennials
from previous generations, have caused us to take notice of them, and
promise to have the greatest impact on the nation's future – including the nation's political future. These factors include the size of the
Millennial Generation, the ethnic diversity of Millennials, their educational attainment and economic status, and their habits and outlook. This exercise highlights the reality that not only do Millennials
have a significant stake in the political process, but that the generation
possesses the size and background to significantly impact American
democracy unlike any generation before them.

Size

As suggested earlier, the Baby Boom generation has loomed large
in the nation's history and much of its power has been a function of
its size. As indicated in Table 1.1, this generation stretched from the
early to mid-1940s to the early to mid-1960s. During that roughly
20-year period, approximately 71–77 million Americans were born
in the United States.[8] The Baby Boom generation has always been
considered the nation's largest generation – until now. When they
christened the youngest generation the "Millennial Generation,"
Howe and Strauss declared not only that the generation would
exceed the Baby Boom generation in size but that they were "on

their way to becoming America's first 100-million-person genera-tion" (2000, 15). As the Pew Research Center points out, this is due less to high rates of fertility than to an influx of immigrants into the United States – including women of child-bearing age (more on the role of immigrants and diversity later in this chapter) (2010, 9).

To be sure, Baby Boomers and their parents still cast a signif-icant shadow over the demographics of the nation. As Figure 1.2 shows, Baby Boomers born between 1948 and 1968 constitute a siz-able portion of the population currently, and when coupled with those members of the previous generation that remain, we see that residents over the age of 45 constitute 40 percent of the current population. In contrast, though, nearly 60 percent of the remainder of the population of the United States is under the age of 45. A mix-ture of Generation Xers and Millennials, those born between 1968 and 1988 account for 26 percent of the population while 33 per-cent of the population is composed of those aged 24 or younger. Interestingly, although American residents under the age of 45 are growing in number, the median age of the United States actually increased between 2000 and 2010 from 35.3 years to 37.2 years.[9] The rise in median age is a reflection of the aging of the very large cohort

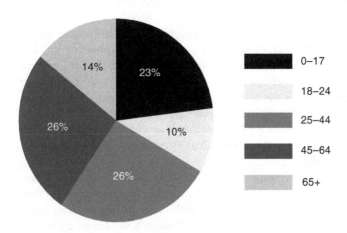

Note: Percentage does not equal 100% due to rounding.

Figure 1.2 Current resident population estimates by age

of Baby Boomers and those who preceded them – another sign of the imprint these age cohorts have left on the nation.

Waiting in the wings, though, is a sizable body of young people who, over the course of the next 50 years, will gradually replace the Baby Boom generation. Population projections from the US Census, presented in Table 1.2, allow us to estimate the size of the Millennial Generation in years to come and the proportion of the population that will consist of Millennials for the next 50 years. These data also allow us to visually depict how the newest largest generation will replace the formerly dominant Baby Boomers.

For example, we see that in 2015, those born between 1971 and 1990 (prime Millennial years) constitute an equal percentage to those born between 1951 and 1970. The dominance of the Millennial Generation will be felt most significantly in 2025 and then 20 years later when Millennials are in their late forties and into their early sixties. Assuming the generational perspective has merit and the era in which one is raised has long-term effects on one's age group's attitudes and behaviors, it's fair to say then that understanding Millennials today will give us a good sense of the traits and behaviors of this age group in 2045 when they make up a sizable proportion of the total population.

Where are the many young people who currently make up the Millennial Generation located geographically? Data from the US Census Bureau allow us not only to isolate states with the greatest concentration of older and younger residents but to consider age distribution in the context of states' political power. This mapping offers at least some rationale for such political realities as get-out-the-vote drives that target certain pockets of the populace or even state-level political actions such as voter identification and early voting legislation.

As Figure 1.3 shows, out of the 50 states, Maine has the highest median age. Two of the ten states with the highest median ages are New Hampshire and Florida – both states considered swing states by *Politico* in the 2012 election.[10] Although New Hampshire doesn't have a large number of Electoral College votes, its high-profile role in the presidential primary season gives the state a certain prominence. The combination of Florida's status as a swing state, its large

Table 1.2 Population projections by age

Age	Number/percentage in 2015	Number/percentage in 2025	Number/percentage in 2035	Number/percentage in 2045	Number/percentage in 2055
Total	321,363	346,407	369,662	389,934	409,873
0–18	74,518 (23%) (1997–2015)	78,190 (23%) (2007–25)	81,509 (22%) (2017–35)	84,084 (22%) (2027–45)	87,744 (21%) (2037–55)
18–24	30,983 (9%) (1991–97)	30,180 (9%) (2001–7)	32,125 (9%) (2011–17)	33,680 (9%) (2021–27)	34,469 (8%) (2031–37)
25–44	84,327 (26%) (1971–90)	91,833 (27%) (1981–2000)	95,013 (26%) (1991–2010)	98,725 (25%) (2001–20)	104,331 (25%) (2011–30)
45–64	83,839 (26%) (1951–70)	81,152 (23%) (1961–80)	83,700 (23%) (1971–90)	92,157 (24%) (1981–2000)	96,020 (23%) (1991–2010)
65+	47,695 (15%) (1950–earlier)	65,052 (19%) (1960–earlier)	77,315 (21%) (1970–earlier)	81,288 (21%) (1980–earlier)	87,309 (21%) (1990–earlier)

Note: Numbers in thousands.
Source: Table 2, "Projections of the Population by Selected Age Groups and Sex for the United States: 2015 to 2060 (NP2012-T2)," US Census Bureau, Population Division (release date: December 2012).

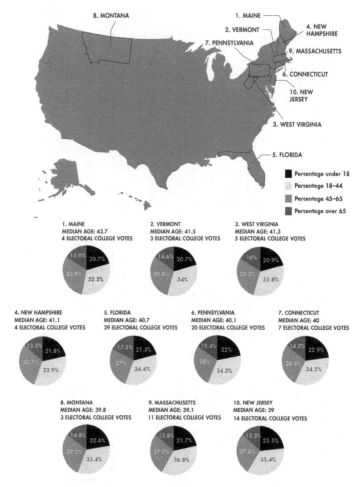

Figure 1.3 States with the highest median age

number of Electoral College votes, and its controversial political history make it a state to watch.

As Figure 1.4 shows, of the ten states with the lowest median ages, Utah ranks at the top (a state not necessarily seen as politically pivotal). On the other hand, two of the ten states with large

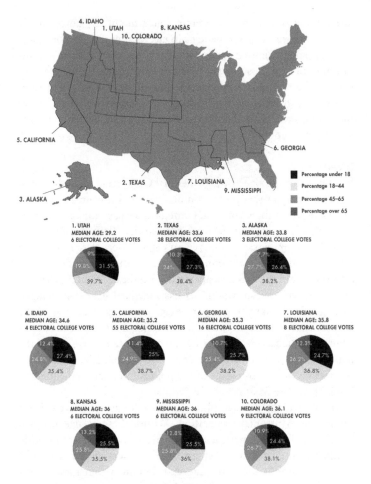

Figure 1.4 States with the lowest median age

numbers of young people are Texas and California – two states that always loom large at election time given their high number of Electoral College votes. Although there are large concentrations of young people in these states, neither was considered a swing state in 2012. On the other hand, Colorado was considered a swing state in 2012 and also has a relatively low median age. Again, distribution of age groups among states might explain strategic decisions as well as discrepancies in electoral practices. For example, campaigns' limited funds require them to target their mobilization efforts to those voters who can be counted on to vote (and vote in their favor). Some candidates might find it worth their effort then to mobilize young adults in those swing states where they can make a difference – especially if it's a state with a number of college campuses.

Diversity[11]

In addition to the size of the Millennial Generation, the ethnic and racial diversity of this generation distinguishes it from all previous age cohorts. On the whole, the United States has undergone a dramatic demographic transformation since the 1990s due to a sizable influx of immigrants. Thirty years ago, African Americans were considered the dominant minority group in the nation. Population estimates from the US Census for 2013 indicate, though, that the percentage of African Americans has remained nearly unchanged since 1980. In contrast, the percentage of Latinos residing in the United States has grown dramatically. Today, members of the population identified as Hispanic or Latino constitute 16.9 percent of the population (a jump of over 10 percentage points). Likewise, Asians represent a larger percentage of the population than they did in the 1980s (Junn and Matto 2008, 2).[12]

To be sure, the demographic changes felt nationally are evident among the Millennial Generation. Within these sizable national blocs of African Americans, Hispanics, and Asians currently residing in the United States are large numbers of young people. Figure 1.5 breaks down the age distribution within these dominant ethnic groups. Currently, the Hispanic population is the most dominant non-White segment of the population and, as Figure 1.5 shows, this slice of the population is dominated by people under the age of 35 (62 percent of Hispanics currently living in the United States can be considered "young"). These numbers suggest that the young Hispanic population possesses the size to be an influential force. When we look at the other dominant non-White populations, Black and Asian, the dominance of young people is evident again. Among Blacks in the United States, 55.7 percent are under the age

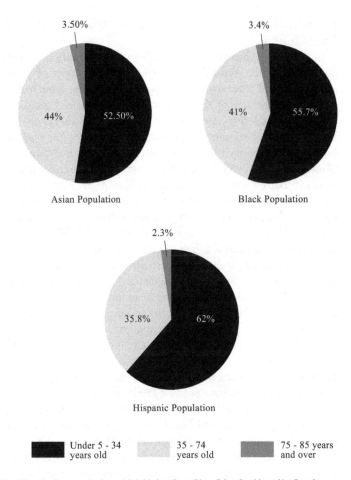

Asian Population

Black Population

Hispanic Population

| Under 5 - 34 years old | 35 - 74 years old | 75 - 85 years and over |

Note: Hispanic refers to people whose origin is Mexican, Puerto Rican, Cuban, Spanish-speaking Central or South American countries, or other Hispanic/Latino, regardless of race.

Figure 1.5 Age composition by ethnicity

of 35. Among Asians residing in the United States, nearly 53 percent are under the age of 35.

The ethnic composition of the nation as a whole is reflected in the Millennial population with the majority of Millennials (61 percent) classified as White, followed by 19 percent categorized as

Hispanic, 13 percent Black, and 4 percent Asian (Pew Research Center 2010, 9).

In light of the increase in the number of immigrants and recent policy discussions regarding the rights and privileges of young immigrants and "dreamers" (those young people who stand to benefit from the passage of the "Dream Act" and similar legislation), it's worth considering naturalization and the contrasting characteristics between young immigrants who are "naturalized" or who "are invested with the rights and privileges of American citizenship" (Junn and Matto 2008, 9) and those immigrants who have not yet been naturalized. Previous research has shown that newly naturalized citizens in the United States tend to possess stronger levels of education, income, and English proficiency than recent immigrants who haven't yet become citizens (Fix and Passel 2003; Fix *et al.* 2003). One's status as a citizen obviously has implications for the extent to which one is eligible to participate in the political process. There are multiple methods of engagement beyond voting, however, and one's likelihood of participating in all forms of engagement are affected by such factors as education and income. For that reason, although they constitute a small component of the overall population, it is worth taking a good look at young noncitizens residing in the United States. As recent data show, they possess a markedly different set of characteristics from citizens under the age of 35 – differences that could have political ramifications.

According to recent US Census data, of the 22 million noncitizens residing in the United States, 10.3 million are under the age of 35 (3.3 percent of the total population) (Acosta *et al.* 2014, 1). Of those under 35 who are not citizens, the vast majority (64.3 percent) were born in Latin America or the Caribbean.[13] Especially in comparison to citizens, most young noncitizens tend to fall between the ages of 25 and 35. As Figure 1.6 indicates, 55 percent of young noncitizens fall between the ages of 25 and 35 and nearly 75 percent of the group of young noncitizens is 20 years of age or older (Larsen *et al.* 2014, 3–4). For the purpose of this text, this is notable given that it is over the age of 18 that citizens are eligible to vote. These data suggest that the vast majority of young noncitizens are of voting age but ineligible to participate in elections due to their citizenship status.

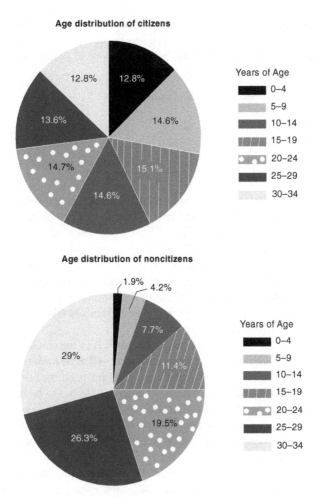

Figure 1.6 Age distribution of population under 35 by citizenship status

Where do young noncitizens reside? Areas of the country such as New York, Los Angeles, San Antonio, and Chicago always have been considered "gateways" for immigrants (Junn and Matto 2008, 2), and "emerging gateway" locations including Las Vegas and Raleigh-Durham also have cropped up (Singer 2004). Recent census data reveal that relative to the total population, these gateways tend to have higher proportions of noncitizens under the age of 35 (Acosta, Larsen, and Grieco 2014, 7). States holding the largest proportion of those noncitizens under the age of 35 include:

- California (22.1 percent of young noncitizens)
- Texas (12.7 percent)
- New York (8.9 percent)
- Florida (7.2 percent)
- Illinois (4.3 percent)
- New Jersey (4.1 percent).

As suggested earlier, the large number of Electoral College votes held by some of these states (California, Texas, and Florida in particular) make this a noteworthy finding from a political standpoint. At the local level, cities such as New York, Los Angeles, Houston, Miami, Chicago, and Dallas have the largest number of noncitizens under the age of 35. Moreover, young noncitizens tend to reside in metropolitan areas with large universities – an interesting finding given that political mobilization of young adults tends to take place in college communities (Acosta *et al.* 2014, 7).

Finally, recently available data suggest differences in the employment status of young citizens and noncitizens, as well as educational differences among young noncitizens from different regions of the globe. For example, citizens aged 25–34 are more likely "to be in the civilian labor force, to have full-time employment, and to be working in management, business, science, and arts occupations or sales and office occupations" than noncitizens in the same age group (Acosta *et al.* 2014, 7).

Additionally, there are stark contrasts between educational attainment and regions of origin of new young immigrants. Of college-age noncitizens (18–24 years of age), approximately one-third are enrolled in college; however, noncitizens from Latin America and the Caribbean are much less likely to be college students than their counterparts from other regions of the world. Specifically, 18 percent of college-age noncitizens from Latin America and the Caribbean are enrolled in college compared to 65 percent of those from Asia, 54 percent from Europe, and 54 percent from Africa (Acosta *et al.* 2014, 9). These educational differences extend to high school education. Specifically, nearly one-half of young citizens from Latin America (aged 25–34) had not graduated from high school while over 50 percent of those born Asia and Europe had attained a bachelor's degree or higher (Acosta *et al.* 2014, 9). Socioeconomic and educational differences effectively explain differences in political participation – those more financially secure and with higher levels of education are more likely to participate in the political process. For these reasons, such findings are meaningful and suggest that large portions of the populace who have a significant stake in the political process are less likely to be favorably situated to engage in it.

Education and economic status

In many ways, the education level and economic status of young people in the United States are inextricably linked in that it's the Millennial Generation that finds itself both highly educated and heavily burdened with student loan debt. Coupled with the weak economy that has accompanied their upbringing, Millennials face steep economic challenges.

The Pew Research Center finds that, compared to previous generations, the Millennial Generation is the most highly educated age group in America's history with 54 percent of Millennials having at least some college education. In contrast, when they were 18–28 years old, only 49 percent of Generation Xers, 36 percent of Baby Boomers, and 24 percent of the Silent Generation had attained at least some college education (Pew Research Center 2010, 10). Data from the US Census allow us to look more closely at the levels of educational attainment not only by age but also by ethnic background.

As Tables 1.3 and 1.4 show, levels of educational attainment are high on the whole but vary based on Millennials' ethnic background. Echoing the data from the Pew Research Center, Table 1.3 shows that most 18–24-year-olds have attended some college while most 25–29-year-olds have attained a high school diploma.

As Table 1.4 shows, these education rates aren't uniform across all groups of young people, however. These data further emphasize

Table 1.3 Educational attainment of 18–29-year-olds, all races, 2010

All races	Total	None	1st–11th grade/2	High school graduate	Some college no degree	Associate's degree (occupational or academic)	Bachelor's degree	Master's degree	Professional/doctoral degree
18 years and over	229,240	849	30,587	71,172	44,354	19,740	41,289	15,357	5,890
18 to 24 years	29,313	67	5,659	8,716	10,693	1,481	2,505	155	37
25 to 29 years	21,453	46	2,362	5,908	4,310	2,033	5,338	1,182	275

Note: Numbers reported in thousands.
Source: US Census Bureau, Current Population Survey, 2010 Annual Social and Economic Supplement.

Table 1.4 Educational attainment of 18–29-year-olds by ethnicity, 2010

	Total	None	1st–11th grade/2	High school graduate	Some college no degree	Associate's degree (occupational or academic)	Bachelor's degree	Master's degree	Professional/ doctoral degree
White alone									
18 years and over	185,781	610	23,959	57,666	35,763	16,182	34,084	12,628	4,890
18 to 24 years	22,698	60	4,246	6,549	8,465	1,204	2,042	100	34
25 to 29 years	16,704	31	1,883	4,498	3,230	1,597	4,386	882	197
Black alone									
18 years and over	27,273	97	4,575	9,643	5,898	2,289	3,259	1,212	300
18 to 24 years	4,304	4	1,030	1,568	1,340	136	210	14	1*
25 to 29 years	2,922	10	313	1,023	736	284	424	96	36
Asian alone									
18 years and over	10,694	111	1,085	2,169	1,392	757	3,250	1,311	619

(cont.)

Table 1.4 (*cont.*)

	Total	None	1st–11th grade/2	High school graduate	Some college no degree	Associate's degree (occupational or academic)	Bachelor's degree	Master's degree	Professional/ doctoral degree
18 to 24 years	1,231	–	346	241	532	84	191	34	1*
25 to 29 years	1,123	5	71	172	170	84	409	182	32
Hispanic (of any race)									
18 years and over	31,845	415	11,067	9,571	4,955	1,945	2,862	745	286
18 to 24 years	5,470	20	1,665	1,757	1,564	236	210	12	6
25 to 29 years	4,219	19	1,272	1,375	688	296	463	96	9

Notes:
– means zero or rounds to zero.
Numbers reported in thousands.

the education gap highlighted earlier between the nation's ethnic groups. Again, given the relationship between education and political engagement, these realities serve as an alarm – warning us that pockets of the Millennial Generation stand the chance of being excluded from the political process.

The importance of a college degree on a young adult's financial future is critical, according to recent research. The Pew Research Center (2014a) found significant disparities in earning levels, rates of unemployment, and poverty levels between those Millennials who had attained a college degree and those who hadn't. In this same report, the Pew Research Center found that:

- Millennials who had earned a Bachelor's degree or higher had a median income of $45,000, averaged an unemployment rate of 3.8 percent, with only a 5.8 percent share living in poverty.
- Millennials who attained some college education averaged a median salary of $30,000 with an unemployment rate of 8.1 percent and a 14.7 percent share living in poverty.
- Millennials with only a high school diploma earned around $28,000, with a 12.2 percent unemployment rate and a 21.8 percent share living in poverty.

Of course, the downside of pursuing a college education is the cost and the debt students and students' families are likely to face in financing a postsecondary education. Yet again, here is an example of how young adults have a stake in the political process. Data from the National Center for Educational Statistics highlight the stark realities of financing a college education, specifically the stark increases that have taken place since the first decade of the twenty-first century:

- The percentage of first-time, full-time undergraduate students at four-year colleges receiving any financial aid has increased from 75 to 85.
- Federal expenditures in the form of student loans have increased from 10 to 38 billion dollars.
- The number of students receiving federal loans has increased from 4 to 11 million students.

- The total outstanding balance of student loans owned by the federal government has grown from 124 billion to 516 billion dollars.
- The percentage of students who defaulted on student loans has risen from 5.3 in 2000 to 9.1 in 2010.[14]

The downside of being the largest and most educated generation in American history, then, seems to be that it also makes it the most indebted generation in American history.

Before leaving the topic of college education, it's important to make mention of the young adults who do not attend college. There has been growing attention paid by organizations such as CIRCLE, Philanthropy for Active Civic Engagement (PACE), the Case Foundation, and the Kettering Foundation to identifying how many young people do not attend college, their socioeconomic background, and the individual and societal ramifications. "Non-college bound youth" or NCBY is defined as "Americans between the ages of 15–29 who have never attended college and are not currently on course to do so. Although most students who graduate from high school go on to college, as many as one in four adolescents do not complete high school."[15] Data analysis reported by PACE holds that NCBY represent about 50 percent of the whole youth population.[16] Any consideration, then, of how Millennials connect to democracy and politics must take into account the reality that a large segment of the generation does not attend college.

Rising rates of student loan debt coupled with an extremely fragile economy have been a potent combination and have made their mark on the Millennial Generation. As a recent report from the Urban Institute points out, the increase in student loan debt has taken place in the context of the "Great Recession," stagnant wages, a weak job market, and a devastated housing market. In addition, ongoing national debt and deficit crises raise the likelihood of rising tax rates for Millennials as they mature. As a result, young adults will find it nearly impossible to save the money necessary to retire when they're older and, therefore, are in much worse shape than previous generations were at this point when it comes to building wealth. As Steuerle *et al.* point out, "Today's adults in their mid-30s or younger – the prime time for career and family formation – benefited little from the doubling of the

economy since the early 1980s and have accumulated no more
wealth than their counterparts 25 years ago" (2013, 1). It's been
asserted that the financial straits of young people have influenced
their buying habits and made them less likely to spend large
amounts of money on such big-ticket items as cars and homes.
As Annie Lowrey wrote in the *New York Times*, "The millennials' relationship with money is quite simple. They do not have a
lot of it, and what they do have, they seem reluctant to spend"
(*New York Times*, May 26, 2013). There's some debate about
whether or not this contention has been borne out in research –
the Pew Research Center found little difference between those
with student loan debt and those without when it came to owning
such items as cars and homes (2014b, 20).

Nevertheless, it's a reality that the financial state of Millennials
is quite different from those generations that preceded them. The
Urban Institute has even argued that older generations have precipitated the situation: "Today's political discussions often focus on
preserving the public wealth and benefits of older Americans and
the baby boomers. Often lost in this discussion is how much of this
preservation comes at the greatest expense of younger generations
who have already been losing out on their share of private wealth"
(Steuerle *et al*. 2013, 1).

In his *New York Times* op-ed entitled "Millennials, We're Sorry,"
Frank Bruni takes this point even a step further, contending that
older generations should take responsibility for the economic mess
young people are in today:

> We conveniently overlook how much more they've had to pay for col-
> lege than we did, the loans they've racked up and the fact that nothing
> explains their employment difficulties better than a generally crummy
> economy, which certainly isn't their fault. They get our derision when
> they deserve our compassion and a political selflessness we've been
> unable to muster. While we're at it, we might even want to murmur an
> apology. (*New York Times*, June 7, 2014)

Habits and outlook
Before addressing how coverage of young people has been framed by
the media or how Millennials have been studied by researchers, it's

worth discussing some key habits of the age group as well as their outlook on life. Clearly, this is a topic vast in scope and impossible to review fully here. Although the topic, in broad terms, is outside the subject matter of this text, our appreciation of youth's engagement in politics and democracy must take into consideration Millennials' connection to technology and cyberspace as well as their "sense of self" (for lack of a better expression). These two features play a prominent role both in how young people are perceived and in our scholarly understanding of youth engagement and, therefore, are worthy of brief discussion.

It may go without saying that the birth and growth of the seemingly endless list of tools of communication such as the Internet, smartphones, instant messaging, YouTube, social media platforms such as Facebook, laptops, and tablets have been revolutionary socially, culturally, economically, and politically – at least for anyone not belonging to the Millennial Generation. For America's youngest generation who have been raised with the Internet, smartphones, and the like, these modes of communication and the accompanying technology don't necessarily signal a revolution but a way of life.

The assumed ubiquity of these communication tools is supported by recent data. Cohen and Kahne (2012, 8) found that, of the young adults they surveyed:

- 81 percent owned a desktop or laptop computer;
- 55 percent owned a handheld device that connected to the Internet;
- 48 percent owned a gaming device that connected to the Internet.

Recent survey research conducted by the Institute of Politics (IOP) at Harvard University indicates the extent to which young adults engage in social media use. As Figure 1.7 shows, although not necessarily overwhelming across all platforms, involvement in social media is extensive.[17] In a representative sample of 18–29-year-olds conducted in the spring of 2014, the vast majority of respondents (84 percent) indicated that they had an account on Facebook. In a subsequent question, 24 percent of the respondents indicated in fact that Facebook was the one website or social network they couldn't live without – although 42 percent indicated that there were no websites or social networks that they couldn't live without.

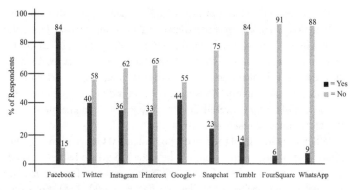

Note: Respondents were asked "On Which Social Media do you have an account?" Decline to answer responses have been omitted.

Figure 1.7 Social media use

Even more interesting were data measuring respondents' feelings surrounding the use of these platforms. The same IOP survey asked respondents to indicate the emotions they experienced in a typical week after signing off Facebook and Twitter. Clearly, among this age cohort, participation in social media platforms invokes feelings of connection, community, and happiness. Regarding Facebook:

- 80 percent felt "connected" after signing off Facebook;
- 80 percent felt "happy";
- 73 percent felt "less anxious."

Responses were similar upon signing off Twitter:

- 76 percent felt "connected";
- 78 percent felt "happy";
- 69 percent felt "less anxious."

Much of these findings echo the extensive data collected by the Pew Research Center (2010, 29) on Millennials and their use of technology and social media. An additional and notable finding by Pew, though, concerns the background of those who utilize tools of social media. In their 2010 research, they found that, among 18–29-year-olds, those most likely to create online profiles were younger, female, White, and college-educated. These numbers suggest a "technology gap" dividing ethnic sub-groups (the Pew data suggest that the gap is felt most strongly by Hispanics) and differing levels of education. More recent research conducted by Cohen *et al.* (2012) offers evidence that this gap might not be as wide as feared, at least along ethnic lines. Given the prevalence of social media in American culture in general but in politics in particular, a divergence in the use of these tools might foretell divergent degrees of engagement, and therefore must be taken seriously.

When they heralded the rise of the Millennial Generation in 2000, Howe and Strauss noted not only how the age group had embraced newly available modes of communication, even referring to the Internet as possessing a "Millennial flavor" (2000, 258), but even predicted that the manner in which Millennials would make use of these tools promised to have a broader impact: "Millennial kids and teens are shaping the culture mainly by picking and choosing from the offerings of others ... American pop culture will experience a Millennial makeover – a reconstruction that will help determine the flavor of the coming decade" (2000, 259). Winograd and Hais pick up this theme and take it a step further, contending that the generation armed with these tools of communication will spur broad political change and alignments (2008). More on this research will be discussed in the following chapters.[18]

The use of these tools of communication is interwoven with a key attitudinal feature of the generation – a strong sense of themselves. Now, whether this outlook has positive or negative consequences has been the source of much debate. There is general agreement, though, among generational scholars that members of the Millennial Generation were raised differently than earlier counterparts. Although the bubble eventually burst, parents of this age group found themselves with more leisure time thanks to a booming economy allowing them to be hands-on and child-focused (Zukin *et al.* 2006, 36–40). As Howe and Strauss point out, this parenting approach was symbolized by the "Babies on Board" and "Have You Hugged Your Child Today?" bumper stickers blanketing the cars of Millennials' parents (2000, 4). As Jean Twenge documents in her book, the hyper-parenting of the 1980s and 1990s placed a good deal of emphasis on building children's sense of confidence and self-worth. Working collectively, parents, schools, and the media disseminated the message that young people could be anything they wanted to be; as Twenge suggests, "they promote the equally powerful concepts of socially sanctioned self-focus, the unquestioned importance of the individual, and an unfettered optimism about young people's future prospects" (2006, 72). Smith *et al*.'s *Lost in Transition: The Dark Side of Emerging Adulthood* (2011) sounds a similar note regarding the role of parents and the larger community: "most of the problems in the lives of youth have their origins in the larger adult world into which the youth are being socialized" (2011, 11).

Again, there is some disagreement over whether the result of intense parental attention has been positive or negative (both in general terms and regarding Millennials' connection to politics). Some would argue that this approach has resulted in a generation of young people who are optimistic and confident problem-solvers (Howe and Strauss 2000). Certainly survey data demonstrate high rates of confidence and optimism among this age cohort – even in the midst of the recent economic crisis. As Pew found in its report "Millennials: Confident, Connected and Open to Change" (2010), young people exhibit higher rates of satisfaction than Americans 30 years or older (2010, 22) and are optimistic about their financial future despite the state of the economy (2010, 41). There are others who have argued that, instead, this approach has led to a generation of narcissists with over-inflated egos. Although Twenge's *Generation Me* (2006) focuses its lens primarily on Generation X, she does turn her attention to Millennials and refutes the rosy claims of Howe and Strauss, contending that "Millennials are the most narcissistic generation in history" (2006, 70).

Smith *et al*.'s study of contemporary youth's progression through the teenage years into adulthood leads them to question the nature of individualism that has been drummed into America's young people, holding that many of the troubles experienced by young people today can be traced to the focus on the self (2011, 235). A far cry from Howe and Strauss, the authors contend that the path to adulthood is "often confusing, troubled, and sometimes dangerous," resulting in young adults who are "disoriented, wounded, and sometimes damaged along the way" (Smith *et al.* 2011, 226).

Resolving this debate isn't necessarily the aim of this text. The reality, though, is that, in addition to the other demographic traits detailed above, these habits and attitudes distinguish Millennials from their generational counterparts. Moreover, these defining characteristics run through both media and scholarly attention dedicated to young people. It's the media coverage of this generation that we'll address next.

Millennials: what we perceive

Thus far, the boundaries of the Millennial Generation have been offered as well as a description of the time period in which members of the generation have come of age and a sketch of their key features. This chapter concludes with a discussion of the perceptions of the nation's youngest set of citizens. Students often have commented to me that they believe members of their generation are misunderstood or are unfairly maligned. This perception isn't necessarily unique to my students. In fact, young residents of Washington, DC recently launched "Millennial Week" to combat this impression. The mission of the movement is "to cultivate, promote and present the most meaningful ideas and trends that reflect the impact of Millennials on culture, enterprise and society."[19]

It's fair to say that the media have offered at least a muddled image of the Millennial Generation. For example, in an August 15, 2013 article, the *New York Times* labeled the age group "Generation Nice," featuring vibrant photos of a diverse and engaging group of young people as well as a selection of stories of young people doing good things. Contrast that to the May 9, 2013 cover of *Time*. Anchored with a photo of a young woman gazing admiringly into her iPhone, the headline of an article written by Joel Stein reads, "The Me, Me, Me Generation: Millennials are lazy, entitled narcissists who still live with their parents – Why they'll save us all." The title itself offers a contradiction, and the photo and accompanying label of "the Me Generation" sends a powerful message.

The last section of this chapter is a systematic take on how Millennials have been covered in the news media. Using a database of well over 300 news articles and op-eds regarding the Millennial Generation, conclusions have been drawn regarding the extent to which the generation has been covered in the news, the nature of the coverage, and the basic tone.

Why does media coverage matter? We know that the media play a critical function, through "gatekeeping," in determining which issues will be brought to the public's attention and which will not. The ability to determine which stories qualify as "news" endows a relatively small number of media "gatekeepers" with a great deal of power (Graber 1997, 99). Similarly, the manner in which the press presents or "frames" the news has a profound effect on the public's perception of politics. As Jamieson and Waldman contend, media frames "continuously shape what citizens know, understand, and believe about the world" (2003, xii). To be sure, the news choices of media elites are influenced by a number of factors including competition between news organizations, news production costs, and the audience appeal of a story (Bennett 2003). In the end, however, it is the people in the newsroom who determine the shape of a news frame.

There are plenty of good reasons to pay attention to Millennials – their size, diversity, and unique features. But to what extent have media outlets turned their attention to this age cohort? I began to answer this question by identifying the nation's leading daily newspapers as determined by the Alliance for Audited Media.[20] The newspapers are listed in Table 1.5. With an average circulation of 2,378,827 (print and digital), the *Wall Street Journal* tops the list of the nation's top leading daily newspapers. The top ten list includes such papers as the *New York Times* and the *Washington Post*, with the *Chicago Tribune* coming in at number ten. The analysis began by visiting each of the newspapers' websites and identifying the number of articles that surfaced when using the search term "Millennial Generation" as far back as the online archive allowed.[21] As Table 1.5 shows, the subject of Millennials has received considerable attention in the popular press over the years, with the *New York Times*, *Wall Street Journal*, and *Washington Post* offering the most coverage.

In order to refine consideration of the media's coverage of young people, a database of nearly 360 articles that address the Millennial Generation was built. The articles were drawn from four of these top ten newspapers: the *Wall Street Journal*, the *New York Times*,

Table 1.5 Newspaper coverage of Millennial Generation

Name of newspaper	Total average circulation*	Number of articles regarding Millennials
Wall Street Journal	2,378,827	428
New York Times	1,865,318	545
USA Today	1,674,306	143
Los Angeles Times	653,868	282
New York Daily News	516,165	128
New York Post	500,521	125
Washington Post	474,767	593
Chicago-Sun Times	470,548	51
Denver Post	416,676	148
Chicago Tribune	414,930	317

Notes: * includes print and digital.
Source: Alliance for Audited Media: www.auditedmedia.com/news/blog/top-25-us-newspapers-for-march-2013.aspx (as of March 31, 2013).

the *Washington Post*, and the *Los Angeles Times*. These four were selected because they have a broad circulation, each had a sizable number of articles with which to work, and they offered both ideological and geographic diversity. This method may be imperfect but it allows for a systematic evaluation of the coverage of the young people. Table 1.6 displays the number of articles from each paper included for consideration.[22]

A fun, although not entirely scientific, method for gleaning the tone of the articles is to create a word cloud of their headlines – see Figure 1.8. Word clouds create images out of text and the size of the words within the cloud reflects how frequently the word occurs. As the word cloud shows, not surprisingly, such terms as "Millennials," "new," "generation," "young" are relatively large because they were mentioned most frequently in the titles of the articles included in my database. Another prominent word is "Obama," suggesting the perceived connection between the Obama campaign and the young people – more on that to come. Finally, it's worth noting other words that are frequently mentioned in the headlines regarding Millennials such as "economy," "work," "Facebook," "ABC," and even words such as "hotel," "Marriott," and "food."

Table 1.6 Articles on Millennials

Newspaper	Arts & Entertainment/ Life & Style	Business/ personal finance	Opinion	Politics – national	Other *	Total articles
Wall Street Journal	24	37	21	2	6	90
New York Times	13	23	9	4	5	54
Los Angeles Times	36	39	13	8	4	100
Washington Post	30	16	36	21	9	112
Total	103 (29%)	115 (32%)	79 (22%)	35 (10%)	24(7%)	356

Note: Other* includes Real Estate, Technology, Autos, Faith, Other.

Figure 1.8 Word cloud of headlines

The prevalence of these words indicates that the impact of this generation is broad and certainly extends beyond politics. Coverage of Millennials suggests that young people are making a noticeable difference in business, marketing, and entertainment – these sectors are paying attention to the generation and adjusting to meet the demographics and behavior of Millennials as well as their demands. Apart from the connection frequently made between young people and President Obama, the impact of youth on the world of politics seems to be less remarkable in the eyes of the media. Instead, relative to other segments of society, attention paid to youth and the impact Millennials have on the body politic appear slight. This impression, made clear through this exercise, certainly is reflected in the way we've studied youth engagement.

In order to get a sense of the nature and tone of media coverage of Millennials, the research began by categorizing each article according to the section and/or subject area in which it appeared, allowing for analysis of the content of each set of articles in order to determine the media frame through which younger citizens were portrayed. The first striking finding was the preponderance of articles on Millennials that appeared in newspapers' business sections or addressed issues having to do with the economy or business. As Table 1.6 shows, 115 articles in the database fell into this category – 32 percent. The articles analyzed tended to hit one of three themes: the business world's efforts to appeal to the demographic, the effects of Millennials in the workplace, or the dire financial straits of this age group.

Most of these business-related articles addressed businesses' efforts to appeal to young people. From well-known and established brands such as Levi, Keds, Mustang, and Calvin Klein to newly opened restaurants and apartment complexes, the message conveyed in these articles is this: the Millennial Generation is a group with a unique set of traits that requires businesses to adjust accordingly in order to woo them. As good business people should, this set of articles suggests that these companies have a very clear sense of who Millennials are and how they spend their money. The list of traits or behaviors ascribed to Millennials as consumers is long and includes: frugality, negligible brand loyalty, heavy use of social media, tendency to take to the Internet to express their opinion, collaborative, expect to be involved in decision-making and to have a wide range of choices and options, desire to express their style and beliefs, optimism, wariness at being fooled or used, and the desire to feel connected to products they use.

Businesses have responded to the Millennial outlook in their marketing and in their goods and services. As the *Wall Street Journal* reported in an article about a restaurant chain's shift in focus to appeal to youth, "Millennials are driving the dining trends, ... eating out isn't just for nourishment, it is a social event" (*Wall Street Journal*, December 19, 2012). A similar tone is struck in an article regarding the restaurant business: "They're not just looking for tasty treats at a good value. What they want is much more complicated: an emotional connection to a brand that is socially responsible and sustainable, using thoughtfully chosen ingredients and considerately employed workers" (*Los Angeles Times*, May 11, 2012). Likewise, greeting card companies are incorporating social media into their business model (*Wall Street Journal*, June 20, 2011) and wedding planners are adjusting their approach to appeal to Millennials. As the *New York Times* reported, "Instead of traditional must-haves like engraved invitations or sit-down dinners, the millennials – people generally in their 20s – seek touches that showcase their interests and personal style" (*New York Times*, November 3, 2010).

Millennials' use of their purchasing power to reflect their values and attitudes is documented in the Brookings report "How Millennials Could Upend Wall Street and Corporate America" (May 2014) and even influenced the *New York Times* to dub Millennials "Generation Nice," noting that "Taken together, these habits and tastes look less like narcissism than communalism. And its highest value isn't self-promotion, but its opposite, empathy – an open-minded and -hearted connection to others" (*New York Times*, August 15, 2014). Business managers also are well aware of the differences between Millennials and their predecessors when it comes to views on work. To be sure, analysis of this set of articles uncovers a good deal of negativity regarding these differences – Millennials are often criticized for being unprepared for the business world, for lacking a strong work ethic, and for possessing an over-inflated sense of their ability and unreasonably high expectations. As one administrator commented, "They tend to be very self-absorbed; they value fun in their personal and their work life … Because they've grown up multitasking on their mobile, iPad and computer, I can't expect them to work on one project for any amount of time without getting bored" (*New York Times*, March 25, 2014). These sentiments aren't universal though. Others point out how these traits might actually be beneficial to managers: "They don't have that line between work and home that used to exist, so they're doing Facebook for the company at night, on Saturday or Sunday … We get incredible productivity out of them" (*New York Times*, March 25, 2014). Even more, the message conveyed in a number of these articles is that the skill set Millennials bring to the workplace, if acknowledged and embraced, can spark great progress: "Millennials work more closely together, leverage right- and left-brain skills, ask the right questions, learn faster and take risks previous generations resisted. They truly want to change the world and will use technology to do so" (*New York Times*, November 10, 2013). As a result, many companies are finding ways to attract and keep Millennial workers that range from designing workspaces that allow for collaboration and connectivity (both virtual and literal) (*Washington Post*, September 1, 2013) to rethinking pay packages and benefits that are attractive to Millennials (*Wall Street Journal*, August 17, 2013) and offering opportunities for meaningful participation. As one firm representative indicated, this approach makes good business sense: "If they don't feel like they're making a contribution to a company overall quickly, they don't stay … If you provide them with the right environment, they'll work forever, around the clock" (*Wall Street Journal*, August 22, 2012). Together with the articles on businesses' efforts to appeal to young people, one comes away from reading this subset of articles with the perception that Millennials are making a difference or are having an impact on the world of business.

As noted above, a number of these business articles focused upon the dire economic straits facing young people. It's worth noting at this point that newspaper coverage of Millennials' financial situation has focused both on how financially conservative Millennials are due to economic conditions (*Los Angeles Times*, January 28, 2014) and yet how optimistic they remain about their economic future (*Washington Post*, March 13, 2014).

Although not as numerous, articles appearing in "Arts & Entertainment" and "Life & Style" sections (a combined percentage of 29 percent of all of the articles) strike a similar chord with an emphasis on how Millennials have impacted culture and the arts and how these worlds are adjusting accordingly. From clothing offerings, to the presentation of operas, to the introduction of social media tools at museums, to the way 5K runs are marketed and administered, to the design of kitchen appliances, and to television and YouTube programming and content that suggests "transparency, authenticity, having an attitude, high self-esteem" (*Los Angeles Times*, November 9, 2013), the common theme is that Millennial tastes are impacting the cultural world around them.

As indicated in Table 1.6, the bulk of the remainder of the articles that addressed Millennials appeared in the editorial or opinion sections of newspapers or in articles addressing political or national news. Of the newspapers included in this search, the *Washington Post* published the most opinion pieces and news or political articles regarding young people. If we assume that the media play a "gate-keeping" function and are responsible for molding public perceptions of current affairs, the distribution of coverage of Millennials certainly leaves the impression that youth influence in the worlds of business and arts and entertainment outweighs their impact in current affairs or politics. That being said, there's much to be learned about the perceived role of Millennials in the democracy by exploring these articles.

The opinion pieces regarding Millennials fell into two broad categories:

- Op-eds that addressed the overall character of Millennials and their effect on the nation at large;
- Op-eds that focused primarily upon the political inclinations and implications of the generation.[23]

The majority of the op-eds (75 percent) fell into the first category and addressed the subject of Millennials in terms of their nature and outlook as well as their impact on society at large – the remaining 25 percent touched upon the political implications of the generation. This seems to underscore the assertion above that youth's political impact is relatively small (at least in the eyes of the media). Not surprisingly, upon drilling down into these articles, views of Millennials ranged from positive to negative to somewhere in between in both of these categories.

In addressing the general impact or role of Millennials, op-ed topics ranged from Millennials' worldview, to their work ethic and job prospects, to their use of social media. More often than not, these opinion pieces were a response to the most recent report released by such institutes as the Pew Research Center or Harvard University's Institute of Politics. Accordingly, the bulk of these articles strike a neutral tone – more often than not, they amount to a summary or analysis of fresh survey data.

Of the remaining op-eds addressing the impact of Millennials in general (not specifically their political impact), more strike a negative tone and thereby offer some support for the contention that they are a misunderstood and underappreciated generation. Specifically, about a quarter of the op-eds discussing the general character of the generation painted an unflattering portrait of Millennials. For example, in a sarcastic reaction to Pew data highlighting young people's lack of attachment to institutions, including religion, Ross Douthat wrote:

> In the future, it seems, there will be only one "ism" – Individualism – and its rule will never end. As for religion, it shall decline; as for marriage, it shall be postponed; as for ideologies, they shall be rejected;

as for patriotism, it shall be abandoned; as for strangers, they shall be distrusted. Only pot, selfies and Facebook will abide – and the greatest of these will probably be Facebook. (*New York Times*, March 16, 2014)

"Entitled to Be a Brat," an op-ed published in the *Washington Post* reacting to a young person's efforts to sue her parents, strikes a similar negative tone regarding Millennials: "She is also the epitome of what is referred to as the Millennial generation but really ought to be rebranded 'Generation E' – for entitlement" (March 11, 2014). The small remainder of the op-eds offer, at the least, a solid defense of Millennials to, at the most, a rousing endorsement of the generation's attributes and their impact on society. For example, in her discussion of Millennials published in the *New York Times* (May 30, 2010), Judith Warner outlines all the positive and less than positive characteristics that have been attributed to the generation (ranging from self-centered and entitled to optimistic and resilient), but contends that not only may these be the traits they need to navigate their future but precisely the sort of skill set their parents have raised them to possess:

These emerging adults may be off-putting to a worried 40-something – their sense of entitlement and their lack of humility are somewhat hard to take – but they're not necessarily maladapted. On the contrary, with their seemingly inexhaustible well of positive self-regard, their refusal to have their horizons be defined by the limitations of our era, they just may bear witness to the precise sort of resilience that all parents, educators and pop psychologists now say they view as proof of a successful upbringing.

Other defenses are even more passionate – not surprisingly, the authors of some of these defenses were themselves Millennials. In a letter to the editor published in the *New York Times* (November 16, 2011) titled "Generation Do," the author writes:

My generation is motivated by impact, not profit. We are products of the political idealism of Barack Obama, the creative genius of Steve Jobs and the globalization of a 21st-century world ... My generation is sowing the seeds of social entrepreneurship and activism that will propel America to success in future generations. We, the millennials, are passionately screaming at the top of our lungs.

Of all of the op-eds that address the topic of young people, 20 (25 percent) touched specifically upon the political implications of Millennials. Again, these pieces offer a range of opinions from positive to negative to somewhere in between about the power of the age group as well as the benefits to be gained by one party or another. Although we're dealing with fairly small numbers here, what's noteworthy is that the bulk of these politically focused op-eds strike a somewhat negative or critical tone that calls into question the power and political engagement of the youth demographic. For example, a few of the op-eds call young people out for undermining their generation's power by not turning out to vote. For example, the *Washington Post*'s Emily Badger argues that Millennials' social views aren't being codified into public policy due to the disproportionate number of older voters showing up at the polls (April 25, 2014). The *Los Angeles Times*' Dan Schnur makes a similar argument, positing that youth engagement at the polls would modulate the extreme partisan views of consistent voters (July 11, 2014).

The remainder of this subset of op-eds focuses squarely on Millennials' disenchantment with the Democratic Party and the Obama presidency. For example, James Freeman writes, "But the man who once dreamed of being a transformative leader in the Reagan mold is inspiring few of those young people to follow his lead … This shift in attitudes among the so-called millennial generation – those born after 1980 – may reflect the fact that the Obama era has been a disaster for them" (*Wall Street Journal*, April 14, 2014).

Nearly equal in number (but not quite) are those op-eds that assert that Millennials represent a potentially powerful political force that shouldn't be overlooked. For example, the *New York Times*' Bob Herbert emphasizes not only the power of the generation but the benefits to be gained by the Democratic Party: "Whether young Americans can shift the balance of the presidential election is an open question. But there is very little doubt that over the next several years they are capable of loosening the tremendous grip that conservatives have had on the levers of American power" (*New York Times*, May 13, 2008). Tim Egan's "Save Us Millennials" (*Washington Post*, June 4, 2010) strikes a similar positive tone, asserting that Millennials have the innate traits that the Obama presidency would be wise to tap into to address the nation's problems: "When an electorate is red-faced and fist-clenched, when the collective national blood pressure is 160 over 100, when the big issues of the day are mired in tired minds, it's time to turn to the great, renewable resource of any vibrant democracy: the kids."

More recently, columnists such as Doyle McManus and Ruth Marcus (*Washington Post*, March 25, 2014) have remarked on the potential power of the generation and assert that it would behoove candidates of both parties to pay attention to them. Making reference to recent survey data from the Pew Research Center, McManus argues:

There are lessons in those numbers for both political parties. Democrats must understand that while the next generation of voters is open to their message, they can't be taken for granted; when they get older and pay more taxes, some will surely bolt. And Republicans had better accept that if they remain a party of social conservatives resisting immigration reform, they're on their way out of business – soon. (*Los Angeles Times*, March 12, 2014)

The few remaining opinion pieces and the bulk of the Millennial-related articles found in the news and political sections strike a more neutral tone and point to either the inclinations and outlook of Millennials (some political and some not) or to the effects of the age group on the political landscape. Like many of the opinion pieces, discussions of young people's political inclinations or political worldview are a response to recently available survey data.

Most interesting for the purposes of this text are those news articles that address how this age cohort is impacting the political world. Specifically, some news reports offer examples of how candidates (or potential candidates) are appealing to Millennials. The *New York Times* reports how Hillary Clinton's discussion of expanding economic opportunities includes references to how her proposals will impact Millennials (May 17, 2014). The *Los Angeles Times* also has reported on Clinton's outreach efforts to young people (possible future supporters) at Clinton Global Initiative events – another example of how Millennials might affect the political landscape (March 22, 2014). There also were reports on how former presidential candidate Rand Paul might reach out to young people, quoting the candidate as stating that "I believe a Republican Party that is more tolerant and dedicated to keeping the government out of people's lives as much as possible would be more appealing to the rising generation" (*Washington Post*, March 13, 2013).

Similar outreach efforts to young voters by President Obama prior to the 2014 midterm elections were covered by the press. For example, the *New York Times* covered a town hall President Obama convened in California for young tech workers to celebrate economic gains during his presidency and economic opportunities for young people (October 8, 2014; October 9, 2014; October 17, 2014). As Kate Zezima of the *New York Times* reported (October 10, 2014), the town hall was part of a larger effort to appeal to Millennial voters for the election – an effort that included significant emphasis on youth's facility with technology, with President Obama remarking, "You're part of the first generation to grow up in the digital age ... Some of you grew up with cell phones tucked into your book bags, while others can remember the early days of landline, dial-up internet. You've gone from renting movies on VHS tapes to purchasing and downloading them in a matter of minutes." Finally, other reports indicate, beyond specific appeals by the president or potential candidates, how the presence of the Millennial demographic has affected and will affect the world of politics. For example, the *Los Angeles Times* reported on the social media campaign launched, with a significant Hollywood presence, in order to encourage young people to sign up for Obamacare (December 12, 2013). Citing research by the Sunlight Foundation, there even have been reports on how members of Congress are utilizing language in their floor speeches that might appeal to Millennials (*Washington Post*, March 9, 2014). These outreach efforts don't necessarily equal the energetic appeals by businesses such as Keds or Calvin Klein mentioned earlier in the chapter, but they offer some evidence of how the political world (at least some of parts of it) might be looking to accommodate the demographic – reaching out to Millennials via their tools of communication and speaking about issues facing their generation uniquely.

This exercise is a useful introduction to an exploration of Millennials – young citizens engaging in democracy and politics. Again, assuming media coverage frames the public's perception of a subject, one comes away from this study of coverage of Millennials with the impression that this age cohort is definitely making an impression on the world around them. The impression may not always be positive and opinions may vary, but it's clear that businesses, marketers, employers, and media outlets are making efforts to accommodate this body of young people and that their presence is being felt in these sectors of society. The same can't necessarily be said when it comes to Millennials' impact on politics. Coverage of the subject is comparatively modest, much of the coverage amounts to a summary of new survey data, and the ramifications of these data tend to be speculative. Unlike coverage of Millennials in the business or arts and entertainment sections, the story of young people's impact on the world of politics seems to be one still waiting to happen.

Conclusion

Much of the rest of this text focuses upon Millennials' interaction with the political world, how well we understand the political participation of young people, and what we still need to learn. The purpose of this chapter was to provide the necessary context for this discussion. By understanding their place in history, their qualities, and the way in which they're regarded, we'll more easily appreciate the high points and the deficits in youth engagement and our study of it.

So much of our scholarly consideration of the Millennial Generation amounts to a comparison between the nation's younger citizens and their generational counterparts – how turnout rates among young people compare to those of older generations, differences in news consumption, and the quality of civic duty and responsibility between generation. The tenor of much of the media coverage is the same. Examining youth engagement through a generational lens has great value. At the same time, such an approach can be limiting and risks us overlooking key differences between age groups. We can only follow this discussion, though, if we know who the key players are – what the difference is between a Millennial, a Generation Xer, a Baby Boomer and members of "the Greatest Generation."

Understanding the generation's defining characteristics is also critical if we're going to fully understand why youth engagement matters and what must be taken into consideration when studying young people. Millennials are impacted by contemporary politics and bring something to the political table that previous generations didn't – ethnic diversity, high levels of education, instant and accessible modes of communication, and a different outlook on themselves and their role in the world. On top of that, the sheer size of the generation (if activated) imbues this body of citizens with the potential for great and unique power.

For these reasons, this is a generation worth studying. Moreover, these features really define our study of young people – both in how we conceive of political participation and how we study it. For example, the increased prevalence of smartphones and social media has sparked new modes of political engagement from fundraising via text to "hashtag activism." Conceptually, scholars must consider the extent to which virtual modes of participation fall under the umbrella of "engagement." Methodologically too, scholars must be careful to consider the realities of the generation when constructing research designs. For example, methodologies heavily reliant on survey research that sample primarily college students overlook the reality that growing numbers of Millennials are "NCBY" or non-college bound youth. Sound findings require methodological approaches that are in tune with the features of the generation – features sketched in this chapter.

Finally, getting a good sense of the Millennial landscape has required not just highlighting the realities of what we know about the age group (the facts and figures) but also considering our collective perception of the generation. Again, the manner in which a phenomenon such as the Millennial Generation is "framed" by news outlets has an effect on the public's appreciation of this phenomenon. The media frame identified here is one that depicts Millennials as a force to be reckoned with in the worlds of business and arts and entertainment but an elusive and uncertain force politically, with little evidence of their political impact. As later chapters explore, this frame is reflected in the scholarly research on the political engagement of young people with a good deal of attention paid to the sorts of political activities Millennials pursue but little attention given either to strategies behind these actions or to the effects of these efforts. So not only might the picture painted of Millennials in the press reflect the extent to which candidates, campaigns, and the public at large view Millennials as relevant political players, it also mirrors the way in which scholars conceive of engagement and go about studying it.

On the other hand, perhaps the relative inattention to youth engagement's effects actually reflects the absence of political impact. Does the relative lack of coverage mean that young adults aren't engaging in the political process to a noticeable degree and, therefore, are having a negligible effect? If this chapter has been about the demographic realities of the Millennial Generation, it is the realities of the political participation of "citizen now" to which we turn our attention in the next chapter.

Think It Out

- Identify a pivotal historical, political, or cultural event in your memory. How has it affected your outlook or behavior?
- If democracy is based on the notion of "We the People," how do the qualities of the Millennial Generation bear on the health of American democracy?

Act It Out

- Interview family members or friends from different generations (parents, grandparents) and ask them about pivotal moments in their memory. Does their outlook or behavior reflect these examples?
- Gather a collection of media products (such as magazine ads, signs, television ads, newspaper articles, Internet graphics). What messages are conveyed about different age groups? Specifically, what images of young people are being conveyed in this content?

Notes

1 For a discussion of the factors influencing the generational perspective and the challenge of distinguishing between generational and life-cycle effects, see Zukin *et al.* (2006, 11–12).

2 The term "Greatest Generation" was popularized by Tom Brokaw's book of the same name.

3 For discussion regarding the insecurity and uncertainty marking this age group, see Zukin *et al.* (2006, 15) and Putnam (2000, 259).

4 According to Horovitz, the term "Generation Wii" was crafted by executives of Taco Bell, "iGeneration" was created by Jean Twenge but forgone for the term "Generation Me," and "Homeland Generation" was the result of a website contest launched by a company owned by the co-author of *Millennials Rising*, Neil Howe *(USA Today*, May 3, 2012).

5 The top ten news events for each of the years selected were gathered from the *World Almanac and Book of Facts* (1986–2013 editions).

6 See Howe and Strauss (2000) chapter 2 in general and table on pages 49–50 in particular.

7 For data strictly on young adults, see the Pew Research Center's Social and Demographic Trends division, "The Millennial Generation": www.pewsocialtrends.org/series/the-millennial-generation; the Center for Information and Research on Civic Learning and Engagement (CIRCLE): www.civicyouth.org; Harvard University, Institute of Politics (IOP): www.iop.harvard.edu/harvard-public-opinion-project; and the US Census Bureau and Current Population Surveys. Other datasets that have been used by scholars to paint a picture of Millennials that are not focused specifically on this age group include the General Social Survey conducted by the National Opinion Research Center, the National Annenberg Election Study, the American National Election Studies, the Bureau of Labor Statistics, and Gallup.

8 Zukin *et al.* place the number of Millennials at 71 million (2006, 14) and the Pew Research Center puts the number at 77 million (2010, 9).

9 Median age is defined as the "age at the midpoint of the population" (Howden and Meyer 2010, 4).

10 *Politico*: www.politico.com/2012-election/swing-state.

11 Much of the data presented in this section of the chapter come from the US Census Bureau and utilize the categorization system established by the Census Bureau that includes: Alaska Native, American Indian, Asian, Black, White, Hispanic.

12 US Census Bureau: http://quickfacts.census.gov/qfd/states/00000.html.

13 Of these residents, 23 percent were born in Asian countries, followed by 6 percent from European countries, and nearly 5 percent from African regions.

14 National Center for Education Statistics: http://nces.ed.gov/fastfacts/display.asp?id=31.

15 This definition comes from J.J. Heckman and P.A. LaFontaine, "The American High School Graduation Rate: Trends and Levels" and is quoted in Zaff *et al.* (2009, 7).

16 Zaff *et al.* (2009) cite Abby Kiesa and Karlo Barrios Marcelo, "Youth Demographics: Youth with No College Experience," in reaching this conclusion.

17 "Survey of Young Americans' Attitudes toward Politics and Public Service 25th Edition," March 22–April 4, 2014, Institute of Politics, Harvard University: www.iop.harvard.edu/sites/default/files_new/Harvard_ToplineSpring2014.pdf.

18 For the most current and extensive research conducted on the connection between the use of new media among young people and its implications, see the "Pew Internet & American Life Project": www.pewinternet.org, and the "Youth Participatory Politics Research Network": http://ypp.dmlcentral.net.

19 "Millennial Week": http://millennialweek.com/about.

20 Alliance for Audited Media: www.auditedmedia.com/news/blog/top-25-us-newspapers-for-march-2013.aspx.

21 Admittedly, this approach is imperfect. By searching only for articles, I excluded other web-based news items such as blog entries and videos. Also, some newspapers' online archives extend much further into the past than others. Moreover, not every site allows for a very refined search, which may result in an inflated count and include articles that utilize the words "millennial" and "generation" but don't match the context of this research.

It is important to note that the number of articles from the *New York Times* and *Washington Post* that emerge from the Westlaw search are far fewer than those that materialize through a search of the newspaper's site. I attribute this to the fact that Westlaw's search is more refined and eliminates duplicates and only identifies those in which the search terms appear in the title or first paragraphs. Articles identified via either Westlaw or web searches that were not applicable, such as those in which the words "millennial" and "generation" were used but unrelated, were eliminated from the database. The last entries to the database were made in November 2014.

22 I utilized a two-pronged approach in gathering these articles. Articles published in the *New York Times* and the *Washington Post* were located

via the Westlaw Database of news articles and, in my query, I searched for all articles in which "Millennial Generation" appeared in the headlines or lead paragraphs. Eliminating duplicates, this search led to a more refined count of articles regarding the subject matter. Westlaw Database does not house complete articles from *Wall Street Journal* or the *Los Angeles Times*, so these articles were gathered from the papers' websites.

23 To be sure, distinctions between these categories were not always clearcut – some articles discussing the nature of the generation in general addressed the politics of the generation and some of the political opeds included discussion of the demographics and outlook. In separating these pieces into these two broad categories, I focused upon what I discerned as the central thesis of the article in question.

## 2

Connecting to politics: expectations and actions

The alarm sounded by Putnam in *Bowling Alone* (2000) regarding the declining political participation of young adults ushered in a wave of research focused upon better understanding youth engagement. Putnam's work and much of the research that followed was sparked by steady declines in young adults' voter turnout rates since the late 1980s – especially in comparison to older generations. Some scholars have argued that this decline is a cause for alarm while others have asserted that the concurrent increase in other sorts of youth engagement, such as volunteering and online activism, signifies that Millennial engagement is simply different and even more expansive. Before evaluating the strength of these arguments and the methodologies scholars have followed in coming to these conclusions, a complete portrait of youth political engagement is needed. That's the purpose of this chapter.

Getting a firm handle on the state of political participation among America's young adults is no easy feat. On the one hand, voter turnout rates have been volatile with relatively high rates of participation in the 2008 electoral contest tempered by considerably lower rates in 2012 and then historically low youth voter turnout rates for 2014's midterm elections. Given these electoral realities, it's understandable that some scholars have focused upon the generational differences in voting rates. On the other hand, young adults seem to be very visible in recent years (both virtually and personally) in expressing their political opinions, and this political action is reflected in their attitudes regarding their efficacy as citizens and voters. Again, these facets of youth engagement explain the body of work generated by those scholars who have celebrated the extra-electoral engagement of Millennials.

In an effort, then, to provide the context necessary to appreciate these competing bodies of work, this chapter pulls together the disparate data on youth voter turnout and participation and offers a picture of the political action of young adults – recent turnout rates, rates of turnout over time, levels of youth participation in relation not only to other generations but to those within their generation, the background of the youth voter, and levels of participation in political activities beyond the ballot box. As this chapter will show, the realities of youth action today don't necessarily match youth attitudes about their power as citizens. Moreover, the realities of youth political participation today don't match the expectations of those who worked for the passage of the 26th Amendment that lowered the voting age to 18 – a history of which is presented in this chapter.

This mismatch of hopes and beliefs regarding youth engagement with the reality extends beyond this exercise and connects to the overarching themes of this text. As the content analysis from the previous chapter demonstrated, Millennials justifiably are garnering a good deal of attention and their impact is clear – except when it comes to politics. Although there have been counter-examples, such as strong turnout rates in the 2008 general election and the recent primary contests, youth engagement in traditional forms of political participation (voting in particular) is unlikely to match the rates of older generations anytime soon. Although other forms of engagement (beyond voting) show great promise and also are gathering attention, we have little evidence as of yet of their palpable effects on the political process. As subsequent chapters will show, conceptualizing youth engagement in such a way that it includes both the demonstrably and questionably effective runs the risk of stripping engagement of its core elements and badly positioning young adults to be effective democratic citizens.

Thoughts behind the action

When we conjure up images of the 1960s – the age of the Baby Boom generation – we often picture protests on college campuses, rallies in the streets, and civil rights demonstrations. It was a period in American history when politics seemed to be closely intertwined with the everyday lives of Americans – young adults in particular. It's fair to say that excitement surrounding the Obama presidency and recent exercises of activism via such movements as "Occupy Wall Street" and "Black Lives Matter" has rekindled the hope that young adults will connect to politics or be infused with a sense of political zeal similar to that of previous generations. Well, what do the data tell us? This section reviews the survey research on the connection between young adults and politics – how relevant the political process is to young adults, how confident they feel as members of the body politic, and the value they see in politics. Like their volatile turnout rates, this review suggests that although young adults don't see much value in the political process, most think of themselves as politically powerful.

Given the busyness swirling around the lives of average 18–24-year-olds (even those in their high school years), it wouldn't be a surprise if politics mattered little to them. Small-scale research conducted with local college and high school students certainly has confirmed this. For example, in focus groups with Rutgers students, most students report that, at this point in their lives, politics plays a minimal role. Looking ahead to the future, they believe they'll be engaged adults – when they own a home, have children, and are more settled. The implicit assumption is that they'll have more of a stake in the political process at that point and will be more apt to care. As one student, a resident of the New Jersey, stated in one focus group: "When you're older you may own a house and then you would pay property taxes in New Jersey and then when you have a voice in your community … that's what property taxes in New Jersey are used for … for schools and so on … I feel like it would be more real for me."[1] The limited interest in politics certainly extends to local high school students. For example, in a pilot of a civics assessment conducted in a handful of New Jersey high schools, most of the students surveyed agreed or strongly agreed with the statement, "Politics is boring compared to other things in my life."[2]

Clearly, these are just snapshots and not highly surprising. The bigger question, though, is the perceived utility of politics in the

minds of young adults. On that front, data derived from representative samples of the generation suggest that sizable segments of
today's youth population question the value of the political process
as a whole. For example, in a survey conducted in the fall of 2014,
Harvard University's Institute of Politics (IOP) asked respondents,
"In general, which do you think is the better way to solve important
issues facing the country – through political engagement or through
community volunteerism?" Of their sample,

- 42 percent answered community volunteerism;
- 18 percent answered political engagement;
- 37 percent indicated that they were not sure;
- 3 percent declined to answer.[3]

In a further endorsement for community engagement, in the same
IOP survey, 67 percent indicated that they were likely to volunteer
for community service if asked by a friend compared to 33 percent
who answered that they were likely to volunteer on a political campaign. At the very least, these numbers suggest that young adults are
more likely to view community involvement as more worthy of their
time than political action. Young adults' propensity to volunteer has
been heralded by some scholars as evidence that they're not nearly
as disengaged as some have accused them of being. That being said,
recent data available via the "National Conference on Citizenship"
indicate that volunteering rates may be weakening across all age
groups – including young adults. In fact, in 2013, Millennials' volunteering rates were the lowest relative to other age groups:

- 30 percent of Generation X volunteered 201.2 million hours of
  service (44 median hours);
- 28 percent of Baby Boomers volunteered 280.3 million hours of
  service (53 median hours);
- 24 percent of older Americans volunteered 187.2 million hours of
  service (92 median hours);
- 22 percent of Millennials volunteered a total of 145.9 million
  hours of service (36 median hours).[4]

Does young adults' expressed preference for volunteering relate to
their feelings regarding the effectiveness of political participation?
Since the mid-twentieth century, the American National Election

Table 2.1 Rates of efficacy, 1992–2008

People don't have a say in what the government does	1992	1994	1996	1998	2000	2002	2004	2008
% that agreed (total)	36	56	53	42	41	29	43	49
% that agreed (born 1991 or later)								43
% that agreed (born 1975–90)	*	54	42	42	40	25	43	47

Note: * fewer than 50 respondents to this question.

Source: American National Election Studies (ANES): www.electionstudies.org/nesguide/toptable/tab5b_2.htm.

Studies (ANES) have been gathering data on the political attitudes and behavior of Americans. Of the many attitudes they consider, these studies measure respondents' sense of political efficacy or their perception of the political impact they can make and allow us to zero in on Millennials' sense of their role in the process.

Table 2.1 presents the percentage of young adults (those born between 1975 and 1990) and those born after 1991 who indicated that they agreed with the statement, "People don't have a say in what the government does." As the data show, since about 1996, less than half of the young respondents have agreed with the statement – signifying that the majority of Millennials do believe that people have a say when it comes to governmental action. As the numbers indicate, the percentage that agreed with the statement was above 50 percent in 1994 and 1996 and dipped in 2002 but fairly consistently has remained either even or below the total percentage agreeing with the statement.

Survey data from the IOP shed light on these rates as respondents headed into the 2012 election. In their spring 2012 survey of a nationally representative sample of 18–29-year-olds (both college and non-college youth), the IOP reported even lower percentages of 18–29-year-olds who agreed with the statement, "People like me

Table 2.2 Rates of efficacy, 2012

People like me don't have any say about what the government does

	Total (18–29)	4-year college
NET: Agree	37	33
Strongly agree	13	11
Somewhat agree	24	22
Neither agree or disagree	34	32
NET: Disagree	29	34
Somewhat disagree	19	24
Strongly disagree	10	10
Decline to answer	1	1

Source: "Survey of Young Americans' Attitudes toward Politics and Public Service, 21st Edition," Institute of Politics, Harvard University: www.iop.harvard. edu/sites/default/files_new/spring_poll_12_topline.pdf.

don't have any say about what the government does" – an even more robust sign of self-efficacy (see Table 2.2). Notably, these rates were more pronounced for those who'd attained some college education. Signifying more confidence were reactions to the statement, "I don't believe my vote will make a real difference," with a plurality disagreeing (see Table 2.3). These rates of efficacy and confidence in one's vote at least suggest that most young people believe they can make a difference and believe it matters whether or not they vote. That being said, the percentage of young adults signifying a lack of efficacy or confidence in his or her vote is by no means negligible.

Whether or not the *sentiments* expressed in these surveys is reflected in the *actions* of the respondents and the generation they represent is the purpose of this chapter. Again, the goal here is to cross-reference perceptions of youth political participation with reality – voter turnout rates primarily but also levels of campaign involvement and other measurements of participation. Although resistant to follow the pattern of those who define today's youth by comparing them to their predecessors, it is worth providing a bit of context. To be sure, much ink has been spilled and plenty of airtime spent decrying the low voter turnout rates of young adults and the

Table 2.3 Importance of voting

I don't believe my vote will make a real difference

	Total (18–29)	4-year college
NET: Agree	29	28
Strongly agree	10	8
Somewhat agree	19	20
Neither agree or disagree	33	31
NET: Disagree	37	40
Somewhat disagree	21	25
Strongly disagree	16	15
Decline to answer	1	1

Source: "Survey of Young Americans' Attitudes toward Politics and Public Service, 21st Edition," Institute of Politics, Harvard University: www.iop.harvard.edu/sites/default/files_new/spring_poll_12_topline.pdf.

disengagement this supposes. Although it's easy to dismiss these criticisms as reprimands or even generational nostalgia, it is worth re-examining both the motivation and the expectations for expanding the franchise and assuring 18-year-olds the right to vote in the early 1970s. This is a history that not many young adults know (not many older adults either, for that matter). Not only does this history help to explain older citizens' consternation with younger citizens, it also provides an important marker against which we can measure the vitality of democratic citizenship among America's younger citizens.

Extending the franchise: lowering the voting age

At the time of this writing, a movement is bubbling to lower the voting age even beyond 18 years of age. In Maryland, for example, city councils in Hyattsville and Takoma Park lowered the voting age to 16, allowing younger residents to vote in local elections. As the *Washington Post* reported, supporters young and old held that "If 16- and 17-year-olds can drive, hold a job and pay taxes, … they should also help decide who represents them in public office" (January 14, 2015).

Proponents of lowering the voting age, such as Peter Levine, argue not only that such an effort is democratic, "If the government affects you, you get to vote" (*Politico Magazine*, February 24, 2015), but also that it heightens the chances of participation. As Levine writes, "At 17, most people are still living at home, where they can see parents voting and probably hear about local issues and candidates. They are still at school, where voting can be encouraged and become a social norm" (*Politico Magazine*, February 24, 2015). In sum, allowing 16- and 17-year-olds to vote not only serves as a valuable civic learning experience but also promises to remedy anemic turnout rates.

This isn't the first time the voting age has been debated, of course. Most discussions of voter turnout rates among young people begin with the first election that took place after the voting age was lowered from 21 to 18 – 1972. But what precipitated that effort? It's worth comparing the arguments for lowering the voting age offered today (that it will boost turnout among 18-year-olds) to those offered when it was passed in the early 1970s. If contemporary efforts are being advanced today as a remedy for poor youth voter turnout, they stand in stark contrast to those offered in the 1970s – that it was the right thing to do.

Given the social and political tumult of the 1960s and the central role that college campuses played in fostering and advancing social movements, it's natural to assume that lowering the voting age in the early 1970s was in part a response to the Vietnam War and the draft. To be sure, this was a motivating factor that spurred the effort. For example, the "National Commission on the Causes and Prevention of Violence," convened in the fall of 1969, advocated reforms both in administering the draft and lowering the voting age to 18 as promising methods for integrating alienated youth and curbing their violent tendencies. As reported in the *New York Times*, the chair of the commission suggested that young people are "highly motivated by ideals of justice, equality, candor, peace," but required outlets to channel these ideals in a productive way (November 26, 1969). However, the roots of the effort to lower the voting age from 21 to 18 can be found in another war – World War II.[5]

In what would be the start of a nearly 30-year effort, Congressman Jennings Randolph from West Virginia first proposed in 1942 that the Constitution be amended to afford those 18 years and older the right to vote. His action was a response to lowering the legal age that one could be drafted from 21 to 18 by President Franklin Roosevelt in October 1942 during the throes of World War II. For the next 30 years, Randolph would be an advocate for lowering the voting age to 18 – an action supported by Presidents Eisenhower and Johnson and unsuccessfully advanced via numerous failed resolutions in Congress.

It wasn't until the late 1960s, though, that the effort to lower the voting age gained traction – not as an amendment to the US Constitution but initially as an extension of the Voting Rights Act by Congress in 1970. By this time, the United States had been embroiled in the war in Vietnam for nearly ten years and had incurred an estimated 48,736 casualties – approximately 40,000 of these deaths occurring between 1967 and 1970.[6] It's clear that the disparity between youth's eligibility to fight but not to vote permeated the debate over lowering the voting age. As one witness at Senate hearings testified, "the brunt of fighting and dying in a prolonged and unpopular war falls with particular force on those between the ages of 18 and 21 ... If taxation without representation was tyranny, then conscription without representation is slavery" (*New York Times*, February 17, 1970).

Rather than try to shepherd the reform through the time-consuming process of amending the US Constitution, in February 1970, Senators Edward Kennedy of Massachusetts and Birch Bayh of Indiana spearheaded an effort to attach as an amendment to the Voting Rights Act of 1965 the proposal to lower the voting age to 18 in all local, state, and federal elections (*New York Times*, February 23, 1970). Although President Nixon had endorsed the idea of lowering the voting age to 18 (at least in federal elections) as a constitutional amendment just days earlier (*New York Times*, February 18, 1970), there was opposition within the administration as well as among members of Congress from both parties to reforming the voting age at all levels via legislation. Specifically, the reform tactic opened up a debate regarding states' rights and the appropriate role of Congress. Hailing the legislative approach as "novel constitutional theory," an op-ed published at the time explained that lowering the voting age via the Voting Rights Act was justified on the grounds that state laws that don't allow 18–21-year-olds to vote violate those citizens' 14th Amendment rights and are, therefore, discriminatory (*New York Times*, March 29, 1970). Others disagreed, including Democratic Senator Sam J. Ervin from North Carolina and Democratic Representative Emanuel Cellar from New York, who held that such a change could only be made via constitutional amendment (*Washington Post, Times Herald*, March 5, 1970 and March 17, 1970).

Other opposition to lowering the voting age seems to have had less to do with the Constitution and more to do with politics. Some legislators and even some civil rights advocates, although supportive of lowering the voting age in principle, opposed the legislative tactic because it threatened the extension of the Voting Rights Act (*Washington Post, Times Herald*, March 5, 1970 and March 23, 1970). Then of course there were concerns over which party would benefit if the electorate included 18–21-year-olds – a debate that has surrounded such recent reforms as the "motor-voter" bill and voter identification laws passed by state legislatures. "Of course, others opposed lowering the voting age to 18 on principle – holding that young people just weren't ready to vote. As Representative Cellar stated, 'Their minds are too malleable,' … 'too subject to the emotional appeals of demagogues'" (*Washington Post, Times Herald*, March 17, 1970).

Despite all of these concerns, the amendment to the Voting Rights Act lowering the voting age to 18 in local, state, and federal elections passed Congress in the spring of 1970. With its passage, 11 million citizens between the ages of 18 and 21 were folded into the eligible voting population (*New York Times*, June 19, 1970). Its passage certainly reflected the will of the people. As the *Washington Post, Times Herald* reported at the time (April 5, 1970), public opinion polling conducted by Gallup indicated clear and long-standing support for lowering the voting age. When asked "Do you think that persons 18, 19, and 20 years old should be permitted to vote or not?," 58 percent indicated that they should be allowed to vote, 38 percent indicated they should not (4 percent expressed no opinion). Public support for lowering the voting age was not novel – in 1953, Gallup found that 63 percent of those surveyed supported lowering the voting age. In all polling on the topic, opposition to the reform tended to cluster among older, more affluent, and more conservative respondents.

Interestingly, despite public approval for lowering the voting age, state by state proposals to extend the franchise to 18–21-year-olds were unsuccessful in the years prior to this legislation's passing. As the *New York Times* reported, some speculated that student protests and youth unrest in the 1960s contributed to the failure of these state efforts (June 23, 1970). In fact, in the same year the voting age was lowered by Congress, proposals on state ballots to lower the voting age actually were defeated in most of the states considering the reform (*New York Times*, November 5, 1970).

Whether or not President Nixon would sign the legislation lowering the voting age into law, though, was far from certain. Upon its passage, the president expressed concerns over its constitutionality, doubting that it would "stand the test of challenge in the courts" given that the Constitution states in "clear and precise terms" that power to change electoral law belonged to the states (*New York Times*, April 28, 1970). He also expressed concerns about the effects on the 1972 elections if the Supreme Court ultimately declared the Act of Congress unconstitutional. Documents made available to the public via the Richard Nixon Library and the National Archives offer a glimpse into the Oval Office's reaction to the legislative action to lower the voting age. Figure 2.1 shows notes from a meeting that took place between President Nixon and John Ehrlichman on March 17, 1970 in which the president's desire to defeat the legislation and line up support for a Constitutional Amendment are clear.

Ultimately, President Nixon signed the legislation into law on June 22, 1970. As an op-ed published in the *New York Times* asserted, linking lowering the voting age to the ultimate legislative achievement of the civil rights movement made it nearly impossible for President Nixon to stand in its way:

> There is no conceivable advantage for Mr. Nixon in a veto that would not be outweighed by the onus he would bear for vetoing also the Voting Rights Act, the renewal of which is a basic part of the bill that approves the eighteen-year-old vote. He cannot veto the one without vetoing the other – the legislation which has done so much to guarantee black political participation in the South. (June 21, 1970)

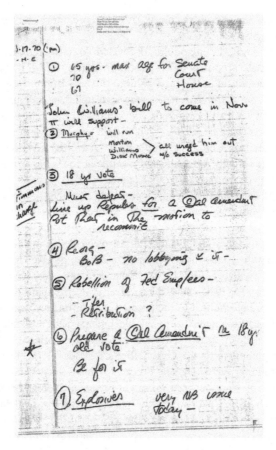

Figure 2.1 Ehrlichman's notes regarding lowering the voting age

Upon signing the legislation though, Nixon tasked his Attorney General to quickly move the legislation through the courts in order to test its constitutional validity and, thereby, avoid future electoral confusion:

> An early test is essential because of the confusion and uncertainty surrounding an act of doubtful constitutionality that purports to extend the franchise. Until this uncertainly is resolved, any

> elections – including primary elections, and even local referenda
> on such questions as school bond issues – could have their results
> clouded by legal doubt. (*New York Times*, June 23, 1970)

At the same time, he urged Congress to prepare and advance a constitutional amendment on the matter in the event of the legislation's voiding by the Supreme Court. This turned out to be sage advice. In December 1970, the Supreme Court in the case *Oregon v. Mitchell* found that, although Congress could lower the voting age to 18 in federal elections, it was beyond the power of the legislative branch to lower the voting age for state and local elections. As the *Wall Street Journal* reported at the time, the decision was divided along ideological lines: "It didn't produce a single opinion of a majority covering the entire matter, but five opinions totaling 150 pages" (December 22, 1970). On the critical issue of states' rights, Justice Black wrote that Congress did not have the authority to "convert our national Government of enumerated powers into a central government of unrestrained authority over every inch of the whole nation."

With the 1972 election on the horizon, Congress and the White House needed to act quickly to thwart any electoral confusion regarding voter eligibility:

> The desirability of speedy action on this amendment should be obvious. Without its adoption and under the laws as they now stand, the 1972 election will be a mess in many states. Voters between 18 and 21 will be eligible to participate in federal but not state and local elections that year. The result will be, in some places, two sets of registration rolls and either two sets of voting machines or ballots. (*Washington Post, Times Herald*, March 8, 1971)

With record speed, an amendment to the Constitution was prepared and advanced. No easy process, an amendment to the Constitution can be passed in one of four ways:

- passed by a two-thirds vote in both the House and Senate and then ratified by a majority vote in three-quarters of state legislatures;
- passed by a two-thirds vote in both houses of Congress and then ratified by conventions in three-quarters of the states;
- as a response to petitions by two-thirds of states, Congress can call a national convention the results of which must be ratified by a majority of three-quarters of the state legislatures;

- passage in a national convention and then ratified by conventions called by three-quarters of the states.

Given the cumbersome and nearly impossible process, it's no wonder supporters opted for a legislative solution. Even more remarkable, given the practicalities of the process, is the speed by which the 26th Amendment that lowered the voting age to 18 was passed. Shepherded by Representative Cellar in the House and Senator Bayh in the Senate, the proposed amendment was approved by two-thirds majorities in both houses of Congress by March 1971 and sent to the states for ratification.[7] It would take majority approval in three-fourths (38) of the state legislatures to ratify the amendment. On July 1, Ohio became the thirty-eighth state to approve the proposal and officially amend the Constitution to extend the franchise to 18-year-olds. With that, the 26th Amendment became the fastest amendment ever to be approved – besting the record six months and six days it took to ratify the 12th Amendment in 1804 that called for separating balloting for president and vice-president (*New York Times*, April 7, 1971).

Just days later, President Nixon held a festive ceremony on July 5 in the East Room of the White House at which the chief of the General Services Administration, Robert Kunzig, certified the amendment. In an unprecedented move, President Nixon invited three young people to join the ceremony and certify the amendment with their signatures: Julianne Jones (Memphis, TN), Paul Larimee (Concord, CA), and Joseph W. Loyd Jr. (Detroit, MI). The three were members of the singing group "Young Americans in Concert" and the group offered a rousing rendition of the "Battle Hymn of the Republic" after the amendment's certification.[8]

Lowering the voting age was an idea whose time had come. As records made available from the National Archives and the Richard Nixon Library make clear, it also was an idea that required subsequent political strategizing. Extending the franchise to 18-year-olds meant that 25 million young adults were eligible to vote in the 1972 election (about 11 million of whom were enfranchised thanks to the 26th Amendment) (*New York Times*, May 18, 1971). Memos prepared by the administration make it clear that President Nixon was keen on both understanding and wooing these newly enfranchised young voters. For example, in a memo they prepared for the president synthesizing survey data regarding youth and their support for Nixon, aides Robert Finch and Charles Colson wrote:

> More than any other previous generation, they resent being talked down to by their elders; hence, it is almost impossible to attack one without attacking them all ... when we even refer to the violent radicals, even the moderates take offense. The wide spread belief among youth is that the President, even more so, the Vice President are hostile to them.[9]

President Nixon himself seems to have been very attentive to how to bring this large number of young adults into the fold in time for the 1972 election – even weighing in on voter registration tactics. In a memo prepared for aide Bob Haldeman, the president advocates targeting outreach efforts to their most likely young supporters – non-college youth:

> In studying the *New York Times* release of the Gallup Poll on youth one lesson comes through loud and clear – it is imperative that we limit our registration efforts wherever possible, without announcing that that is our tactic, to the non-college youth ... generally speaking we have to realize that there is about a two to one chance that college youth will vote for McGovern. There is about an even chance that the non-college youth will vote for us.[10]

Of course, such strategizing begs the question that was asked at the passage of the 26th Amendment and continues to be asked – "But will they vote?" Reporting at the time indicates that experts were dubious about the effects. In the absence of a uniting issue to mobilize them, conventional wisdom was that adding 18–21-year-olds to the rolls would have only a slight impact on voting behavior and vote choice. Referencing an adage used by political scientist David B. Truman, R.W. Apple wrote that "lowering the voting age to 6 would make no great difference in election results unless free bubble gum were a major issue" (*New York Times*, December 22, 1970). Mobility promised to keep turnout low among youth and, despite assumptions at the time, differences within the cohort made it unlikely that one party would benefit substantially (*New York Times*, June 28, 1970). There are echoes of these themes in current discussions of youth political participation.

"Old enough to fight, old enough to vote" was a rallying cry initiated during World War II and brought back into the national rhetoric during the Vietnam Era. Whether or not it would result in a politically engaged group of young citizens probably was beside the point at the time. Given the number of 18–21-year-olds fighting and dying abroad, it was generally agreed that giving them the power to vote was the right thing to do. The passage of the 26th Amendment also made the dream conceived by Senator Randolph some 30 years earlier a reality. As the *New York Times* reported at his death, upon seeing his legislative goal come true, Randolph stated, "I believe that our young people possess a great social conscience, are perplexed by the injustices which exist in the world and are anxious to rectify these ills" (May 9, 1998). The extent to which young adults actively sought to address these ills and the methods they've pursued is the focus for the remainder of this chapter.

The youth vote

In the next few chapters, a good deal of attention will be dedicated to exploring various, often conflicting, conceptualizations of political engagement. To be sure, much of this discussion involves the importance of voting or where voting ranks in the "hierarchy of engagement." It is worth acknowledging at the outset then that voting is not the only method available to citizens if they want to effect change, or even always the most effective. At the same time, it goes without saying that voting plays a pivotal function in a representative democracy and is one important measure of the health of a democracy. Moreover, the voting behavior of a group (an age group in this case) is a reflection of how well it is being represented in the halls of power. As this chapter makes clear, there is reason to be concerned about young adults' representation politically given their current rates of participation on Election Day.

From a research standpoint, consistent data availability also makes this indicator a productive method for documenting political participation over time, comparing participation rates between sub-groups, and discerning the qualities of the average voter – the young voter in our case. Much like the previous chapter, this chapter offers a depiction of the Millennial as a member of the political community – a view of how young people today engage in the political process and the degree of their involvement. Given that it took 30 or so years to extend the voting age to 18, a good place to begin is voter turnout rates of young people since the passage of the 26th Amendment.

With data available from the US Census Bureau, we're able to track the extent to which young adults today and young people over time have exercised their right to vote. Figure 2.2 offers a voting history of the total percentage of the population that voted since the passage of the 26th Amendment.[11] As we see, in presidential election years, turnout rates for America's youngest voters (those aged 18–24) have averaged about 40 percent. Rates peaked in a few elections – to nearly 50 percent the first year following the passage of the 26th Amendment and then again in 2008 in the election contest between Barack Obama and John McCain. These rates also have experienced noticeable drops – most dramatically in 2000 when turnout rates for the total population of 18–24-year-olds hovered at 32 percent. Keeping in mind the discussion in the previous chapter, if we use 1976 as the starting point for the beginning of the Millennial Generation, the election of 1996 was the first presidential election year in which members of this age cohort were eligible

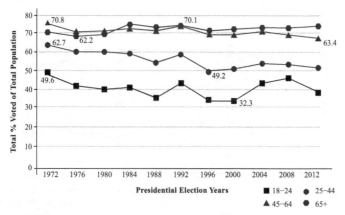

Notes: Prior to 1996, the CPS did not collect information on citizenship in a uniform way. Estimates for the citizenship population presented in this table prior to 1996 should be interpreted with caution, as they are not directly comparable to estimates from 1996 and after.

Figure 2.2 Voter turnout rates by age, presidential election years

to vote. As we see, turnout rates for America's youngest voters that year stood at 32.4 percent.

These data also allow us to compare the voter turnout rates of America's youngest voters to older age cohorts. As we see, on average, voter turnout rates for older age groups are markedly higher than younger citizens. Over the course of this 35-year period, voter turnout rates for 25–44-year-olds average 55 percent among the total population. For both the 45–64-year-olds and those aged 65 and over, the average voter turnout rate over this same period of time was 65 percent. As these numbers suggest, voting seems to be a behavior most popular among those who are middle-aged and older, with decreasing popularity the younger voters get.

Not surprisingly, the same can be said for voting in off-year elections. Figure 2.3 displays voter turnout rates over the same period of time for the midterm election years and demonstrates that patterns are fairly similar to turnout levels in presidential contest years. On average, turnout rates in midterm elections for the total population have been 19 percent for 18–24-year-olds since the voting age was lowered. All age groups outpace the youngest cohort by fairly hefty

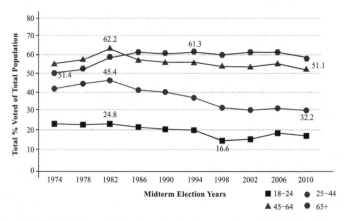

Notes: Prior to 1996, the CPS did not collect information on citizenship in a uniform way. Estimates for the citizenship population presented in this table prior to 1996 should be interpreted with caution, as they are not directly comparable to estimates from 1996 and after.

Figure 2.3 Voter turnout rates by age, midterm election years

margins – 25–44-year-olds voting at an average rate of 35 percent, 45–64-year-olds voting at an average 51 percent, and those aged 65 and over voting on average at 54 percent.

As the note in Figures 2.2 and 2.3 indicate, it's only been since 1996 that citizenship data have been collected in a uniform way. Figures 2.4 and 2.5 offer the rates of voter turnout for presidential and midterm elections for these age groups since then and compare the turnout numbers for total versus citizen population. Not surprisingly, for all age groups, this careful calculation results not only in a more accurate accounting of voter turnout but also slightly higher rates of turnout. For the presidential election years

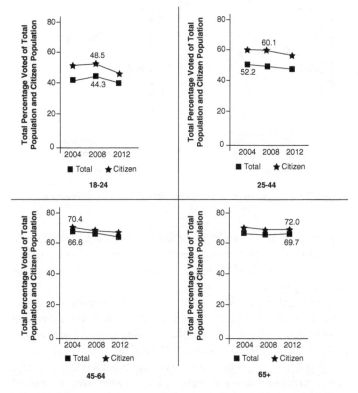

Figure 2.4 Voter turnout rates citizen population, presidential election

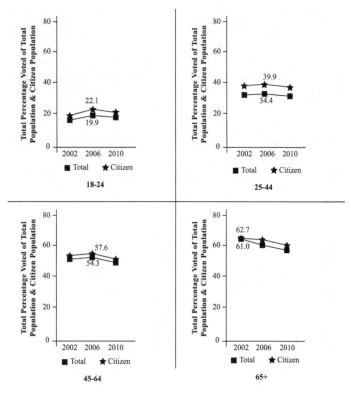

Figure 2.5 Voter turnout rates citizen population, midterm election

in particular, there seems to be the most notable distinction between total and citizen population among 18–24 and 25–44-year-olds – evidence most likely of the high numbers of immigrants among the younger age cohorts.

A reasonable question to ask is whether comparatively lower voter turnout rates among young people simply are a function of their age. Perhaps such factors as voting inexperience, mobility, and the busyness associated with settling into college and/or adulthood hamper youth turnout now but, once these burdens have eased, turnout rates will increase with age. Essentially, we're faced with the question of whether political behavior, voting in this case, is a function of one's generation or their stage in life – a topic discussed in the previous chapter. One way to address this question is to look at the voter turnout rates of traditionally strong voters (older citizens) when they were young. Like young people in the last 30 or so years, did Baby Boomers and members of the "Greatest Generation" also vote at lower levels when they were young?

Available turnout data offer at least a partial answer to these questions. Via the US Census Bureau, we have voter turnout data for various age groups (in both midterm and presidential election years) as far back as 1964. These data allow us:

- to compare the voting rates of older citizens against their younger selves and
- to compare the turnout rates of the young people of the 1960s to the young people of the 1970s and beyond.

These comparisons are imperfect, of course. First, these data stretch back only to 1964 – voter turnout rates from earlier years certainly would enhance this effort. Second, as we know, from 1964 to 1972, not all 18–21-year-olds were eligible to vote. State law in only a selection of states (Georgia, Kentucky, Alaska, Hawaii) allowed voting under 21, and it wasn't until the passage of the 26th Amendment that 18–21-year-olds nationwide could go to the polls. The census data available for those aged 18–24 then actually is for those between 21 and 24 years of age. Third, some of these age ranges are quite broad and don't allow us to discern differences between younger and older members of these age groups. Despite these limitations, the comparisons are enlightening.

Table 2.4 provides the turnout rates for 18–24 and 25–44-year-olds in the presidential and midterm elections that took place between 1964 and the lowering of the voting age to 18 in 1972. This table also includes the ages of the young voters of the 1960s in recent elections (the 2010 midterm and the 2012 presidential elections). Again, these data allow us to compare the voting rates of today's most dependable voters to their rates when they were young as well as compare the voting behavior of young voters across decades.

As we see, today's strongest voters (those aged 45 and older) certainly didn't vote when they were younger at the rates they do now.

Table 2.4 Youth voter turnout rates, 1964–70

Presidential election year	Total % voted total population (18–24 years old)	Total % voted total population (25–44 years old)
1964	50.9	69
Age in 2012	66–72	73–92
1968	50.4	66.6
Age in 2012	62–68	69–88
Midterm election year		
1966	31.1	53.1
Age in 2010	62–68	69–88
1970	30.4	51.9
Age in 2010	58–64	65–84

Source: US Census Bureau, Current Population Survey, November 2012 and earlier reports.

As we saw in Figure 2.2, for the 2012 election, more than 70 percent of voters aged 65 and older turned out on Election Day. The youngest of today's oldest voters (those who fell in that 18–24-year-old bracket in the 1960s) didn't vote at the rates they voted in 2012 back when they were young. Instead, turnout rates stood at about 50 percent. The same can be said about this group's voting behavior in midterm elections in the 1960s. In 2010, voter turnout rates among the 65 and over age cohort was 59 percent. In 1966 and 1970, these same citizens' voter turnout rates stood at about 30 percent. To be sure, then, voter turnout rates increased for this age group (the youngest of today's oldest voters), thereby offering some support for the argument that life-cycle effects are at play when explaining voting behavior.

That being said, it's also worth comparing the voter turnout rates of the young voters of the 1960s to the young voters of today (and those in between). Although their turnout rates in the 1960s didn't match their rates of voting in 2012, the voting behavior of Baby Boomers and the World War II generation when they were young outpaced today's youth vote. As shown in Figure 2.2, 38 percent of all 18–24-year-olds voted in the 2012 election, 12 percent lower than their counterparts in 1964 and 1968. Certainly the same can be said when we compare turnout rates for midterm elections. In 2010, about 20 percent of all 18–24-year-olds voted – about 10 percent less than young voters of the 1960s. These comparisons then offer some support for the generational argument – voting rates certainly increased over time for many of those first voting in the 1960s, but the voting history of Baby Boomers and the World War II generation started stronger than subsequent generations.

A close look at the long-term voting behavior of the oldest members of the nation's oldest age cohort is even more interesting and offers more support for the generational explanation. Voters who fell in the 25–44 age range in the 1960s currently are in their late sixties, seventies, eighties, and even nineties – mostly members of the World War II generation. Interestingly, their strong turnout rates today mirror their rates of voting when they were young. In 2012, rates of turnout for those aged 65 and over stood at 70 percent. In 1964, 25–44-year-olds (those who were between the ages of 73 and 92 in 2012) voted at the same rate – 69 percent. Comparisons between 2012 and 1968 also are consistent – the 25–44-year-olds of 1968 voted at a rate just 2 percent lower than in 2012 when they voted as 70- or 80-year-olds. Nearly the same can be said when it comes to the midterm elections recently and in the 1960s. At least according to these comparisons, life-cycle explanations don't seem to apply here.

Comparisons between voting counterparts also reveal further generational differences. The voter turnout rates of the older members of the oldest age cohort (those who fell in the 25–44-year-old bracket in the 1960s) certainly voted at stronger rates in the 1960s than 25–44-year-olds did in 2012 and 2010. In 2012 and 2010, 25–44-year-olds' voter turnout rates were nearly 20 percent lower than those of the same age in the 1960s. Again, these comparisons offer stronger support for the argument that voting behavior is a function primarily of one's generation as opposed to stage in life.

Given that the thrust of this text is looking at the political behavior of young adults now, what's the relevance of these generational comparisons in voter turnout rates? The relevance lies in how these differences in voting behavior affect representation. Census data makes clear that, relative to their eligibility, younger voters consistently under-vote (File 2014, 7–8). In contrast, older Americans "vote at higher rates than their share of the eligible population" (File 2014, 7) with a noteworthy gap in voting rates between younger and older voters in 2012. Given differences in policy preferences, this reality means that youth views will not be realized in public policy. As the *Washington Post*'s Emily Badger noted,

> Younger and older Americans have divergent views on a number of public policy questions, from gay marriage to legalized marijuana to immigration. And, particularly on social issues – where older voters tend to be more conservative – policy could shift more slowly than public opinion data would suggest if the demographic driving attitude change in America doesn't turn out to vote at rates in line with its full potential influence. (April 24, 2014)

Generational comparisons, then, are about more than highlighting the weaknesses of one generation versus another but about documenting the effects of these differences. As Badger correctly states, "To the extent that younger would-be voters have very different views than their parents and grandparents on these questions, they're currently not translating those views in the voting booth as loudly as they could" (*Washington Post*, April 24, 2014).

Another approach for gaining some insight on this topic is to look at voting patterns of Millennials themselves as they've matured. As indicated in the previous chapter, the oldest members of the youngest generation are approaching 40 years of age and have been eligible to vote for nearly 20 years now. Again, thanks to Census data, we can track the voting rates of Millennials as they've aged. Tables 2.5 and 2.6 lay out the voter turnout rates of a selection of Millennials for all of the presidential and midterm elections in which they've been eligible to vote. In addition, their age at the time of the elections in question is documented. For example, Table 2.5 shows that the first presidential election in which those born in 1976 voted were the 1996 elections. That year, those born in 1976 were 20 years old and their voter turnout rate was 33.4 percent.

Is there any reason, then, to believe that Millennials' turnout numbers will improve as they get older? The rates presented here suggest that, for each of the years selected throughout this time period, the voting history for that set of voters improved with each election with only minor exceptions. For example, just under

Table 2.5 Millennial voter turnout rates by year of birth, presidential elections

Year of birth	% turnout 1996/ year of age	% turnout 2000/ year of age	% turnout 2004/ year of age	% turnout 2008/ year of age	% turnout 2012/ year of age
	33.7/18 to 20 years of age**	36.1/18 to 24 years of Age**	48.6/18 to 28 years of age**	52.4/18 to 32 years of age*	49.2/18 to 36 years of age*
1976	36.2/20 years of age	41.9/24 years of age	55.4/28 years of age	58.6/32 years of age	59.7/36 years of age
1978	31.6/18 years of age	42.8/22 years of age	50.9/26 years of age	58.4/30 years of age	56.1/34 years of age
1980		32.7/20 years of age	49.8/24 years of age	54.9/28 years of age	57/32 years of age
1982		29.3/18 years of age	46.2/22 years of age	55.4/26 years of age	54.7/30 years of age
1984			46.5/ 20 years of age	52.8/24 years of age	52.1/28 years of age
1986			42/18 years of age	50.7/ 22 years of age	48.8/26 years of age
1988				46.8/20 years of age	46.5/24 years of age
1990				42.7/18 years of age	44.3/22 years of age
1992					42.3/20 years of age
1994					33.4/18 years of age

Source: US Census Bureau, Current Population Survey, November 1994–2012.

Table 2.6 Millennial voter turnout rates by year of birth, midterm elections

	% turnout 1994/year of age	% turnout 1998/year of age	% turnout 2002/year of age	% turnout 2006/year of age	% turnout 2010/year of age
	14.8/18 years of age**	**16.9/18 to 22 years of age****	**20.5/18 to 26 years of age****	**26/18 to 30 years of age***	**26.9/18 to 34 years of age***
1976	14.8/18 years of age	19.2/22 years of age	27.2/26 years of age	33/30 years of age	36.5/34 years of age
1978		17.1/20 years of age	24.4/24 years of age	32.9/28 years of age	35.5/32 years of age
1980		11/18 years of age	21.3/22 years of age	27.6/26 years of age	32/30 years of age
1982			18.3/20 years of age	28.7/24 years of age	28.7/28 years of age
1984			14.5/18 years of age	23.6/22 years of age	24.8/26 years of age
1986				21.9/20 years of age	25.3/24 years of age
1988				16.5/18 years of age	23/22 years of age
1990					20.7/20 years of age
1992					14.8/18 years of age

Source: US Census Bureau, Current Population Survey, November 1994–2012.

14 percent of the Millennials born in 1976, whose first election was the 1994 midterm election, showed up to the polls that year. By the time this same group of voters reached the age of 34, their turnout rate had improved to nearly 36.5 percent. The same held true for this group when it comes to presidential elections. In 1996, about 33 percent turned out to vote. By the 2012 election, nearly 60 percent of this subset of Millennials (36 years of age by this point) was voting. As the data show, it was only in the 2012 presidential election that rates dipped slightly or at least held steady. Certainly, this gives credence to the notion that maturation heightens the likelihood of improved voter turnout rates.

This exercise also indicates that, as the generation as a whole has matured, Millennials' baseline voting rates have fluctuated but have not shown consistent and marked improvement. For example, 1994 was the first year those born in 1976 were eligible to vote, and barely 14 percent showed up on Election Day. As Millennials have turned 18 and been eligible to vote in midterm elections, rates have ticked upwards (to 16.5 percent in 2006) but then dipped again (to 14.8 percent in 2010). The same can be said regarding the presidential elections. For example, 18-year-olds voting for the first time in 1996 showed up at a rate of 29.8 percent. The rates of 18-year-olds casting their ballots in subsequent presidential contests dipped to 26.7 percent in 2000, peaked at 42.7 percent in 2008, and then dipped again to 33.4 percent in 2012. These numbers amplify earlier findings – although young adults' voting history shows signs of improvement as they get older, maturation of the generation as a whole doesn't seem to be improving baseline rates of involvement. Not only does this buttress the generational explanation for youth engagement, it underscores the reality that, given their starting point, Millennials have little likelihood of matching the voting rates of older generations.

By looking at the data from the 2012 elections, this section on voting concludes by exploring who votes – what are the demographics of youth voters, what sort of background do they share, and do those states heavily populated by Millennials also exhibit strong voting behavior? This examination echoes themes planted in the first chapter – although this is the nation's most diverse generation, these differences often aren't reflected in their behavior.

Figure 2.6 displays the voting behavior of young voters according to their ethnic background. As the US Census Bureau reports, there have been inconsistent patterns in voter turnout rates by age and ethnic background in elections since 1996 (File 2013, 6–8). For example, from 1996 to 2004, White voters between the ages of 25 and 44 voted in increasingly larger percentages but then reversed those patterns between 2004 and 2012. Among young Black voters, rates of turnout have shown increases of varying degrees since 1996 until 2012, when rates among all young voters dropped except among Blacks between the ages of 25 and 44. Young Hispanics also have shown volatility. Between 1996 and 2008, all young Hispanics experienced increases in voting rates (some modest and some more dramatic). From 2008 to 2012, though, Hispanics aged 18–24 and 25–44 experienced drops in voter participation.

A close look at 2012 in particular (Figure 2.6) shows that among all voters of the citizen population, Whites and Blacks voted at higher rates than Asians and Hispanics. This was a trend that extended into the younger age cohorts. Of 18–24-year-olds, nearly 49 percent of young Blacks turned out compared to 42 percent of Whites, 34 percent of Hispanics and 31 percent of Asians. Patterns

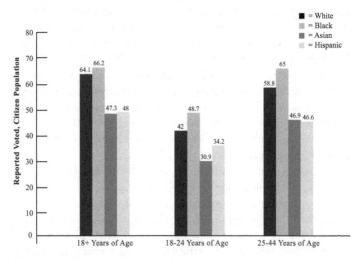

Figure 2.6 Youth voter turnout by ethnicity

Table 2.7 Percentage voted by educational attainment and age, 2012

Selected characteristics	18 to 24		25 to 44	
	% registered	% voted, US citizen population	% registered	% voted, US citizen population
Total	53.6	41.2	68.7	57.3
Less than 9th grade	6.1	0.5	24.2	16.6
9th to 12th grade, no diploma	33.0	24.9	43.4	28.1
High school graduate	42.1	29.1	56.4	42.1
Some college or associate degree	63.7	50.1	71.0	58.2
Bachelor's degree	74.7	63.0	79.4	71.0
Advanced degree	67.5	55.9	85.0	79.1

Source: US Census Bureau, Current Population Survey, November 2012.

were similar among 25–44-year-olds but with some of these racial gaps diminishing.

In addition to racial differences, educational attainment and economic status also seem to be reflected in the voting patterns of young people. The data presented in Table 2.7, for example, show that among both 18–24-year-olds and 25–44-year-olds, attaining some college education seems to be an important threshold when it comes to voting – 50 percent of 18–24-year-olds who've attained some college education showed up to the polls in 2012 compared to the 29 percent of this age group who'd only attained a high school education up to that point. The pattern is similar among 25–44-year-olds.

Level of family income also seems to be related to the voting behavior of young people. As seen in Table 2.8, as income levels rise, voter turnout rates increase among both 18–24-year-olds and 25–44-year-olds. These findings certainly are consistent with plenty of research demonstrating the links between educational and

Table 2.8 Percentage voted by family income and age, 2012

Selected characteristics	18 to 24		25 to 44	
	% registered	% voted, US citizen population	% registered	% voted
Total	52.9	41.2	70.5	59.3
Under $10,000	49.9	33.8	63.4	45.4
$10,000 to $14,999	48.2	37.0	58.9	40.7
$15,000 to $19,999	51.3	39.0	56.8	42.4
$20,000 to $29,999	44.1	33.8	63.3	49.9
$30,000 to $39,999	46.8	34.4	65.8	52.1
$40,000 to $49,999	52.5	38.7	68.8	54.1
$50,000 to $74,999	55.6	43.3	74.9	62.8
$75,000 to $99,999	63.4	51.7	81.1	70.8
$100,000 to $149,999	62.9	49.4	84.7	75.6
$150,000 and over	72.2	58.7	87.4	79.3
Income not reported	38.5	31.6	48.4	41.8

Source: US Census Bureau, Current Population Survey, November 2012.

economic status and voting behavior. Much of the previous chapter was dedicated to highlighting the Millennial Generation's unique features – from its diversity to its size to its levels of education. These numbers suggest that, despite these unique qualities, the role of education and income persists when it comes to explaining voting behavior.

To round out this picture of youth voting trends, data in Figure 2.7 documents the voter turnout rates in 2012 in states identified as those with the largest concentrations of young people. As discussed in Chapter 1, some of these states are notable not just for their youth population but for the number of Electoral College votes they hold. As Figure 2.7 shows, Mississippi has the strongest voter turnout rates among 18–24-year-olds and Louisiana has the strongest turnout rates among 25–44-year-olds. For both age groups, Texas's rates of turnout are lowest – noteworthy given the large number of Electoral College votes it holds. Although it isn't

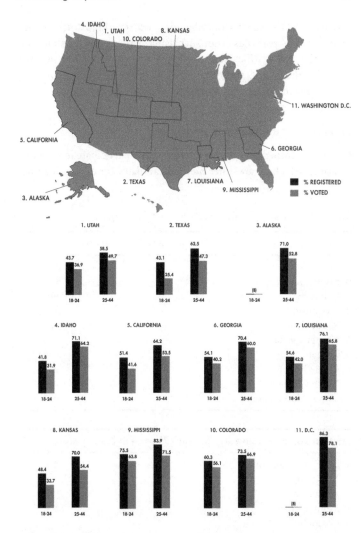

Note: The symbol (B) means that the base is less than 75,000 and therefore too small to show the derived measure.

Figure 2.7 Voter turnout rates in states with lowest median age, 2012

a state, the District of Columbia also has very high turnout rates among 25–44-year-olds – not surprising perhaps given its location. Of all the states, which had the highest rates of turnout in 2012? Table 2.9 documents those states in which young adults showed up to the polls in the highest numbers.

Engaged in other ways

Of course, voting isn't the only way citizens participate in the political process. There are other methods available for expressing one's

Table 2.9 States with highest voter turnout rates, 2012

Highest voter turnout rates for ages 18 to 24 in 2012 by state	
1. Mississippi	63.8
2. Minnesota	59.4
3. Colorado	56.1
4. Wisconsin	56
5. South Carolina	54
6. New Hampshire	51.9
7. Oregon	51.1
8. Rhode Island	50.3
9. North Carolina	50
10. Iowa/Massachusetts	49.9

Highest voter turnout rates for ages 25 to 44 in 2012 by state	
1. District of Columbia	78.1
2. Mississippi	71.5
3. Wisconsin	70.1
4. Minnesota	68.7
5. Colorado	66.9
6. North Carolina	66.9
7. Massachusetts	65.8
8. Louisiana	65.8
9. Maryland	65.1
10. Virginia	64.7

Source: US Census Bureau, Current Population Survey, November 2012.

candidate choice or policy views. As indicated above, a good deal of attention in the next few chapters will be paid to exploring both the breadth of these methods and their role in the life of the democratic citizen. At this point though, it's worth just getting a sense of what sorts of activities, beyond voting, are part of the "political toolkit" of young adults and the extent to which Millennials engage in such traditional methods of engagement as volunteering for a candidate as well as new methods that are available thanks to advances in digital media. Although turnout rates may increase as they get older, it's clear that Millennials' voting behavior pales in comparison to older generations' current and even their past voting patterns. Is it possible that, when we look at a broader range of political activities, Millennials shine? That's the question addressed in this section.

In addition to chronicling Americans' political attitudes and voting behavior since the middle of the twentieth century, the ANES also has collected information on the other ways citizens engage in a campaign and participate in elections. These activities include making a campaign contribution and wearing a sticker or button in support of a candidate or simply following a campaign in the news. Table 2.10 presents some of these data for those born between 1975 and 1990 and those born after 1991 – specifically, the percentage of young people who participated in a selection of "beyond voting" activities. For comparison, the percentages of all of the respondents who answered "yes" to these questions in the study are also presented.

When we look at the participation of those born between 1975 and 1990, we see that in most instances, rates of participation in these activities have increased over the years. These improvements aren't necessarily perfectly linear but, in most instances, the rates of participation that they exhibited in 2008 were higher than their rates of activity in 1992. For example, when it came to working for a party or candidate, fewer than 50 respondents in this age category participated in this activity in 1992 but by 2008, rates of participation matched the total number of respondents. It bears emphasizing that 2008 was a remarkable political year – both the nomination campaign between Barack Obama and Hillary Clinton as well as the presidential contest between Obama and McCain and the selection of Sarah Palin as the Republican vice-presidential candidate may account for

Table 2.10 Political activities beyond voting

Tried to influence how others vote[a]	1992	1994	1996	1998	2000	2002	2004	2008
% that answered "Yes" (total)	37	22	28	19	34	29	48	45
Born 1991 or later	**	**	**	**	**	**	**	41
Born 1975–90	*	11	19	11	33	19	56	45

Attended political meeting[b]	1992	1994	1996	1998	2000	2002	2004	2008
% that answered "Yes" (total)	8	5	5	5	5	5	7	9
Born 1991 or later	**	**	**	**	**	**	**	9
Born 1975–90	*	1	3	4	4	3	8	7

Worked for a party or candidate[c]	1992	1994	1996	1998	2000	2002	2004	2008
% that answered "Yes" (total)	3	3	2	2	3	3	3	4
Born 1991 or later	**	**	**	**	**	**	**	3
Born 1975–90	*	0	0	2	2	1	3	4

Wore a button or put a sticker on the car[d]

	1992	1994	1996	1998	2000	2002	2004	2008
% that answered "Yes" (total)	11	7	10	6	10	9	21	18
Born 1991 or later	**	**	**	**	**	**	**	18
Born 1975–90	*	10	5	5	8	3	23	18

Gave money to help a campaign[e]

	1992	1994	1996	1998	2000	2002	2004	2008
% that answered "Yes" (total)	7	6	8	7	9	11	13	13
Born 1991 or later	**	**	**	**	**	**	**	8
Born 1975–90	*	1	0	0	2	5	4	12

Watched campaign on TV[f]

	1992	1994	1996	1998	2000	2002	2004	2008
% that answered "Yes" (total)	89	**	74	**	82	62	86	86
Born 1991 or later	**	**	**	**	**	**	**	80
Born 1975–90	*	**	67	**	76	51	83	86

(*cont.*)

Table 2.10 (*cont.*)

Read about campaign in newspapers[g]

	1992	1994	1996	1998	2000	2002	2004	2008
% that answered "Yes" (total)	65	**	55	**	56	**	67	68
Born 1991 or later	**	**	**	**	**	**	**	59
Born 1975–90	*	**	48	**	44	**	56	64

Notes:

a "During the campaign, did you talk to any people and try to show them why they should vote for [1984 and later: or against] one of the parties or candidates?"

b "Did you go to any political meetings, rallies, [1984 and later: speeches,] [1978, 1980, 1982: fund-raising] dinners, or things like that [1984 and later: in support of a particular candidate]?"

c "Did you do any [other] work for one of the parties or candidates?"

d 1984 and later: "Did you wear a campaign button, put a campaign sticker on your car, or place a sign in your window or in front of your house?"

e 1988 and later: (2 questions) "During an election year people are often asked to make a contribution to support campaigns. Did you give money to an individual candidate running for public office?"; "Did you give money to a political party during this election year?"

f 1978, 1980, 1982, 1984, 1986, 1990, 1992, and later: "Did you watch any programs about the campaigns on television? (1978, 1980, 1984, 1990, 1996, 2004, 2008 only: If "Yes" – "Would you say you watched – a good many, several, or just one or two?")

g 1988, 1992, and later: (If R has read a daily newspaper in the past week:) "Did you read about the campaign in any newspaper?"

* indicates 50 or fewer total respondents within group.

** indicates question not asked or no cases within group.

2008 note: open-ended coding of occupation is not yet complete.

Source: American National Election Studies, table 6B, "Campaign Participation" (table generated August 5, 2010): www.electionstudies.org/ nesguide/gd-index.htm (NOTE: variable used for race grouping has changed. See table 1A.3).

these relatively higher numbers. Even so, for most of these campaign indictors, the rates of participation for either young people or the total population aren't overwhelmingly high. Although their history isn't as long, the rates of behavior of the younger Millennials (those born after 1991) offer an interesting contrast. At least for the 2008 election, this subset of Millennials seems to have started at a higher level than their older counterparts. For example, in 1992, a negligible number of total respondents in the 1975–90 group indicated that they tried to influence others on how to vote in that election. In comparison, 41 percent of those respondents born after 1991 tried to influence others on how to vote in the 2008 election. The higher rates of involvement among younger Millennials compared to older members of their age cohort are evident across a range of activities.

Table 2.10 also presents data on how "tuned in" young adults have been to recent campaigns and shows fairly similar patterns to their campaign activities. Again, although not in a linear fashion, those born between 1975 and 1990 seem to exhibit a growing propensity to follow campaigns (via television and newspapers) as they've matured – rates certainly are higher in 2008 than they were in 1992. Again, these findings certainly are tempered by the unique features surrounding the 2008 campaign.

With recent survey data from the IOP, we can explore the nature and extent of young adults' political participation beyond voting since the 2008 election. In their spring 2013 survey of a nationally representative sample of 18–29-year-olds (both college and non-college youth), the IOP found that:

- 8 percent of 18–29-year-olds had participated in a government, political, or issue-related organization (most of them less than once a month);
- 11 percent had donated to a political candidate or cause;
- 7 percent had volunteered on a political campaign for a candidate or issue.[12]

Once again, we see that campaign activity beyond voting wasn't remarkable among Millennials during that presidential contest. As explained earlier, tepid campaign activity during that period mirrored the decline in voter turnout rates among younger voters for the 2012 elections.

What about political activities beyond the electoral arena? What are the other ways, if any, that Millennials involve themselves in the political process? In light of such attention-grabbing movements as "Occupy Wall Street," the protests surrounding the deaths of Michael Brown and Eric Garner, and the rise of digital activism, it's worth looking not only beyond the voting booth but also beyond the bounds of campaigns when measuring youth engagement. If voter turnout rates lag behind those of older generations and if, relative to their size, young adults don't seem to be heavily engaged in campaign activities, perhaps demonstrations and other expressions of political opinion is where they focus their attention.

Since its inception, Harvard's Institute of Politics' survey of Millennials has gathered data on youth participation in protests or demonstrations – these results are presented in Table 2.11. One of the more interesting findings revealed by these data is the downward trend in participation in protests and demonstrations among Millennials. The first time the IOP asked the question "Have you ever attended a political rally or demonstration?" in 2002, 20 percent of the total respondents indicated that they had. By spring 2013, that percentage had dipped to 13 percent. As Table 2.11 shows, the survey registered upward ticks in participation in rallies or demonstrations in 2003 and 2005. As the timeline provided in Chapter 1 indicates, those years marked significant US military involvement in Iraq and may account for these increases in such political behavior. Interestingly, the data gathered in this series of surveys indicate that, despite the attention it garnered, relatively small percentages of Millennials participated in the "Occupy Wall Street" protests. As their fall 2011 survey found:

- 2 percent of the respondents indicated that they themselves had participated in any of the Occupy Wall Street protests and 11 percent knew someone personally who had participated;
- 70 percent indicated "no" – they hadn't themselves participated or didn't know anyone personally who had protested at Occupy Wall Street.[13]

The other interesting finding from these data on youth participation in protests and demonstrations is the marked difference in the behavior of college and non-college students. In 2006, the

Table 2.11 Political rallies and demonstrations

Question	Survey date	Have participated (total) (%)	Have not participated (total) (%)	Have participated (college) (%)	Have not participated (college) (%)	Have participated (non-college) (%)	Have not participated (non-college) (%)
Have you ever attended a political rally or demonstration?	Fall 2002	20	80				
	Spring 2003	35	64				
	Fall 2003	26	73				
	Fall 2004	32	68				
	Fall 2005	36	64				
	Fall 2006	21	79	28	73	19	81
	Fall 2007	21	79	26	74	19	81
	Fall 2008	22	78	31	69	19	81
	Spring 2010	16	82	24	73		
	Spring 2011	15	83	22	77		
	Spring 2012	12	88	18	81		
	Spring 2013	13	87	14	86		

IOP survey began to pay close attention to the differences between
those respondents who were enrolled in a four-year college at the
time they completed the survey and those who weren't. The "non-
college" sub-sample is composed of those not currently enrolled
and includes respondents of varying educational background, from
those in high school to those in community college to those with
no college experience. As the results show, the imbalance between
college and non-college-educated youth evident at the voting booth
on Election Day is apparently just as prevalent when it comes to the
public square. Given the growing number of "non-college-bound
youth" among Millennials documented in Chapter 1, this is a noteworthy finding.

As detailed in Chapter 1, America's youngest citizens have tools
of political expression available to them that were not only unavail-
able to but unheard of by previous generations. Discussions regarding the potential of digital media to serve as a method of political
engagement and participation have intensified as the Millennial
Generation has come of age and seem to have reached a crescendo
in recent years with such digital milestones as:

- the YouTube phenomenon of "Kony 2012" – a video documenting Joseph Kony's "Lord's Resistance Army" that had 100 million viewers in less than a week;[14]
- the "#BringBackOurGirls" Twitter campaign launched in
  response to the kidnapping of over 270 Nigerian schoolgirls by
  Boko Haram (a campaign joined even by First Lady Michelle
  Obama, who posted a photo of herself holding a sign reading
  "#bring back our girls");[15]
- the "#BlackLivesMatter" effort sparked by the acquittal of
  George Zimmerman in the killing of Trayvon Martin and by the
  police shootings of African American men that have taken place
  since that time.[16]

Much of the data presented thus far suggest that, when it comes to
campaign activities and even protests, Millennial behavior is rather
unremarkable but no less remarkable than the behavior of other age
groups. It's in the use of social media as a political tool, though,
where America's youngest citizens have the greatest potential to
distinguish themselves and shine. For example, the Pew Research

Center's Internet & American Life Project (2013) found that young adults were much more likely than older generations to be politically active on social networking sites including Facebook and Twitter, that political activity via social networking had deepened in recent years, and that expression via social media often translated into enhanced participation. For instance, they found that political discussions on Facebook and Twitter prompted younger adults to more deeply study the issues debated on these sites (2013, 7).

Work by the MacArthur Research Network on Youth and Participatory Politics offers a similar assessment of the potential of youth political engagement thanks to new media – not only through social media but through such forms of "participatory politics" as starting political groups online and composing and sharing politically oriented blog posts (Cohen *et al.* 2012). These researchers offer evidence that large segments of the young adult population engage in this sort of online political behavior, that these acts typically augment rather than replace other forms of political engagement, and that the distribution along ethnic groups is less divided when it comes to participatory politics than when it comes to such traditional methods as voting.

Although all of these findings suggest that this is one area of political participation that youth might dominate, there are some important caveats. The effects of a person's income level and education that for so long have been linked to political participation certainly persist when it comes to digital engagement – the Internet isn't necessarily the great equalizer. For instance, the Pew Research Center found that education and income (although to a somewhat lesser degree) have a greater effect on a person's propensity to participate in "online traditional political activities" than a person's age (Pew Research Center, Internet & American Life Project 2013, 6). Similarly, Cohen *et al.* concluded that level of education is an important predictor of a person's participation in participatory politics – participation is highest among those currently in college and very low among those who either left high school early or never attended college after high school (2012, 28). Again, this finding is meaningful given the growing number of "non-college-bound youth" documented in the previous chapter. Although they do find an equal distribution among ethnic groups in access to the Internet and less of a gap between such groups in participatory politics compared to the gaps in voting rates, it bears mentioning that Latino youth in particular lag behind when it comes to both traditional political engagement and digital and participatory politics (Cohen *et al.* 2012, 26).

A final caveat that bears emphasizing, not only for its importance but also its connection to findings presented in the previous chapter, involves the impact of online activism. As Cohen *et al.* point out, one possible risk associated with participatory politics based in digital media is the failure to distinguish between "voice" or expressing one's opinion and "influence" or actually effecting change: "we recognize that the promise of a democratic society is predicated on the belief that political actors have more than voice. They must have influence" (2012, 37–38). To reference a contemporary example, although millions may have tweeted and retweeted "#BringBackOurGirls" or changed their profile picture on Facebook since the kidnapping of hundreds of Nigerian schoolgirls, 230 of the 270 or more girls kidnapped remain missing.[17] Herein lies the distinction between voice and influence.

The impact, then, of such activism is uncertain. As a result, the promise and excitement surrounding the use of digital media or "hashtag activism" as a means of engaging young adults has been criticized as a diversion from real action and even tagged "clicktivism," "slacktivism," or, as Dana Milbank defined it, "a uniquely American form of engagement in which statements are made without any real sacrifice" (*Washington Post*, December 30, 2014). Milbank continues, in reference to the ALS "Ice Bucket Challenge" and the release of the movie *The Interview* (a film critical of North Korean dictator Kim Jon-Un):

> The Slacktivist gets icy water over the head to fight Lou Gehrig's disease, or tweets out hashtags to fight kidnapping in Nigeria (#BringBackOurGirls). The Slacktivist wears color-coded bracelets for causes, 'likes' causes on Facebook, and goes to see a Seth Rogan film to defy Korea.

For Milbank and others, such forms of participation are insufficient. Regarding the protests surrounding the "#BlackLivesMatter" effort, the *New York Times*' Charles Blow makes a similar argument and urges young protesters not to lose sight of the importance of the vote: "Voting is not some fruitless, patrician artifact from a bygone era. It is not for those devoid of consciousness and deprived of truth. It is an incredibly important part of civic engagement" (December 14, 2014). Touching upon the risks involved with confusing "voice" with "influence," Blow goes on to write: "We are the young people in the streets, who shout out and die-in for the right to be treated equally and to live freely. We are people who must know that the voice and the vote are mutual amplifiers, not mutually exclusive."

Conclusion

The topic of results or impact is a theme that was posited in the first chapter, emerges here in this chapter, and will be extended in later chapters when the academic literature on youth political participation is reviewed and case studies of youth-led organizations are offered. The impact of the Millennial Generation has been and continues to be palpable in the worlds of business, the economy, the arts, and entertainment. The impact of the generation on the world of politics has been uncertain bordering on negligible, though. That's not to say that there aren't counter-examples – both at the ballot box and in cyberspace. For example, energized young voters are credited with playing a pivotal role in the 2008 Iowa caucuses – sealing an important victory for Barack Obama and a stinging defeat for Hillary Clinton at the start of the nomination fight (Kirby *et al.* 2008a). In 2012, three young women from Montclair High School in New Jersey launched an online petition via Change.org to urge the Commission on Presidential Debates to select a woman to moderate one of the presidential debates that campaign. Their digitally rooted campaign was a success – Candy Crowley was selected to moderate the debate that took place between Barack Obama and Mitt Romney.[18] Certainly, there are other examples. As the *Washington Post*'s Caitlin Dewey pointed out in her blog about Internet culture, raising awareness ought not to be dismissed: "Despite the oft-repeated claim that awareness does nothing, it almost always does something – something small, perhaps, but something measureable" (May 8, 2014).

Once again, it's important to distinguish perception from reality – expectations from actions. This chapter shows that when it comes to voting, younger voters indeed are increasing their voting rates, but they don't match and likely will never match the turnout rates of older Americans. Juxtaposing these turnout numbers with the history of the lowering of the voting age, it seems that the hopes of proponents of the 26th Amendment have not been realized. This set of turnout data also help to explain the generational approach taken by some scholars and the dire conclusions they've drawn as a result of focusing upon voting rates of Millennials compared to previous generations.

For those scholars embracing a broader conception of engagement – one that extends beyond voting – this chapter also highlights the reality that campaign activity beyond voting among Millennials, though unremarkable, is no less remarkable than the actions of other age groups. The information presented here also suggests that, although promising, these extra-electoral (often virtual) realms of engagement have their drawbacks. Like voting, participation in such activities as protests and online activism aren't equally pursued by all segments of the generation, with levels of education in particular serving as a determinant of engagement. Broadening the conceptualization of engagement to include these forms of engagement also risks confusing voice with influence and diminishing an essential element of engagement – its impact. Moreover, the case studies of youth-led organizations centered on issues of concern to young adults suggests that scholars' nearly exclusive focus on youth actions (whether traditional or not) overlooks the politically oriented motivations of these groups – to make a difference.

Think It Out

- Imagine the 26th Amendment to lower the voting age to 18 was being considered today, and you have been tasked to make a recommendation to your representative on whether she should support its passage. Consider all of the arguments for and against lowering the voting age to 18 today and offer a well-supported recommendation.[19]

Act It Out

- Organize a voter registration drive on your campus or in your community. Begin by contacting your local Board of Elections to confirm local electoral regulations and deadlines and consult the following resources for information on how to run a successful drive:
  - Campus Compact (http://compact.org/?s=voter+registration)
  - Rock the Vote (www.rockthevote.com/get-involved/register-voters)
  - National Voter Registration Day (http://nationalvoterregistrationday.org).
- Organize a mock social media campaign around a public issue that matters to you. Working with others, identify a particular cause or issue around which you want to mobilize the public; create a name for your movement and a two-sentence mission statement; create a fake Twitter or Facebook account (see www.classtools.net for templates); create a hashtag to get your message out and brainstorm who you would tweet in order to convey your message; and think about how you might take this viral campaign further (i.e., organizing a protest, meeting with a public official, etc.).

Notes

1 "What RU Thinking?: RU Voting Focus Group Project, 2010–2011," by Elizabeth C. Matto, Bobby Irven, Harini Kidambi, and Evan Lehrer. The protocol for this research was reviewed and approved by the Institutional Review Board of Rutgers University, Protocol #E10–295.

2 "The Eagleton Assessment" was piloted in 2007–8 in three high schools in New Jersey. The research protocol for the pilot was reviewed and approved by the Institutional Review Board of Rutgers University, Protocol #E07–355.

3 "Survey of Young Americans' Attitudes toward Politics and Public Service, 24th Edition," October 29–November 11, 2011: www.iop.harvard.edu/likely-millennial-voters-grabs-upcoming-midterm-elections-harvard-youth-poll-finds.

4 Corporation for National and Community Service & National Conference on Citizenship, "Volunteering and Civic Life in America": www.volunteeringinamerica.gov/demographics.cfm.

5 In addition to those sources specifically cited, I relied upon information available via the National Archives: http://blogs.archives. gov/prologue/?p=12964, and the National Archives' "Presidential Timeline": www.presidentialtimeline.org/#/exhibit/37/03.

6 "Statistical Information about Fatal Casualties of the Vietnam War": www. archives.gov/research/military/vietnam-war/casualty-statistics.html.

7 See Appendix B for a copy of the joint resolution passed by Congress on March 23, 1970 approving the amendment to lower the voting age.

8 Video of the signing ceremony can be found here: www.youtube.com/ watch?v=Spe_-rqugD8. See Appendix C for a copy of the signed amendment.

9 Memo prepared by Robert Finch and Charles Colson, March 15, 1971. Richard Nixon Library. Rights Status: Unrestricted: www.presidentialtimeline.org/#/object/1513.

10 Memo from President Nixon to H.R. Haldeman, July 23, 1972. Richard Nixon Library. Rights Status: Unrestricted: www.presidentialtimeline. org/#/object/1518.

11 The US Census Bureau, when calculating turnout rates, distinguishes between the total voting age population and the eligible or citizen population. Voting age population (VAP) refers to the population of residents who have reached the minimum voting age. Voting eligible population (the United States Election Project uses the acronym VEP: www.electproject.org/home/voter-turnout/faq/denominator) refers to the population that is eligible to vote and, thereby, does not include noncitizens. Voter turnout rates that account for eligibility generally result in more accurate findings (at least since 1996, when the Census Bureau gathered such data consistently). See File's (2014) report for the US Census Bureau.

12 "Survey of Young Americans' Attitudes toward Politics and Public Service, 23rd Edition," March 20–April 8, 2013: www.iop.harvard.edu/ spring-2013-survey.

13 "Survey of Young Americans' Attitudes towards Politics and Public Service 20th Edition," November 23–December 3, 2011: www. iop.harvard.edu/sites/default/files_new/fall_poll_11_M_topline. pdf.

14 Kony 2012: http://invisiblechildren.com/kony-2012.

15 Bring Back Our Girls: http://bringbackourgirls.us.

16 Black Lives Matter: http://blacklivesmatter.com.

17 Bring Back Our Girls: http://bringbackourgirls.us.

18 Yahoo News: http://news.yahoo.com/blogs/the-ticket/high-school-girls-launched-campaign-female-debate-moderator-234222119--election.html;_ylt=A0LEVimxkTdVWoIApsQnnI1Q;_ylu=X3oDMTEzdHV0M20zBHNlYwNzcgRwb3MDMgRjb2xvA-2JmMQR2dGlkA1lIUzAwMl8x.

19 This activity is adapted from the learning resources regarding the 26th Amendment offered by the National Archives: www.presidentialtime-line.org/#/educators/RMN/26th_amendment/index.

3

What does it mean to be an "engaged citizen"?

Up to this point, we've considered who Millennials are as well as their participation in the political process. The demographics and habits of the generation – their size, background, educational status – have been laid out, as well as their place in the succession of generations preceding them. Armed with this information, we've considered the role of young adults in the world of politics – the ways in which they exercise their political muscle and the degree to which they exercise it. With this information as a foundation, then, this chapter and the next will address how scholars have studied youth engagement.

The demographics and unique features of the Millennial Generation understandably have sparked scholarly interest. Given its distinguishing features and its potential for power, the Millennial Generation's engagement in the political process is a topic worthy of study. At least at the ballot box, it's clear that young adults are "underrepresented" – their political power doesn't reflect their demographic power. That being said, the presence of young adults is felt in the world of digital media, and if directed appropriately, could be a source of political power for this age group. The juxtaposition, then, between unsteady turnout rates that fall behind those of older generations and growing participation in other modes of engagement has served as fertile soil for a wide range of scholarship on the subject.

As this chapter and the next one will show, more recent study on Millennials extends a scholarly trend to reconsider the concept of "engagement." Specifically, the way the idea has been depicted has evolved over the years from one fairly squarely focused on direct forms of political action (namely voting) to something broader and inclusive of a range of activities. This reconceptualization has informed scholars' opinions on the health of youth political engagement – some argue that today's young adults are "disengaged," some assert that they're "engaged differently," and still others claim that Millennials are "better engaged." As these chapters will argue, there are strengths and weaknesses in these assessments. Those who define engagement narrowly risk overlooking promising avenues of participation that might serve as political entryways for young adults. Scholars who advocate a broader rendering of engagement risk stripping the idea of its core political elements.

In the end, though, most scholarly attention has focused upon defining and quantifying the various facets of youth engagement, uncovering the variables influencing their behavior, and rendering a conclusion as to the vitality of youth engagement. What's been lost is a careful consideration of the other essential political elements of youth engagement including targets of youth political action, the issues prompting such action, and the impact. Either these elements don't exist – there are no targets of youth action, nor issues that spark youth engagement, nor any intended impact – or scholars aren't considering them. The case studies offered in Chapters 5 and 6 offer support for the latter assertion rather than the former. Of the considerable amount of scholarship that has been generated on engagement, specifically among young adults, scholars have pursued a fairly common approach and utilized a fairly common methodology. As a result, our understanding of youth engagement isn't nearly as rich as it needs to be.

Defining "engagement"

In discussions of youth political involvement specifically and participation of the populace in general, the term "engagement" is frequently used imprecisely. "Civic engagement" and "political engagement" are often employed interchangeably or are casually intermixed with such terms as "political participation," "volunteering," or "political activism." For some scholars, these notions are one and the same or at least closely related, while for others they are mutually exclusive. The purpose of this section is to synthesize the literature that addresses the concept of "engagement," paying special attention both to the ways in which the idea has been conceptualized and the different categories and measures that have been used to characterize "engagement."

Why undertake this exercise? It's worth remembering that the health (or lack thereof) of American democracy has been the object of discussion and even debate among scholars prior to recent considerations of the Millennial Generation. In their volume *Civic Engagement in American Democracy* (1999, 3–7), Skocpol and Fiorina assert that a confluence of such factors as disillusionment with government, innovations in research, and nostalgia for the "good old days" prompted popular and academic discussions of the state of civic engagement as the twentieth century was coming to an end.

Fifteen years later, many of these same factors cited as sources of concern regarding the health of democracy remain – historically low voter turnout rates, a lack of public trust in government, and minimal involvement in shared or communal endeavors. Moreover, sources of unease and anxiety that focused attention on the health of democracy at the turn of the century have only been amplified – economic uncertainty, social and cultural changes sparked by an influx of immigrants, and an explosion in mass media (Skocpol and Fiorina 1999, 3–7).

An additional element has come to the fore, though – a generational shift. The nation is adjusting to the coming of age of a generation that is large in size, more diverse than any in American history, and possessing a unique set of attitudes and abilities. Likewise, the body politic needs to adjust. Much like the re-examination of civic engagement Skocpol and Fiorina undertook, the shifting demographics of the nation attributed to Millennials is forcing both scholars and the public to consider the ways in which young people engage in their communities and the political process. The first step, though, is understanding what we mean by the concept "engaged."

Concepts serve as the foundation of the social sciences and can be understood as an "abstraction representing an object, a property of an object, or a certain phenomenon" (Frankfort-Nachmias and Nachmias 1992, 27). In the context of this chapter, then, "engagement" is the core concept under investigation. Concepts are vague, though, and can be interpreted differently by different people. The role of the social scientist is to make them less vague, more precise, and more commonly appreciated – to make concepts useful tools for understanding the world around them (Frankfort-Nachmias and Nachmias 1992, ch. 2). An important step in advancing understanding of a concept, engagement in our case, is to enunciate conceptual and operational definitions.

A conceptual definition is a description of a concept (Frankfort-Nachmias and Nachmias 1992, 30–31). For example, political scientists typically define the concept "politics" as the process of acquiring and utilizing power. Operational definitions link these concepts to reality and can be understood as "a set of procedures that describe the activities to perform to establish empirically the existence or degree of existence of a phenomenon described by a concept" (Frankfort-Nachmias and Nachmias 1992, 31). Building upon the example above, the conceptual definition of politics as the process of acquiring and utilizing power spurs numerous operational definitions from election outcomes to a president's legislative successes and failures.

Untangling the conceptual web of engagement comes down to getting a firm handle on the difference between the concepts of *civic* and *political* engagement – terms that often are used interchangeably and even haphazardly. To what extent are they separate and distinct and to what extent are they interrelated? As the discipline has progressed, this distinction has become more and more difficult to discern, but that wasn't always the case. Some more contemporary depictions of engagement conceptualize political participation as a component of civic engagement or as a category that falls under the broader *umbrella* of civic engagement. For others, political engagement is viewed as a mode of engagement in and of itself, with its own set of indicators, that can be distinguished from (even balanced against) civic engagement – each of them in their own *box*. These conceptualizations stand in contrast, though, to more classic understandings of engagement – ones that place political participation as the focal point or the *bulls-eye* of engagement. The evolution of scholarly thought on the concept of engagement reflects the overall tendency of those studying youth participation to focus on what sorts of actions young adults are pursuing and the extent to which they're pursuing these actions rather than exploring why they pursue these activities, the issues that spark such efforts, and the desired impact. Moreover, this evolution in thinking is suggestive of a relocation, even diminishment, of traditional political elements in our appreciation of engagement – a trend that has extended into our understanding of youth engagement.

Civic and political engagement: umbrellas, boxes, and bulls-eyes

Broad in scope, much of the recent scholarship promotes an umbrella-like view of engagement and envisions civic engagement as a sort of umbrella under which a number of diverse activities, including overtly political activities, fall. With this conceptualization, we see the challenge of enunciating conceptual and operational definitions in such a way that they make the concept, engagement in this case, less vague and more commonly understood. For example, referring to the text's conception of civic engagement as "capacious," the editor of *Democracy at Risk* asserts that "civic engagement includes any activity, individual or collective, devoted to influencing the life of the polity" (Macedo 2005, 6). Here civic engagement is an expansive term that includes a wide spectrum of activities from acquiring political knowledge, to expressing your political voice, to talking to others about politics, to voting, to non-electoral activities such as attending informational forums about an issue, to joining a volunteer or community group (2005, 7). Arguing that "politics and civil society are interdependent," the text's editor eschews the idea of making a sharp distinction between civic and political engagement (2005, 6).

Similarly, Peter Levine offers a fairly broad definition of "civic engagement" in his text *The Future of Democracy*, in which he conceives of "civic engagement" as influencing public matters through the use of legitimate methods, either for selfish or altruistic reasons (2007, ch. 1). Levine offers, then, a fairly broad umbrella under which numerous methods of community involvement can legitimately be considered as "civic engagement," holding that those actions taken to influence public matters can include actions that take place in the "civil society" or via associations or they can

Figure 3.1 Umbrella-like conceptualization of engagement

involve direct or indirect political actions (Levine 2007, 46–50). According to Levine, such actions as running for office or holding office, serving as a juror, serving on a board or as a civil servant represent "direct, personal involvement in the government itself" (2007, 48). Indirect methods of influencing the government are numerous and include "voting, organizing or persuading other people to vote, petitioning or lobbying the government, and suing for changes in policy ... open-ended efforts to influence the state by ... organizing public deliberations or educating young people to be effective participants" (2007, 48–49).

In addition, numerous examples of expressing one's "political voice" qualify as political participation, including submitting a letter to the editor of a newspaper, displaying a button or sign to express political views, or participating in a boycott or "buycott."[1] Levine also advocates that such efforts as verbally confronting or challenging someone when they've said something offensive falls under the category of expressing one's political voice (Levine 2007, 50–51).

There are other scholars for whom the lines of distinction between different forms of engagement are more definitive or can be assigned to different boxes – especially the distinction between civic and political engagement. One example of this approach is *Educating Citizens* by Colby *et al.* In this text, the authors make it clear that not all political activities fall under the umbrella of civic engagement. Instead, the authors conceive of a "civic domain" that includes political and non-political activities. Non-political civic activities are those that "enhance community life" and require individuals to "work collectively to resolve community concerns" (Colby *et al.* 2003, 18). Such activities might include volunteer work, social or club activities, and personal commitments to such public concerns as the environment or animal welfare (2003, 19).

Although they recognize that non-political and political activities occasionally overlap, the authors make a strong case for delineating the two types of behaviors, arguing that political and non-political involvement often are "independent of one another in terms of both motivation for and modes of involvement," and

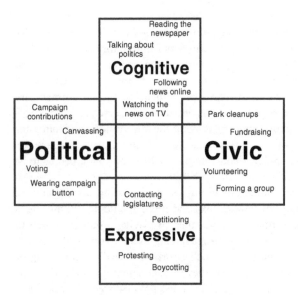

Figure 3.2 Box-like conceptualization of engagement

define political engagement as "activities intended to influence social and political institutions, beliefs, and practices and to affect processes and policies relating to community welfare, whether that community is local, state, national, or international" (Colby *et al.* 2003, 18). For these authors, there is a clear emphasis on political change when defining political involvement that is separate and distinct from civic engagement. For them, the defining feature of political engagement is a focus on public policy and involvement in governmental affairs. For that reason, not all civic activities should be considered political and not all political activities should be considered civic.

A New Engagement? by Zukin *et al.* offers a similar approach and argues that, although civic and political engagement can be conceived of as separate modes of engagement, the line of distinction can be "porous" (2006, 59). Holding that public engagement is "multi-faceted," the authors assert that American democracy requires a balance of different types of public participation and that this balance fluctuates (2006, 52). Rather than those who define engagement broadly or with laser-like precision, Zukin *et al.* take the "middle ground," stating, "We acknowledge the necessity and value of diverse participation, while remaining cognizant that civic engagement can not substitute for political engagement or vice versa" (2006, 9).

Acknowledging the blurry lines of distinction, *A New Engagement?* offers a four-part typology of engagement that not only provides clear conceptual and operational definitions of the different modes of participation (civic, political, public voice, and cognitive),[2] but also has served as a template for much of the research that has been conducted on youth participation, specifically the work conducted by CIRCLE.[3]

Civic engagement is conceptualized as "participation aimed at achieving a public good, ... usually through direct hands-on work in cooperation with others," while political engagement is defined as "activity aimed at influencing government policy or affecting the selection of public officials" (Zukin *et al.* 2006, 51). In the authors' view, these types of participation are distinguishable – civic engagement represents a direct way individuals and groups can address public problems, while political engagement, reliant upon a formal and representative system, constitutes an indirect approach to dealing with public problems.

Although the authors enunciate a distinct set of indicators for "public voice" (including contacting officials, contacting the media, protesting, petitioning, boycotting), they envision this facet of engagement as highly related to both civic and political engagement. Regarding cognitive engagement via news consumption or discussing current events, the authors hold that it can be both a precursor and an offshoot of political and civic participation. More importantly, Zukin *et al.* assert that, although cognitive engagement has its own set of operational definitions or indicators, they alone are not a sufficient expression of citizenship (2006, 54).

When scholars conceive of engagement broadly, including activities that range from voting to volunteering for a cause to challenging an offensive comment, at what point do we deem someone "an engaged citizen"? A review of those scholars who characterize engagement as either umbrella or box-like makes it clear that the focus is entirely on the individual engaged in the activities rather than the effects of the activities. For example, the authors of *A New Engagement?* develop a standard of measurement to weigh or assign a value to one's engagement (Zukin *et al.* 2006, 63–65):

- respondents were categorized as *civically engaged* if they participated in two or more *civic* activities;
- *politically engaged* respondents were those who participated in two or more *political* activities;
- *dual activists* were those respondents who indicated that they engage in two or more civic activities and two or more political activities;
- respondents were classified as *disengaged* if their survey results showed that they engaged in fewer than two civic or political activities.

The most salient component of this measure of engagement is the parity between civic and political participation – a so-called "civic specialist" who raises funds for a charity, regularly volunteers for a non-political organization, and works with others to solve a community problem is just as "engaged" as a "political specialist" who votes regularly, canvasses for a candidate, and contributes money to a political campaign. Clearly, a dual activist excels in both political and non-political participation and, thereby, stands as the "gold standard" of active citizenship. These broadly conceived notions of engagement and corresponding measures exemplify, then, the tendency to place the emphasis nearly completely on the actions of individuals rather than any other factors, such as their political effects, and to equate traditional political actions with non-traditional ones.

In contrast, there are other scholars for whom engagement isn't a catch-all phrase or an idea that can be segmented into different modes or boxes but something very specific, or the bulls-eye of our attention – political action. This certainly is the case with Verba and Nie's classic *Participation in America* that asserts that political participation is "at the heart of democratic theory and at the heart of the democratic formula in the United States" (1972, 3). The authors enunciate a long list of activities that can be categorized as political engagement and even group them in distinct modes: voting, campaign activity, citizen-initiated contacts with public officials, and cooperative efforts that take place outside the context of an election or cooperative efforts to influence the actions of the government (1972, 46–47). Although the authors consider a broad range of activities, their focus is squarely on activities that "are more or less directly aimed at influencing the selection of governmental personnel and/or the actions they take" (1972, 2).

Although not quite as narrowly focused on political action as *Participation in America*, the authors of *Voice and Equality* view political efforts (direct or indirect) meant to affect the government as the essence of engagement. As the authors state in the first paragraph of their text, "Political participation provides the mechanism by which citizens can communicate information about their interests, preferences, and needs and generate pressure to respond" (Verba *et al.* 1995, 1). Voting, working on a campaign, contacting officials, serving on a local board or committee are the tools citizens use to exercise power. In addition to its political nature, the authors' conceptual definition of engagement has a dynamic quality – it involves action. As the authors state, "we are concerned with doing politics, rather than with being attentive to politics" (1995, 39). Such activities as consuming or discussing the news or expressing

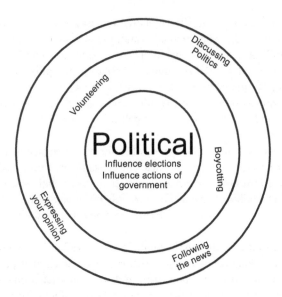

Figure 3.3 Bulls-eye conceptualization of engagement

one's opinion to a newspaper or radio call-in show don't qualify as political engagement under this conceptual framework. Clearly, this approach stands in sharp contrast to the broad conceptualization enunciated by scholars of the "umbrella" approach.

For those who view political behavior as the focal point of engagement but whose conceptual framework includes an array of activities, engagement isn't necessarily measured by the consistent completion of a particular act, such as voting in every election, but by what one puts into one's political activity and the effects of that activity on political institutions. For example, Verba and Nie's (1972) rich conceptualization of political participation (that extends beyond voting) is based on the supposition that different types of political behavior influence the political system in different ways. As they write,

> The votes of citizens in a Presidential election are a major force in shaping the direction of the nation for a four-year period – though in such circumstances the vote of a single individual is of very marginal

importance. Other citizen activities may affect only some narrow decision of a local government, or of a particular bureau or official. These activities, though much narrower in the scope of their impact, are important to consider if one wants to gauge the overall impact of participation. (Verba and Nie 1972, 10)

For them, then, the preferred governmental outcome often dictates the appropriate method of political participation. The mark of an engaged citizen is more than a consistent voting pattern; it lies in pursuing an effective method or collection of methods for influencing the political process. Just as important as method choice for Verba and Nie, though, is the impact of these methods. Their conceptual framework holds that meaningful engagement involves effectively conveying policy preferences, via an appropriate choice of political activity, to those public officials responsible for seeing to these preferences and then achieving a "concurrence" or agreement with public officials that affects that official's actions. In sum, one's political activity is meaningful if it sends a message to the appropriate officials in charge, results in a "concurrence" with these officials' outlook, and then influences the officials' actions (Verba and Nie 1972, Part III, 267–343).

In *Voice and Equality*, the authors advance this approach and construct a method for identifying which political acts stand out from the rest. Again, no one form of political participation is seen as the "end all, be all" of engagement. Instead, political activities are distinguished by what people put into these efforts and what they get out of these efforts (Verba *et al*. 1995, 43–48). Each political activity, whether it's voting or serving on the Board of Education, requires an investment of a certain amount of "time, money, or skills" (1995, 44). Some activities require a fairly modest amount of time or expertise (such as voting or making a campaign contribution) while others require a significant amount of time, ability, and resources.

For Verba *et al*., the information conveyed in these activities and the pressure they exert on public officials also allow us to distinguish some political activities as more meaningful than others. As the authors note, a letter to a public official or a sign at a demonstration offer a much clearer indication of what's on a citizen's mind than his or her vote does (1995, 45). These acts can be further distinguished by the extent to which they can be multiplied, or the "volume of the activity," in an effort to put pressure on public officials and influence their actions. As the authors document, interactions with public officials via letters, volunteer work, contributions, or even demonstrations can be multiplied again and again, yet "each citizen has one and only one vote" (1995, 46). Although the act of voting is the essence of democracy, it may not have the impact of other forms of political engagement.

This review of the literature suggests a shift in the way the rather abstract concept of engagement has been defined. The number and nature of the activities associated with being a participative member of the community haven't necessarily changed between the publication of *Participation in America* in 1972 and *Democracy at Risk* in 2005. What has changed, from a conceptual standpoint, is the prominence those activities considered "political" holds in the panoply of activities constituting "engagement." For some, political activities or actions taken to influence government action are the essence of democracy and the most prominent feature when defining engagement. In some recent considerations of engagement, though, political activity doesn't hold a central role in the conceptual definition of engagement – it either is one mode of participation among many or is viewed as a subset of a broader form of participation. This shift parallels the changing nature of youth participation that was documented in the previous chapter. As rates of traditional political participation such as voting have decreased, the conceptual focus has broadened beyond purely political acts. As the next section will show, in the scholarship of youth engagement that has emerged in recent years, scholars' assessment of the health of youth engagement seems to derive from the conceptual framework of engagement utilized – narrow or broad.

Explaining, predicting, and understanding youth engagement

As demonstrated in Chapter 1, the topic of the "Millennial Generation" has prompted plenty of discussion in the popular press – occasionally high in volume and intensity and often contradictory. The same holds true in scholarly circles, though. In recent years, a wide range of research has been conducted and published, both within political science and beyond, on the topic of youth engagement – the nature of youth engagement, the degree to which young people participate in the civic and political community, and the implications of their engagement (or lack thereof). On the one hand, we have scholars such as Robert Putnam characterizing those born after World War II as having been "exposed to some anti-civic X-ray that permanently and increasingly rendered them less likely to connect with the community" (2000, 255). Similarly, Smith *et al.* conclude as a result of their research that "Most emerging adults ... feel apathetic, uninformed, distrustful, or disempowered when it comes to politics and public life" (2011, 213). In contrast, utterly hopefully, Winograd and Hais portray Millennials as a new, positive, accomplished, and group-oriented "civic generation" that will "change the course of history and remake America."[4] Equally upbeat, Dalton credits the nation's youngest age cohort as responsible for the rebirth of the democratic process: "America is witnessing a change in the nature of citizenship and political participation that is leading to a renaissance of democratic participation – rather than a general decline in participation" (2009, 55).

As this section will show, these contrasting opinions reflect the different conceptual stances of the authors: those holding a broader view of engagement are more apt to render a positive assessment of youth participation and those with a more traditional stance are more inclined to offer a negative assessment. What's remarkable, though, is that scholars have come to these conflicting conclusions despite the fact that they've approached the subject in a fairly uniform manner – one that looks nearly exclusively to youth actions and not to other elements commonly associated with political participation, such as the issues spurring action, the strategy behind such actions, and the desired effects. As a result, the current scholarship on youth engagement amounts to a back and forth between competing viewpoints rather than a comprehensive picture of the way the youth population today, or "citizen now," is engaging in politics and democracy.

Young adults: disengaged vs. engaged
differently vs. better engaged

The bulk of the existing scholarship on youth political participation basically addresses two overall research questions: in what activities are youth engaging and what explains their behavior? Scholars' contrasting responses to these questions help to explain disagreement among researchers on the health of youth engagement and can be organized into three categories – those who assert that young adults are "disengaged"; those who argue that they are simply "engaged differently"; and a third groups that contends that, in fact, young adults are "better engaged" than previous generations. Dalton's (2009) argument rests on the idea that different assessments of young adults as citizens are rooted in different conceptions of citizenship. The continuum outlined below is consistent with this argument yet offers a new take by focusing less on one's depiction of citizenship and more on one's view of "engagement" and by calling into question the grounds upon which this rendering of citizenship is based.

Those who argue that today's young adults are "disengaged," authors such as Putnam (2000), Wattenberg (2012), Twenge (2006), and Smith *et al.* (2011), conclude fairly definitively that the state of engagement among young people is not only a cause for concern but even speaks "poorly of the condition of our larger culture and society" (Smith *et al.* 2011, 225). Their dire assessment is due in no small part to their common conceptual outlook – one that is closely aligned to traditional definitions of political engagement.

Although he points to the emergence of the Baby Boom generation as the starting point of the decline, Putnam sounds an alarm in *Bowling Alone* and warns that those generations following Boomers promise to continue a downward decline in engagement. When holding stage in life constant and looking solely at generational

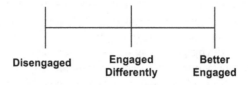

Figure 3.4 Conclusions on youth engagement

differences, Putnam concludes that, when comparing engagement in the early 1970s to levels in the late 1990s, in every instance declines in rates of engagement in various forms of participation have been concentrated among younger age groups. As Putnam concludes, "the more recent the cohort, the more dramatic its disengagement from community life" (2000, 251).

Given the time period of his research, much of Putnam's focus on young people is placed on Generation X – he makes it clear, though, that he believes the trends he sees among Boomers and Generation Xers most likely will continue with Millennials. For Putnam, the changes that began with Baby Boomers and worsened with each generation will have long-term and dire effects, "Unless America experiences a dramatic upward boost in civic engagement in the next few years, Americans in the twenty-first century will join, trust, vote, and give even less than we did at the end of the twentieth" (2000, 256).

The picture Putnam paints of Generation Xers as members of the civic and political community is far from flattering. He writes that they "have an extremely personal and individualistic view of politics" and "have never made the connection to politics, so they emphasize the personal and private over the public and collective" (2000, 259). Moreover, they feel less guilty about not voting than older generations, and

are less interested in politics, less informed about current events (except for scandal and personality, and sports), less likely to attend a public meeting, less likely to contact public officials, less likely to attend church, less likely to work with others on some community project, and less likely to contribute financially to a church or charity or political cause (2000, 261).

Putnam's consideration of engagement is multi-faceted and this view is reflected in the measures he uses. Not all indicators of engagement are traditionally "political" and there is no hierarchy of engagement proposed in which voting is viewed as the be-all and end-all of political participation. That being said, Putnam utilizes the 12 measures of engagement included in a series of the Roper Social and Political Trends surveys – measures that do not include such non-traditional forms of engagement as boycotting and buycotting, protesting or demonstrating, or other acts of civil disobedience. On the one hand, the absence of these measures has a methodological

explanation – in order to engage in longitudinal analysis, one needs
to use the same measures over time. It may also reflect a conceptual outlook. Although he views engagement as multi-dimensional,
Putnam views political participation in traditional terms. For him,
engagement is active and takes place in the context of associations
and democratic institutions: "Just as one cannot restart a heart with
one's remote control, one cannot jump-start republican citizenship
without direct, face-to-face participation. Citizenship is not a spec-
tator sport" (2000, 341). Make no mistake, the importance Putnam
places on the most traditional form of engagement, voting, is quite
clear. For him, voting "embodies the most fundamental democratic
principle of equality. Not to vote is to withdraw from the political
community" (2000, 10).

Wattenberg approaches the topic of youth political participation
from a similar perspective. Like Putnam, he recognizes that there
are other forms of engagement that have a role in the political process, but it's quite clear that voting is the "sine qua non" or the
essential ingredient of democracy. He explores the role that other
forms of engagement among young people play in their political
life and entertains the contention that extra-voting methods such
as protesting, boycotting, and volunteering have become their preferred mode of action, but Wattenberg doubts both their vitality and
their effectiveness (2012, ch. 7). Instead, he worries that voting is a
habit that has become "the province of the elderly" (2012, 1) and
even offers compulsory voting as a method for securing "generational equality at the polls" (2012, 6). This suggestion alone is indic-
ative of Wattenberg's conception of what it means to be an engaged
member of the political community – like Putnam, his assessment of
youth engagement is in no small part a reflection of how he defines
participation.

In *Generation Me*, "personality psychologist" Jean Twenge offers
a forceful statement on the attitudes and personalities of younger
generations, the roots of these attitudes, and their overall effects
on the behavior of young people. Although Twenge does comment
on youth political engagement, her focus certainly extends beyond
the world of politics, and it's quite clear that, for her, "Generation
Me's" unflattering traits and behavior pervade all aspects of the
culture – including political and civic communities. Utilizing a

generational lens as Putnam and Wattenberg do, Twenge's depiction of the political and civic inclinations of "Generation Me" stands in stark contrast to the so-called "Greatest Generation": "The days when young Americans marched in the streets to change the world are, for the most part, gone. Although some protests still draw crowds and collective action, the young person who believes that she can make a difference in world events, national politics, and sometimes even her own life is more and more rare" (2006, 137–138). Especially in comparison to previous generations, it's Twenge's view that "Generation Me's" overwhelming cynicism, lack of faith in government and institutions, and their sense that they can't make a difference has resulted in diminished voting rates, disinclination to engage in protests or demonstrations, and inattention to news and current events (2006, ch. 5). Like Putnam and Wattenberg, her critique of youth engagement is centered on mostly traditional forms of participation – voting in particular.

Taken together, Putnam, Wattenberg, and Twenge offer a fairly similar take on youth political engagement and use similar approaches in reaching this conclusion. Although they may account for such extra-political modes of engagement like volunteering when quantifying youth's activities, this set of researchers gives most careful consideration to the most traditional forms of engagement – with voting ranking high on the list.

Like Twenge, the authors of *Lost in Transition* are not political scientists and their text is not focused solely on the political and civic behavior of young people or what they refer to as "emerging adults" – 18–23-year-olds. Instead, they approach the topic of young people from the "sociological imagination" approach, which "seeks to understand the *personal experience of individual people*, on the one hand, and *larger social and cultural trends, forces, and powers*, on the other, by *explaining each in terms of the other*" (Smith *et al.* 2011, 4; emphasis original). If Twenge is focusing on the effects of attitudes on youth behavior, Smith *et al.* are interested in the sociological roots of the "outlooks, experiences, and practices in emerging adult life today" (2011, 3).

Their consideration of the political and civic behavior of "emerging adults" does lead them to the rather definitive conclusion that most of the youths they studied were "highly civically and politically disengaged, uninformed, and distrustful. Most in fact feel disempowered, apathetic, and sometimes even despairing when it comes to the larger social, civic, and political world beyond their own private lives" (Smith *et al*. 2011, 196). In order to reach this conclusion, Smith *et al*. establish a typology to categorize the nature and extent of youth engagement including: the apathetic, the uninformed, the distrustful, the disempowered, the marginally political, and genuinely political. They find that only 4 percent of their interviewees are genuinely political – a small minority possessed "substantive knowledge of political matters, genuine interest in participating in politics, and specific descriptions of meaningful ways that they are civically and politically engaged" (2011, 208). This small handful of young people place importance on being informed and "having a voice in politics," are concerned about the state of the nation, and wanted to "help create change" (2011, 209).

Those who fell outside this category weren't entirely apathetic but apathetic about politics (and even felt somewhat guilty about it), possess little to no knowledge about the political process, may have notable levels of knowledge but are so distrustful of the system that they stay out of it, feel alienated from the process given its great complexity, or have some interest in and knowledge of the political process but are terribly vague about their involvement in it. It's fair to say then that the authors of *Lost in Transition* approach the topic with an ideal of democratic participation. For them, participation is predicated upon political knowledge and political action:

> A thriving republic depends upon its citizens becoming civically informed and active in order to exercise the informed public stewardship needed to sustain communities of responsibility and freedom. Effective government – to the extent that such a thing is possible – requires an attentive and informed public that can envision a common good, interact with the political system, and hold government officials accountable. (Smith *et al*. 2011, 213)

For this group of scholars, then, those who characterize young people as "disengaged," the notion of engagement is narrow in focus (reflecting the *bulls-eye* depiction) and closely aligns with the definition of political participation articulated at the outset – active, undertaken by average citizens, traditionally political in nature, with an aim towards directly or indirectly influencing outcomes – particularly electoral outcomes. Young people's failure to meet these standards leads them to their dire prognosis of democracy's health.

Anchoring this continuum are those scholars who don't necessarily agree with the characterization of young adults as "disengaged." Instead, they assert that they're "engaged differently." Zukin *et al.*'s *A New Engagement?* perfectly exemplifies this outlook on youth participation. Like Putnam and Wattenberg, they find that, indeed, traditional measures of political engagement such as voting are lower among younger citizens compared to their older counterparts. They also point out, though, that other measures such as volunteering and consumer activism are robust among younger Americans. In fact, the authors assert that young Americans tend to see business rather than government as the focal point of power (2006, 114–115) and are more likely to view their purchases (or lack thereof) as an expression of their preferences. This finding certainly coincides with the research presented in Chapter 1 regarding Millennials' impact on the economy.

Countering Putnam and others, Zukin *et al.* assert that the aging of the "Greatest Generation" and Baby Boomers and rise of Generation X and Millennials hasn't necessarily resulted in vast disengagement but has ushered in a change in the nature of engagement: "citizens are participating in a different mix of activities from the past, and that this is due largely to the process of generational replacement. We believe the volume of citizens engagement has not declined so much as it has spread to a wider variety of channels" (2006, 3).

The "middle ground" approach that pervades *A New Engagement?* is evident in the way they conceive of engagement (compartmentalized or balanced among various boxes) and the ramifications of young people being "engaged differently." Whether the nature of youth engagement should be viewed with hope or dismay is still to be seen or is in the eye of the beholder for them. As they write in the preface, "In the end, we're not sure if the glass is half-empty or half-full. In some measure, it depends on whether one is pouring or drinking. We will let our readers judge for themselves" (Zukin *et al.* 2006, viii). This measured tone certainly stands in stark contrast to those placed at the "better engaged" end of the continuum. For them, the generational differences manifested in youth engagement are to be celebrated and indicate that young people actually are "better engaged."

Those scholars in the "better engaged" category offer a much rosier take on the quality and quantity of youth participation than those on the opposite end of the continuum. Moreover, they're not as bound to the traditional definitions of political participation and, as such, are apt to view a wide range of activities not only as meeting the threshold of engagement but also as evidence of a healthy democratic spirit among Millennials.

Around the same time that Robert Putnam published *Bowling Alone* and issued dire warnings about the impact of youth disengagement on democracy, Howe and Strauss were celebrating the arrival of what they referred to as "The Next Great Generation" with the publication of *Millennials Rising*. As documented in the first chapter, Howe and Strauss are credited with naming this age cohort the "Millennial Generation" and are unapologetically Millennials' champions. As the authors admit, they're not exactly objective in approaching their subject matter: "We're both fathers, and we freely admit that we share a prokid bias. We root for our kids, their teams, and their generations" (2000, 369). Howe and Strauss successfully offer readers a vibrant depiction of young people as they are – or at least as the authors see them.

Unlike Twenge and the others, Howe and Strauss see Millennial behavior as something to celebrate. Belying the labels placed upon them, young adults, according to Howe and Strauss,

> are beginning to manifest a wide array of positive social habits that older Americans no longer associate with youth, including a new focus on teamwork, achievement, modesty, and good character. Only a few years from now, this can-do youth revolution will overwhelm the cynics and pessimists. Over the next decade, the Millennial Generation will entirely recast the image of youth from downbeat and alienated to upbeat and engaged – with potentially seismic consequences for America. (2000, 4)

Given that *Millennials Rising* pre-dates the age cohort's first vote (the authors set the beginning of the generation at 1982), Howe and Strauss aren't able to react to or comment on youth voting or many other forms of political engagement. That being said, the authors assert that the political process does not play a central role in youths' lives: "During the Millennial childhood, politics has become increasingly irrelevant" (2000, 103). In their mind, though, this reality doesn't diminish Millennials' capacity to effect change or to be a positive social and political force. Herein lies the difference between Howe and Strauss and the previous set of scholars – for them, Millennials need not be confined by strict definitions of engagement. Instead, young people's interest in community and helping those around them has forged a new form of engagement: "A new Millennial service ethic is emerging, built around notions of collegial (rather than individual) action, support for (rather than resistance against) civic institutions, and the tangible doing of good deeds" (2000, 216). Howe and Strauss also predict that, if committed, Millennials can also unleash their power in the political world: "When Millennials focus on a political problem, they can be smart, persevering, and adept at high-tech research skills" (2000, 233). Moreover, when properly directed and when ready, Howe and Strauss see Millennials as ushering in an age of greatness:

> Once this new youth persona begins to focus on convention, community, and civic renewal, America will be on the brink of becoming someplace very new, very 'millennial' in the fullest sense of the word. That's where the 'end of history' stops, and the beginning of a new history, their *Millennial* history, starts (2000, 6).

Sweeping in language and outlook, Howe and Strauss's optimism stems from both the timing of their writing and the breadth of their focus. Again, Howe and Strauss published *Millennials Rising* just as Millennials (according to their generational lines of demarcation) were turning 18 and, consequently, their work consists mainly of predications of future behavior rather than assessment of actual behavior. Their views of engagement also distinguish Howe and Strauss from the others. For example, they see increased rates of volunteering as a sign of a deeper service ethic rather than a by-product of increased service-learning efforts in schools. More importantly, they're pointing a very wide lens at youth behavior and are not looking solely at traditional political behavior. This may be because they define "engagement" broadly and as extending beyond voting, or it may be that Howe and Strauss aren't political scientists and their primary interest isn't politics. It's worth noting that Winograd and Hais's *Millennial Makeover* (2008) and *Millennial Momentum* (2011) follow in Howe and Strauss's footsteps both in outlook and methodology and offer a similarly hopeful set of conclusions.

The other authors from this end of the spectrum are political scientists, though, and share both the breadth of focus and enthusiasm towards Millennials that Howe and Strauss and others convey. Their approach, both conceptual and methodological, allows us to further account for the discipline's efforts explaining, predicting, and understanding youth political behavior. The heart of Rimmerman's *The New Citizenship* is an explanation of an alternative method of looking at engagement – a conceptualization of engagement that goes beyond voting and that encompasses various forms of "participatory democracy" including service, activism, and various unconventional forms of political action. Using the civil rights movement as a model, Rimmerman enunciates various indicators or examples of "participatory democracy" such as boycotts, marches, demonstrations, and civil disobedience (2005, 64–65).

The overriding quality that these activities share is that they represent, in Rimmerman's mind, unconventional forms of political engagement or a form of politics "that required participants to go outside the formal channels of the American political system and embrace the politics of protest and mass involvement" (2005, 64). Why pursue this route? For civil rights activists, these methods of participatory democracy brought media attention and shone a light on racial injustice, mobilized and attracted others to their cause, and disturbed those with political and economic power (2005, 64–65). Rimmerman's overall contention is that participatory democracy, as exemplified by civil rights activists, provides a useful model of how to revive and renew American democracy – among the population as a whole and young people in particular.

Although he holds that voter turnout rates are not a sufficient measure of a democracy's health, Rimmerman argues that they reflect, among youth and the remainder of the population, a sense of alienation or indifference. Rimmerman sees "participatory democracy" as a promising approach for engaging youth who feel that traditional methods such as voting and signing petitions aren't effective. According to this research, "students can imagine a different politics" and are receptive to a "different politics … rooted in bringing people together at the community level to 'find ways to talk and act on problems'" (Rimmerman, 2005, 54). For Rimmerman then, looking at political engagement differently and educating young people to be participatory citizens offers a promising route for bringing youth into the democratic process and, thereby, enlivening democracy as a whole. Pointing to renewed activism and the emergence of issue-based organizations on college campuses, Rimmerman holds that younger generations are fertile ground for such an approach to take hold.

If Rimmerman holds that a broader vision of engagement will serve as a promising mode of animating young people and restoring democracy, Dalton's work takes that argument a step further with his assertion that youth outlooks on engagement will change American politics for the better. This chapter began with the dire assessments of Putnam and others on the state of youth engagement. Dalton's disagrees heartily and asserts, "The good news is … the bad news is wrong" (2009, 3).

The heart of Dalton's argument is that, due to generational replacement, a significant shift in citizenship norms is taking place and that this shift in norms is producing a different type of engagement among younger citizens. The "duty based model" of citizenship, embraced by older generations, emphasizes traditional responsibilities of citizens and, thereby, produces traditional modes of engagement such as voting and abiding by the law. Instead, according to Dalton, young people are embracing a "engaged model of citizenship" that "includes participation, but in non-electoral activities such as buying products for political reasons and being active in civil society groups" (2009, 28). Broad in comparison to those enunciated by the "disengaged" group, Dalton's model also encompasses efforts to understand others, "a moral and empathetic element," and "solidarity" with others both domestically and internationally (2009, 28).

This multi-faceted conception of youth engagement, one that extends beyond purely active and purely political behavior to include such actions as following the news and participating in community service projects, certainly overlaps with Zukin *et al.* (2006) and Levine (2007). Dalton holds that young people, operating under an "engaged model of citizenship," have expanded the engagement repertoire to include methods of engagement (such as contacting officials directly and protesting) that are more direct than voting. In the end, Dalton holds that this enlarged vision of citizenship and the wide range of activities it spawns produces more positive democratic results than the alternative:

> duty-based citizenship produces a more restrictive image of democracy based on conformity and acceptance of authority. The good citizen is a loyal subject. In contrast, engaged citizenship reinforces Americans' commitment to norms of autonomous action and inclusion. Engaged citizens stress minority rights and the social dimensions of democratic politics in keeping with their self-definitions of good citizenship. (Dalton 2009, 130–131)

As this section and the one preceding it show, the conceptual frameworks that have been used to understand the phenomenon of engagement have evolved. The scholarly literature regarding the Millennial Generation extends this trend, with some broadly envisioning the notion of engagement while others have remained faithful to the more traditional version. As documented with the "disengaged" to "better engaged" continuum, evaluations of youth engagement are intertwined, then, with how the idea is conceived – narrowly or broadly.

The role of political participation in engagement

This chapter began with a discussion of concepts and the role of conceptual and operational definitions. Although definitions of "engagement" have undergone a transformation in the last 40 or so years and consequently have influenced considerations of youth engagement, it's worth considering the stability of the notion of "political participation." As modes of participation have multiplied and younger generations have replaced older ones, those elements of political participation that have remained consistent have been overlooked as scholars have broached the subject of youth participation from the same approach – one focused nearly exclusively on the actions undertaken by young adults.

If the notion of engagement has expanded from one grounded strictly in terms of traditional political engagement (such as voting) to a much broader conceptualization, political science as a discipline has maintained a fairly constant definition of "political participation" – a concept with a few essential features:

- the participation in question needs to involve action – it can't merely be interest in politics or a sense of efficacy;
- these activities must be voluntary and undertaken by average, ordinary citizens and not elites;
- the action must be political and, therefore, be directed at a governmental policy or activity;
- the participation must be geared towards influencing an outcome or result.

This definition has its roots in Verba and Nie's *Participation in America* (1972) and has been reaffirmed more recently by scholars such as Brady (1999) and Schlozman (2002). To be sure, applying this definition isn't always straightforward. As Schlozman warns, "the domain of behavior known as 'voluntary political activity' has porous, ill-defined borders" (2002, 434). Nonetheless, depictions of engagement that don't meet the above criteria may be termed engagement, but that doesn't necessarily make them *political participation*.

Another useful guidepost in assessing the body of literature that has emerged on youth political participation is a classification system of the phenomenon of political activity. In the social sciences, there's value in labeling and categorizing the ways in which we conceptualize and operationalize a phenomenon. In addition to providing a useful classification system of political activity, Brady's synthesis of the study of political participation provides a compelling argument for the use of taxonomies:

> Naming, distinguishing, and counting things are thought of as pedestrian scientific tasks ... This perspective has changed as philosophers of science, linguistics, cognitive psychologists, and practicing

scientists has shown how our classifications underlie our world view. How we name and classify things has a lot to do with how we understand them. (Brady 1999, 739)

In his taxonomy of political acts, Brady outlines two overall considerations when categorizing the actions in question: what are their "core characteristics" and what are the "proximate causes and effects" of the actions? When looking at the core characteristics, Brady holds that key questions to consider are:

- what is the "nature of the act"?
- "what political level and what actor or agency are the targets?"
- what are the "characteristics of the issue involved"?

When thinking about causes and effects of political participation, Brady urges that one considers:

- "reasons for doing it?"
- "did it have an impact?"
- is there "satisfaction with result"? (1999, 769, table 13–15)

This classification system and the key questions it encapsulates serve as essential tools when mapping the research that has been conducted and the conclusions drawn regarding youth participation. For the most part, research on the political engagement of young people has focused upon defining and quantifying various incarnations of youth participation, identifying those factors that impact youth behavior and weighing their effects on the behavior, and attaching meaning to all of these findings. A cross-reference of this literature with existing classification systems of political participation highlights those elements that haven't been given serious attention thus far in studies of youth political participation – *targets of youth political action, issues prompting such action, and the effects or impact of these efforts*. This reality compounds the risks already involved with relocating and even diminishing the role of politics when we broaden conceptions of engagement.

The review of the literature on youth engagement presented in this chapter, then, highlights the conceptual shortcomings in the way the phenomenon has been studied up to this point. The next chapter extends this discussion by exploring the theoretical frameworks scholars have utilized to explain youth engagement and also points out the limits and potential flaws involved with the methodologies we've pursued in studying young adults. Taken together, this critique suggests the need for a new approach – one grounded more in the experiences of those actually engaging in these activities today.

Think It Out

- Consider the ways in which you and your peers typically engage in your community and in politics. Does your manner of engagement come closest to the "umbrella," "box-like," or "bulls-eye" conceptualization described in this chapter? If none of these fit, create your own description and name for the sort of engagement most common among your peers.

Act It Out

- Working alone or with a group, write and film a short public service announcement (PSA) encouraging your peers to be "active citizens." What actions might you encourage your peers to undertake? Are they a mixture of activities discussed in this chapter ("civic," "political," "expressive," "cognitive," to use Zukin *et al.*'s terminology) or do they lean more heavily on a certain type of activity?
- Create a poster that represents young adults as citizens today. The poster can be a drawing or collage but should depict the manner in which young adults engage in politics or democracy.

Notes

1 "Buycotting" refers to purchasing a product or service to signal that you agree with the social or political values of the company providing or producing it (Zukin *et al.* 2006, 58).
2 See Table 3.1 in *A New Engagement?* for a listing of all the core indicators of engagement (Zukin *et al.* 2006, 57–58).

3 The research presented in *A New Engagement?* grew out of the 2002 report, "The Civic and Political Health of the Nation: A Generational Portrait," by Scott Keeter, Cliff Zukin, Molly Andolina, and Krista Jenkins: www.civicyouth.org/special-report-the-2002-civic-and-political-health-of-the-nation (accessed August 6, 2014).

4 Website promoting *Millennial Momentum: How a New Generation Is Remaking America*: http://millennialmomentum.com.

4
Where we've been: where we need to go

Scholarly diagnoses on the health of the political behavior of young adults range from positive to neutral to negative. How have scholars come to these conclusions? What theoretical frameworks have they used and what methods of study have they undertaken to come to these divergent judgments? These conflicting opinions have emerged despite a fairly common approach and similar methodologies. This leads to the conclusion that it's time to reframe our discussion and our approach when it comes to studying youth political participation – with less of an emphasis on how today's youth engage in politics compared to their parents and grandparents along with a conscious effort to look at the matter from "citizen now's" perspective. Such a shift, reflecting where we've been, is necessary in order to get to our desired destination – a complete and accurate understanding of Millennials as political actors.

Explaining youth engagement: theoretical frameworks

In the previous chapter, the role of concepts was discussed in the context of our consideration of engagement. It's fair to say that concepts serve as the building blocks of the social sciences, and these building blocks are utilized to construct the theoretical frameworks around which research takes place. What's a theory and what are theoretical frameworks?

The goal of all sciences, including the social sciences, is to improve our understanding of how things work. For us then, the goal of political science is to help to explain the world of politics. Constructing

theories regarding politics goes beyond simply describing or reporting on various aspects of politics such as campaign contributions or
voter turnout rates. Instead, we seek to develop theories to explain
these phenomena (Etheridge 1990, 4), and how we approach our
study of these phenomena relates to our theoretical framework.
Theoretical frameworks serve as the "underlying structure, the
scaffolding or frame" of a scholar's study and are "derived from
the orientation or stance that you bring to your study" (Merriam
2009, 66).

The contrasting scholarly camps outlined in the previous chapter offer an opportunity to more carefully explore the theoretical
frameworks utilized to study youth political participation. For the
most part, the study of youth political engagement has been viewed
through a generational lens – differences in the way Millennials
engage in their communities and the political process have been
undertaken by comparing "citizen now" to "citizen then." By studying a phenomenon via a "generational lens," one assumes that a
shared set of historical, cultural, and political milestones make a
mark on those raised in the shadow of these milestones and that
these factors affect an age cohort's outlook and behavior. A generational perspective also assumes that the effects of a generation
endure – there's no "growing out of it."

Scholars from all three camps outlined in the previous chapter – those who assert that young adults are "disengaged," those
who label them "differently engaged," and those who claim they're
"better engaged" – bring a generational orientation to their study of
the nature and intensity of youth engagement. As discussed in the
last chapter, scholars' conception of engagement (whether narrowly
political or broad in scope) has been interwoven in this orientation.
In applying this generational lens, scholars have utilized various
theoretical perspectives – social capital, historical, sociological, psychological, and rational choice. Interestingly then, it's the different
application of a common generational approach that leaves us with
competing theories of youth political participation. This result calls
for a new approach to the study of youth engagement and a new
theory to explain it.

Some have explored how historical factors have made an imprint
on the outlook and behavior of today's young citizens compared to

those of the past. For example, although he identifies a number of factors that explain the disengagement of young people relative to older generations, Putnam points to World War II as having a profound and enduring influence on that generation's sense of duty and civic-mindedness (2000, 275–276) that has fostered consistent and traditional political behavior (voting in particular). At the "better engaged" end of the spectrum, Howe and Strauss's work on Millennials addresses not only how history shapes a generation (from their sense of membership to their beliefs and behaviors) but also how a generation shapes history (2000, ch. 2). From the "engaged differently" zone, Zukin *et al.* also employ a historical theoretical perspective by sketching a detailed timeline of the various generations and speculating how the collective events and various "technological, economic, cultural, and political shifts" have contributed to "generation differences in political attitudes, opinions, and behaviors" – one that has fostered less traditional engagement but a greater interest in volunteering (2006, 18–19).

Understandably, the impact of Millennials' history on their outlook and behavior has been given less attention than the effects of previous cohorts' history on their generation. Obviously, the history of the Millennial Generation is still being written and, therefore, has been studied less than subjects such as the effects of World War II on "the Greatest Generation" or the Vietnam War on Baby Boomers. In order to consider the effects of Millennials' history on their behavior, more is needed than simply time. There must also be a purposeful effort among scholars to frame both their research questions and their research designs in such a way that such an exploration can be undertaken. Given the significant cultural, economic, political, and technological changes that have occurred throughout this generation's history, there's good reason to consider the imprint it's made on its citizens.

Generational comparisons have offered scholars a setting to employ other theoretical perspectives. For example, Putnam asserts that generational differences in levels of social capital offer the most robust explanation for levels of (dis)engagement between younger and older Americans. As Putnam writes, younger generations have felt "less connection to civic communities – residential, religious, organizational – without any apparent offsetting focus of belongingness, beyond the ties to family, friends, and co-workers that they shared with the older generation" (2000, 275). Weakening social and communal ties or a decline in social capital among younger generations, then, thwart the civic virtue necessary to foster civic and political engagement. Elizabeth S. Smith makes a similar argument regarding the importance of connections to others in predicting the political behavior of young adults, concluding that "social capital serves as an important resource in the socialization of politically relevant norms and behaviors, including the desire to cooperate for the benefit of society through participation in political and civic activities" (1999, 554).

Unlike the others, Smith *et al.*'s primary interest is not measuring one age group against another but understanding and explaining youth today: "We frankly do not ultimately care what former generations did or did not do that might not have been good. We care about emerging adults *today*, what *they* believe, think, and do, and what of significance that may tell us" (2011, 7–8). Although they do not utilize a generational lens as the others do, Smith *et al.*'s "sociological imagination" approach takes social conditions and culture into account. Specifically, they consider how such "macrosocial" issues as the growth of higher education, the delay of marriage, economic changes, prolonged parental support, and readily available birth control intersect with youth's experiences and influence their behavior (2011, 13–15). The authors conclude that, among other things, these conditions have prompted a disengagement from the political process. Moreover, given the study's roots in sociology, the authors view young adults' behavior as a reflection of culture and, therefore, unlikely to change with age:

> the lives and experiences of youth are great barometers of the condition of the adult world that is socializing them, into which they are being inducted. So if we see problems in emerging adult culture, with some exceptions, we do not expect them to simply change or disappear when those who inherit and sustain that culture settle down, have kids, buy houses, and become "real" adults. (Smith *et al.* 2011, 12)

The explanations Wattenberg (2012) offers for levels of youth engagement (or lack thereof) are rooted in generational differences. His focal point isn't the generational difference in social capital or culture between older and younger citizens but different levels of news consumption and resulting political knowledge. For Wattenberg, changes in news consumption have resulted in a disconnect from politics that has precipitated a decline in political knowledge and, as a result, low voter turnout.

Wattenberg's argument exemplifies other scholarly works, from *What Americans Know about Politics and Why It Matters* (1997) by Delli Carpini and Keeter to Bauerlein's *The Dumbest Generation* (2009), that explore the extent to which deficits in political knowledge among younger generations compared to older generations explain divergent levels of engagement. This line of reasoning taps into a very broad strain in the academic literature regarding youth political participation that looks at the role of political socialization that takes place in the home and in the school. For instance, Verba *et al.* find that "political stimulation in the home" is one significant determinant of young adults' future engagement (1995, 448). Others, such as Andolina *et al.* (2003), Jennings and Niemi (1968, 1974), and Jennings *et al.* (2009), also have studied the role that parents play in socializing their children to be politically active (or not). Schools also have been shown to be an important factor equipping young people with political knowledge (Niemi and Junn 1998) that, in turn, makes it more likely that they will be active citizens (Delli Carpini and Keeter 1996, Torney-Purta 2002).

Attitudes also play a prominent role in the theoretical approach of Wattenberg and others. For Wattenberg, younger generations' lack of a sense of civic responsibility distinguishes them from older citizens and helps to explain their disengagement and their comparatively weak voter turnout rates. Psychologist Twenge also offers an attitudinal explanation for youth disengagement. She asserts that, thanks in no small part to a culture rooted in boosting children's self-esteem and hyper-parenting, today's young adults have grown up speaking "the language of the self as their native tongue." For "Generation Me," "The individual has always come first, and feeling good about yourself has always been a primary virtue" (2006, 2). In her mind, this has led to a whole host of alarming behaviors including political disengagement.

On the "better engaged" side, a generational lens also is utilized to highlight the importance of citizenship norms – the role of

civic duty in particular – in explaining the nature and intensity of
youth engagement. According to Dalton, changing social conditions
that have taken place as younger generations have replaced older
generations have altered citizenship norms. With each successive
generation, living standards and levels of education have increased
and work experiences have changed, along with greater diversity
and changing gender roles. Using generations as context, Dalton's
model holds that social conditions influence citizenship norms that
ultimately determine the nature of youth behavior (2009, ch. 3).
Bucking the trend of the others who employ a generational lens,
Dalton asserts that generational differences, in citizenship norms
and the sort of behavior they spark in particular, have fostered
positive democratic consequences. Again, Dalton's conception of
engagement extends beyond the traditional modes emphasized by
those on the other end of the continuum.

According to Dalton, citizenship traditionally has been conceived
as a balance between public participation in traditional democratic
acts, such as voting, and an acceptance of the authority of the state.
As a result, the assumption that American citizens have a duty to
participate in these traditional acts has pervaded the nation's history and even is drilled into new citizens: "The centrality of obedi-
ence is quite clear in what the United States tells its new citizens"
(Dalton 2009, 23). Dalton holds, though, that this outlook on citizenship overlooks a facet with which young adults identify – "social
citizenship."

Pointing both to demographic changes and the expansion of civil
and political rights, Dalton asserts that there's been an emergence
of "a new category of social rights, such as social services, providing
for those in need, and taking heed of the general welfare of others"
(2009, 23). As such, "Citizenship thus includes an ethical and moral
responsibility to others in the polity, and beyond" (2009, 23) and
manifests itself in caring "about those less fortunate at home, as
well as issues of global inequality and the conditions of the global
community" (2009, 24) and "non-electoral activities such as buying products for political reasons and being active in civil society
groups" (2009, 28). As a result, "instead of seeing political participation primarily as a duty to vote, engaged citizenship prompts
individuals to be involved in a wider repertoire of activities that give

them direct voice in the decisions affecting their lives" (2009, 29). It's fair to say that this mindset of an expanded understanding of citizenship is in line with the broader definition of engagement.

As Dalton himself acknowledges, the notion of "social citizenship" or concern for "social responsibility" is resonant with European social democratic traditions (2009, 29). An argument could be made that the "engaged model" that Dalton outlines reflects Rousseau's notions regarding "general will" and social contract – one that envisions all citizens playing an equal and active role in providing consent of the governed and, thereby, ensuring popular sovereignty. The normative shortcomings of this thinking are discussed in the concluding chapter.

One of the few studies that constructs a model of youth engagement that is inclusive of nearly all of these features is the one offered in Zukin *et al.*'s *A New Engagement?* The authors' multivariate path analysis weighs the direct and mediated effects of several variables on engagement including sociological factors, social capital, political capital (political knowledge, sense of efficacy, civic duty), political attitudes, and mobilization. In the end, the authors find that depressed levels of political capital (such as civic duty) and the unlikelihood of being mobilized offer the most definitive explanations of youth engagement (or lack thereof) (Zukin *et al.* 2006, ch. 5). On the generational question, the authors conclude that the differences in engagement of younger generations compared to older citizens is due partly to unique features of their generation and partly to their stage in life – some behaviors (or lack thereof) will change with time and others won't. For example, younger generations' political knowledge most likely will improve as they age but the limited amount of political discussion taking place in their homes is a function of their upbringing.

By arguing that the "costs" of voting are high enough to affect a young person's decision-making and outweigh the benefits of participating, Zukin *et al.*'s conclusions support an explanation mostly in line with the rational choice theoretical perspective. It's worth mentioning that similar rational choice arguments are advanced in works such as Green and Gerber's *Get out the Vote* (2008) and Rosenstone and Hansen's *Mobilization, Participation, and Democracy in America*

(2003) that highlight the positive effects of contacting and mobilizing young people for elections – by lowering its cost, youth participation is more likely. Other work by Fitzgerald (2003), Wolfinger
et al. (2004), Kirby *et al.* (2008b), and Kawashima-Ginsberg *et al.*
(2009) also has explored the effects such institutional factors as voter
registration laws and Election Day practices have on the cost–benefit
analysis involved in youth participation.

Although all of these works make use of their own theoretical
perspective – by emphasizing historical or social conditions, by considering attitudes, by looking at cost–benefit analysis, or by some
combination of a few of these approaches – they nearly all utilize
a common theoretical framework by considering the engagement
of today's youth in relation to that of older citizens. The authors'
conception of what it means to be "engaged" really marks the division between scholars in their assessment of the political behavior
of young adults. An examination of these contrasting camps also
highlights noteworthy gaps in each theoretical structure that render
them incomplete explanations of youth participation.

Those who narrowly conceive of engagement, using this as the
foundation of their criticism of young people's political behavior, run the risk of overlooking the political possibilities that have
emerged thanks to technological advances and the rise in new media.
As Putnam himself wondered, might the Internet provide a sense of
connectedness and even social capital approximating the social ties
of previous generations (2000, 410–411)? Research by Cohen *et al.*
(2012) explores the potential of these digital tools to bring people
closer to politics – in its traditional form. For example, "Countable"
is a mobile app and website that tracks and explains legislation
under consideration and allows users to express their opinion on
the issues not only to each other but to their individual representatives.[1] This digital tool then promises to perform the same function
as such traditional political acts as making a statement at a public
meeting or writing to a congressperson. Often, the methods used
to study political engagement, longitudinal surveys specifically,
hamper inclusion of this angle in research (more on this in the next
section). If our purpose is to develop theories to explain behavior,
then explanations will be incomplete if they don't consider different

iterations of traditional political behavior – especially in light of Millennials' facility with new media.

If the "disengaged" set have failed to absorb new modes of engagement in their theoretical structure, those who embrace a less traditional definition of engagement have sacrificed key elements of past frameworks that are intrinsic to defining "political engagement." Much like the inattention to targeting and issues that mobilize young people, the literature on youth engagement does little to account for the results (or lack thereof) of less traditional forms of participation. It's worth remembering that classic research regarding political participation, such as that conducted by Verba and Nie (1972) and Verba *et al.* (1995), pays close attention to both targeting and outcomes. Again, Verba and Nie's theory of political participation is based on the supposition that different types of political behavior influence the political system in different ways. For them, the preferred governmental outcome dictates the appropriate method of political participation, and the mark of an engaged citizen lies in pursuing an effective method or collection of methods for influencing the political process.

Just as important as method choice for Verba and Nie is the impact of these methods. Their framework holds that one's political activity is meaningful if it sends a message to the appropriate officials in charge, results in a "concurrence" with these officials' outlook, and then influences the officials' actions (1972, 10 and Part III, 267–343).

For those on the "better engaged" end of the continuum, we see little attention being paid to these factors in considerations of youth engagement. Is this because youth political involvement today has not produced any results as the content analysis of newspaper coverage presented in Chapter 1 suggests? Or is it because we as scholars aren't including these factors in theoretical frameworks? In fact, the implicit assumption for scholars who assert that youth participation today is healthier than in the past is that traditional scholarly images of political behavior are outdated and have limited relevance given the changes the nation has undergone (Dalton 2009, 8). Interestingly, although Dalton offers "the engaged model" of citizenship as a healthier version of democracy, there is little consideration as to whether this enlarged version of engagement will produce anything. In actuality, as Dalton admits in his consideration of the tolerant attitudes of Millennials, this model of citizenship may not always have results:

> Although expressions of tolerance have grown over the past several decades, we know there is a gap between statements and behavior. The change in public sentiments has not been fully matched by the reality of public actions or public policy (2009, 100).

It seems, then, that scholars such as Rimmerman and Dalton, who assert that an "engaged model" of citizenship which is less bound to tradition and duty is the more preferable manifestation of democracy, must demonstrate that this model produces results or is able to effect change for those for whom the model is designed. Specifically, if engagement includes a wide range of activities from the traditional to the non-traditional, to what extent is the public sphere responsive to such modes of engagement? Dalton argues that the vote is "a limited tool of political influence" (2009, 78), especially compared to more direct and individualized activities that "allow citizens to focus on their own issue interests, select the means of influencing policymakers, and choose the timing of influence" (2009, 79). In order for such an approach to be held up as a new and improved model of engagement, there needs to be some evidence that it produces results.

In contrast, Howe and Strauss do point to the impact of the engagement – not as a result of Millennial engagement but due to the engagement of their parents. As they point out, due to more attentive (possibly overly attentive) parenting, parents of Millennials successfully pursued a number of public policies in an effort to protect the physical and moral well-being of their children, including policies regarding product safety, car safety, and regulation of the Internet (Howe and Strauss 2000, 112–113). This is evidence of results. Rimmerman's admonition to use civic rights organizations and their actions as models for a reconfigured contemporary democracy also is instructive. Both our collective memory and the examples Rimmerman cites point to the considerable strategizing that took place among civil rights activists and the end goals they sought – changes in public policy to eradicate institutionalized racial segregation and the suppression of minority rights.

Political impact, of lack thereof, has been a recurring theme in this text. The newspaper content analysis presented in Chapter 1 demonstrated that, when it comes to politics, Millennials haven't been perceived to have made much of an impression. In Chapter 2's discussion of the use of new media in politics, Cohen *et al.*'s warnings regarding confusing "voice" with "influence" were highlighted. It may well be that young people engage in politics differently than older people, according to arguments advanced by those who believe that young people are "better engaged." What's not clear, though, is whether politics has changed to accommodate this Millennial approach. Popular opinion certainly has tried to make that case. For example, as part of an NPR series on the Millennial Generation, Selena Simmons-Duffin stated,

> Because millennials look different en mass than generations past, the future is going to look different too. They've already led the country to massive shifts in opinion on social issues over the past ... Millennials have already steered the country to a place where diplomats tweet, gay marriage is turning mainstream, and running a blog can be more financially secure than a company gig. (*National Public Radio*, October 6, 2014)

Ashley Spillane, president of "Rock the Vote," made similar assertions regarding the political impact of young adults and even mirrored the "better engaged" argument that young people's power lies in methods of engagement beyond voting:

> Beyond exercising our power at the ballot box in recent elections, and as an extension, support for marriage equality, young people are also being credited for lobbying and changing the minds of the older generation by simply forcing a dialogue about how our generation approaches this debate. In fact, it has been reported that many politicians have altered their position on marriage equality in large part because of conversations they've had with their millennial children, a fact that highlights how these conversations are just as important as voting in elections. (*Huffington Post*, May 4, 2015)

Do such diffuse forms of engagement (even conversations with parents) have an effect on the political process? Should they be considered political if they don't have political effects? We can't answer these questions if we don't turn our attention not only to the target-ing of youth engagement but also to the outcome of their efforts in both our theory and in our method.

Studying youth engagement: methodologies

Theoretical frameworks do more than shape our explanation of a phenomenon – they also play a role in determining the way in which we study it. A research design serves as a researcher's plan for the methodology he or she will utilize to address those questions still in need of an answer. Methods come in all shapes and sizes and include experiments, observation, survey research, secondary data analysis, and qualitative methods (Frankfort-Nachmias and Nachmias 1992). As stated earlier, despite the vary-ing opinions on the health of young adults' political participation, a fairly uniform approach has been pursued when studying youth political participation. This is due most likely to the generational angle used by many of the scholars considering the subject. As this section makes clear, although the methods commonly used have great value, there are drawbacks to considering youth politi-cal participation through a narrow methodological lens. Moreover, the need for new theory to explain today's young people, or "cit-izen now," necessitates the use of new means of cultivating that theory.

Although it may seem counter-intuitive, research regarding political participation does not necessarily need to have behavior or activity as its primary point of focus. Instead, scholars can focus on those settings or contexts in which political activity often occurs (Brady 1999). For example, scholars could focus upon institutions such as trade associations and membership groups in which cit-izens often practice their political skills and utilize these skills when petitioning the government. Such an approach allows the researcher to identify potential locations for political action (1999, 743). Or the focus of study might be on issues or problems that prompt political action – gathering information about one's con-cerns and then enumerating the political actions one has taken to address these concerns.

As Brady points out, scholars frequently use a combination of approaches but the most popular by far is the political action approach. This certainly has been the case when it comes to the study of youth political participation. To be sure, there are exceptions here and there. For example, Putnam includes a number of measures of group membership in his indicators of engagement including union membership and holding a leadership position in a local organization (2000, 248–257). In this way, Putnam's work does employ an institutional as well a "political activity" approach. Putnam also includes measures of social trust and interest and attention to politics. The combination of looking at youth engagement through a generational lens and making their behavior the object of study has resulted in heavy use of survey research – this certainly has been the case with those scholars on the "disengaged" to "better engaged" continuum.

The methodologies used by scholars such as Putnam, Wattenberg, and Twenge center on secondary analysis of survey research and is reflective of their theoretical outlook. Given that Putnam's research question centers on generational effects on civic and political behavior, it is critical that he utilizes longitudinal data – data that measure the same sort of information (such as attendance at public meetings or contacting elected officials) over several points in time. Such data allow researchers to track changes, changes in civic and political behavior from one generation to another in this case, to determine whether these changes are due to differences in age groups or simply one's stage in life. In order to conduct longitudinal analysis, Putnam utilizes not only records of group membership but such social surveys as the National Election Studies and General Social Surveys, Roper Social and Political Trends and the DDB Needham Life Style surveys (2000, appendix I). Wattenberg's empirical approach mirrors Putnam's in that he relies on existing survey data in order to conduct longitudinal analysis – a comparison between the behavior of older age groups and that of younger age groups. These secondary data include surveys from the American National Election Studies, General Social Surveys, Pew Research Center and the National Annenberg Election Study. Again, this is an entirely appropriate methodological approach when trying to explain differences between generations. It's not without its flaws, however.

Clearly, survey research offers a powerful method for measuring what has been the most popular approach to studying political participation – the political activities and behavior of subjects. As Brady (1999, 742–743) and Skocpol and Fiorina (1999, 7) point out in their respective reviews of political scientists' studies of engagement, survey research offers an avenue for gathering a large amount of data from a representative sample that then can be subjected to careful statistical analysis. As suggested earlier, surveys that are regularly conducted over a long period of time also allow for comparisons between age cohorts.

If the purpose of survey data is longitudinal analysis, it is necessary that questions be worded in the same way with every iteration of the survey. However, there's often a downside to identical wording of surveys year after year. As Skocpol and Fiorina point out, category systems that might have made sense at the survey's origin may be less applicable to contemporary respondents (1999, 7–8). The availability (or lack thereof) of survey data that adequately measure the researcher's research question and allow for comparisons between age groups or nations often requires researchers to make difficult decisions. For example, in his consideration of news consumption between generations, Wattenberg was unable to identify recent survey data on news consumption of national political stories and was forced to utilize a close approximation (2012, 15–16). Brady identifies a number of other shortcomings associated with survey research, including the burdens it places on respondents not only to remember past events but to consider them in the terms that the researcher utilizes and the inability of surveys to capture information about respondents' lack of activity (1999, 742–743).

Also like Putnam and Wattenberg, Twenge relies on longitudinal survey data in order to make generational comparisons – specifically, she relies on a large set of psychological data gathered from the 1960s and 1970s (Baby Boomer data) and compares it to data gathered in the 1980s, 1990s, and 2000s. As she explains in her introduction and appendix, the psychological data is then supplemented by other works including survey data collected from the Higher Education Research Institute – surveys of American college freshmen that have accumulated approximately 50 years' worth of information.

Twenge's reliance on data from college students to advance her argument is apparent throughout the text – including her analysis of youth engagement. For example, in her discussion of young people's sense that they are powerless to control outside or external forces, Twenge points to data collected from college students during the 1960s and compares that to data gathered from college students 40 years later (2006, 139). In her discussion of a lack of interest in political acts such as voting and protesting, it's college students Twenge is considering. She cites low levels of interest among college freshmen in protesting and following the news, asserting that "Even staying informed is now apparently too much work" (2006, 141). Non-college youth are given little attention in Twenge's research.

So, why is this problematic? When conclusions regarding an entire age cohort are drawn on the basis of data gathered from a subset of the cohort (college students in this case), one wonders how representative are the data of the entire population of young people and how can one compare the composition of college populations in 2000 to those in 1960? Twenge anticipates the second criticism and addresses it in her appendix by asserting that the median income levels of college students' parents (when adjusted for inflation) haven't changed considerably between 1960 and 2000 and even concedes that "College students come from middle-class and upper-middle-class families, and this has not changed much over time" (2006, 244). Additionally, changes in racial composition have changed only modestly, according to Twenge, and "Most college student samples remain mostly white just as they were in earlier eras" (2006, 245). Although this explanation addresses the concern about comparing contemporary college data to information gathered 40 or so years ago, it only underscores the other methodological concern – how well do college campuses approximate the realities of an entire age group?

For a few reasons, there are significant shortcomings to this methodological approach when considering the Millennial Generation. First, as demonstrated in Chapter 1, not all young people are enrolled in college. As the burdens associated with financing a college education increase, the middle-class and upper-middle-class environment Twenge references most likely will become even more pronounced. Moreover, census data reported in Chapter 1 also indicate that young

African Americans and Hispanics currently are not enjoying the same levels of educational attainment as Whites and Asians. To draw conclusions about an entire population from data drawn from college campuses that are predominantly White and middle–upper class is to overlook a significant portion of the populace.

Second, there is good reason to believe (and now good data to demonstrate) that those enrolled in college may have a different set of attitudes and may engage in their communities differently than those young people not enrolled in college. Although survey data gathered from non-college-youth is not nearly as prevalent as data coming from college campuses, a greater effort is being made among researchers to gather their perspective. For example, CIRCLE's *That's Not Democracy: How Out of School Youth Engage in Civic Life and What Stands in Their Way* takes a systematic look at the gap in political and civic behavior between those who have attained a college education and those who have not (Godsay 2012). Similarly, Harvard University's Institute of Politics (IOP) has increased efforts since the inception of their biannual poll of Millennials to gather data and make comparisons between those enrolled in a four-year college and those who are not. These comparisons have highlighted differences in political attitudes and experiences. For example, in their spring 2008 survey, the IOP survey found that higher percentages of those enrolled in four-year college programs were registered to vote and, possibly more importantly, being offered opportunities to register to vote than those not enrolled in such programs.[2]

Third, there is a body of research that indicates that young people educated in lower-income communities that are highly ethnically diverse and composed predominantly of "non-college-bound youth" don't tend to be offered the same sorts of civic opportunities that instill skills, attitudes, and knowledge associated with political engagement such as in class discussions, simulations, and debate (Kahne and Middaugh 2008). Thanks to this "civic opportunity gap," the education system hasn't equipped this subset of young people to be informed and engaged citizens, thereby making it unlikely that they will be engaged citizens once they're adults. Twenge's assertion, then, that generational differences account for contemporary youth political disengagement may be misplaced. Instead, the education system may be at least partially to blame.

Unlike the others on this end of the continuum, Smith *et al.* utilize primary data – interviews and original survey questions – to study "emerging adults." The questions posed in the surveys and interviews are not replicated from previous surveys but an original attempt to learn more about young people's "typical assumptions, beliefs, norms, values, hopes, worries, goals, relationships, patterns of speech, and life experiences" that mark their culture (2011, 17). The authors seek to learn about the "established categories, expectations, explanations, and concerns that structure emerging adult culture" (2011, 17). Unlike the other scholars, there is no effort to impose a generationally tested standard of measurement on the objects of study. Instead, the research subjects themselves generate the standards. As the authors clearly state at the outset, they are not interested in making comparisons to previous generations: "We are less interested here in relative historical change over time than in the reality and meaning of the absolute facts today" (2011, 7).

Secondary analysis of survey research isn't confined to those who find young adults "disengaged." In his study of citizenship norms and their effects on behavior, Dalton utilizes data from the General Social Survey, Citizenship, Involvement, and Democracy Project, and the International Social Survey Program. This secondary analysis leads to his conclusion that there are different generationally based norms of citizenship that result in different types of behavior and that the "engaged model" of citizenship prevalent among young adults is a richer and more meaningful rendering of democracy.

Like Twenge, Rimmerman is highly reliant upon secondary data from college students – focus groups of college students and survey data gathered from the Higher Education Research Institute. In fact, he sees college students and college campuses as playing a key role in the future success of "New Citizenship." Of course, this brings up the same critiques directed towards Twenge – college campuses aren't necessarily the best representation of the youth population and those not receiving these lessons in citizenship stand to be further alienated from the political process when these efforts are centered on college campuses.

Like the other scholars reviewed, Rimmerman's primary approach in studying participation is to examine behavior – traditional and non-traditional. What distinguishes his work methodologically, though, is the attention he pays to the role of groups and their response to issues or public problems. As stated at the outset, organizations can serve as educative venues for citizenship. Additionally, groups are often the setting in which political participation exists and their vitality can be a reflection of the health of the populace and, thereby, a promising method for studying participation. Rimmerman points to civic rights organizations such as Southern Christian Leadership Conference (SCLC) and Student Nonviolent Coordinating Committee (SNCC) as performing these functions – organized efforts to address public problems that not only enliven democracy but teach people how to be active citizens. To him, grass-roots organizations such as ACORN (Association of Community Organizations for Reform Now) and campus-based organizations such as Public Allies and COOL (Campus Outreach Opportunity League) offer contemporary examples of organizations to foster participatory democracy. In these ways, Rimmerman offers an alternative approach not only to consider youth engagement but to study it.

The work by Zukin *et al.*, like its position on the continuum, is methodologically "middle of the road." Although it does give great consideration to the differences between generations, it's carried out through an original and multi-method design that includes holding conversations with panels of experts on youth engagement, conducting focus groups and the creation of a survey instrument that reflects the findings of the focus groups, subsequent web-based probability and nationwide telephone surveys, as well as a follow-up telephone survey. Like the study conducted by Smith *et al.*, the questions asked of young people were grounded more in their own experiences than those of previous generations, promising findings that are more reflective of young people as a generation.

Identifying and addressing the gaps

The bulk of this chapter has addressed where we've been in our consideration of youth engagement. To be sure, not all routes have been included in this effort but at least the major ones have been mapped. A final step, though, is to consider the paths that still need to be taken in order to address the gaps in our understanding – namely, a full consideration of the core characteristics of youth political participation and not only their causes, but their effects. Readjusting our research questions as well as our research designs is an essential first step. Paying close attention to such factors as which issues foster youth engagement, among which segments of the population these issues raise interest, preferred strategies and targeting of these efforts, and ultimately their effects and results must be included in careful considerations of youth engagement *today*.

The emphasis on youth *today* also is suggestive of shifts in research that might be considered. One of the ongoing questions both scholars and the public at large have pondered is whether the current state of youth engagement is a function of their stage in life or their generation itself. The data presented up to this point as well as the review of the scholarship lend strong support to the generational argument. Some, such as Wattenberg and Putnam, who argue in fairly absolute terms that the quality of youth engagement is generational, see this as a source of concern. Scholars on the other end of the spectrum, such as Dalton, who agree that young adults' political behavior is rooted in their generational features, see this as a cause for celebration. As Dalton posited and this text has amplified, scholars' assessments seem to be rooted less in approach than how "engagement" is defined. This reality underscores the need for a new theoretical framework – one that blends the key components of each of these approaches as well as a blended methodology to study the political behavior of young adults today – "citizen now."

What gets lost in debates regarding the definition of engagement and the health of youth political participation is a clear and complete appreciation of how youth are engaging in the world of politics, why they are taking the actions they're taking, and what they're accomplishing. The critical assessment of the literature offered in this text suggests that this is due mainly to our tendency to study youth engagement in a limited manner – nearly exclusively utilizing the "political actions" approach by comparing the actions of youth today to those of previous generations. Although generational analysis is an essential element in the consideration of youth engagement, it has its limits. As suggested, confining such studies to survey instruments that bear little relevance to young people today renders them less than meaningful. Instead, methodologies that are "grounded" in the experiences of young adults promise to offer a more accurate depiction of where young people are today – not necessarily in comparison to their parents or grandparents. Studies such as those conducted by Smith *et al.* and Zukin *et al.* that base their large representative surveys on the impressions and experiences of the subjects themselves serve as useful models.

Overuse of a generational lens also risks, as Dalton suggests, the perpetuation of outdated norms or expectations. For example, Wattenberg's lament that young people don't consume news or vote as much as older generations once did reads more as one yearning for the "good old days" rather than one seeking solutions to advance democracy today. Like it or not, youth conceptions of citizenship are rooted less in duty than in choice. Moreover, we know that these differences in civic duty have significant effects on political partic-ipation. Acknowledging these realities and seeking to understand them is a more productive approach than chastising Millennials for not being more like their elders.

Finally, much like the integration of qualitative measures in sur-vey research design, there's value in scholars taking a more "gran-ular" approach to their study of youth engagement – designing studies that allow careful attention to the details of the specifics of youth engagement. Research conducted on youth activism might inform these sorts of research designs. In recent years, such works as Clay's *The Hip-Hop Generation Fights Back: Youth, Activism, and Post-Civil Rights Politics* (2012), Haenfler's *Straight Edge: Clean-Living Youth, Hardcore Punk, and Social Change* (2006), and Taft's *Rebel Girls: Youth Activism and Social Change across the Americas* (2011) have offered rich and detailed explanations of how certain segments of the youth population have addressed issues of concern via activism. For the most part, these works utilize an ethnographic approach – one that is lacking in existing research but serves as a valuable addition.

Putting ourselves in the shoes of young people – in the questions we ask and the way we answer them, and considering engagement from the perspective of the problems or issues prompting behavior as well as the groups of young adults concerned with these problems – will allow us to better integrate the experiences of young people into our understanding of youth engagement. This is the task taken up in the next few chapters.

Think It Out

- Consider the ways in which you participate in politics and the democratic process. What factors have had the greatest impact on the manner and extent of your participation (parents, schools, peers) and how?

Act It Out

- Designate three locations in your classroom and assign the first "better engaged," the second "engaged differently," and the third "disengaged." In this variation on the game "four corners," when prompted, students should position themselves in the location they think best represents the quality of young adults' engagement in politics and democracy. Students should be prepared to explain their stance. Conduct the exercise again but in respect of the engagement of older citizens. Are the results any different?
- Write an editorial for publication in your school or local newspaper regarding young adults' engagement in politics. In your editorial, take a stand on the nature of youth engagement – is it something to applaud or criticize? Based on your stance, offer recommendations to educators, scholars, policymakers, and young adults themselves on appropriate steps to be taken to engage Millennials in politics.

Notes

1 Countable: www.countable.us.
2 Harvard University, Institute of Politics, Public Opinion Project: www. iop.harvard.edu/spring-2008-survey.

5

Citizen now: organizing
for action

Although it may run counter to common assumptions, younger and
older adults share a similar set of public concerns. Young adults care
just as much as older cohorts about "pocketbook" issues and foreign
affairs. This certainly has been the case when it comes to the economy. Since the early years of this century, the state of the nation's
economy has been a top concern to both the public at large and the
young adult population. As such, the reaction of young adults to the
dire economic situation they face offers an excellent opportunity to
pursue underutilized research methods – systematic study of how
youth organizations have offered a political response to the effects
of a poor economy on their generation.

This chapter and the next offer a rich description of three organizations whose actions (mostly political but not exclusively) have
been motivated by this pressing issue. By situating the research
from the point of view of these three groups and their leadership,
the intention is to address what's been lost in the study of youth
engagement thus far – careful consideration of the factors that foster youth action, the segments of the youth population responsive
to these issues, preferred strategies and targeting of their efforts,
and ultimately the effects and results of youth efforts regarding the
economy.

These case studies promise not only to guide the future research
efforts of youth political participation but to underscore the value
of inductive qualitative methodologies in the face of conflicting
theoretical frameworks – a situation we find ourselves in today.
In addition, this effort offers readers compelling models of young

adults engaging in the political process that even might inspire such engagement not only regarding the economy but on a whole host of issues facing this generation. But first, it's important to sketch out the problem motivating such action and its impact on young adults.

The "problem": the economy

Although there are risks involved with scholars overusing the generational theoretical framework, there is a good reason to believe that the context in which a group comes of age will have a long-term impact on the outlook and the actions of that segment of the population. To be sure, the state of the nation's economy is a critical element when considering generational context and, when it comes to the Millennial Generation, the economy has played a prominent role in this group's upbringing.

According to Gallup, in eight of the 14 years since the turn of the century, the economy has been identified as "the most important problem facing the U.S." With "government, Congress, and politicians" identified as the most important problem facing the country, 2014 was the first year since 2007 that the economy was not the top issue of concern. It's worth noting, though, that the economy came a very close second to "government, Congress, and politicians" in the 2014 poll.[1] These sentiments are reflected among the youth population specifically. In surveys of Millennials conducted by Harvard University's Institute of Politics, the economy was identified by most respondents as the "issue that concerned them the most" from 2008 to 2014. In the 20 surveys the IOP has conducted since 2000, the economy was identified as most important issue 11 times.[2]

It makes sense that the state of the economy has made an impression on those coming of age at the turn of the millennium – they're the members of the populace experiencing the effects most profoundly. The ripple effects of the "Great Recession" – years of anemic economic improvements, underemployment, the crisis in the housing market, ballooning student loan debt – have significantly burdened younger Americans. As Ross Pomeroy and William Handke from "RealClearPolitics" write, it's a burden unique to this

generation: "For the first time in America's history, an entire generation of her citizens are poorer, more indebted, and less employed
than the preceding generation" (*Business Insider*, January 8, 2015).
Research from the Pew Research Center supports this sentiment,
finding historically low rates of employment among young adults, a
historically wide gap in employment between youth and the remainder of "working-age adults," and greater drops in wage earnings
among young adults compared to other age groups in recent years
(2012).

Although the same research from the Pew Research Center
also reports that the majority of young adults continue to possess
a sense of optimism about their future (financial and otherwise),
that doesn't mean the generation is free of stress or frustration
regarding their economic circumstances. As Alexandra Petri
writes, citing survey data on young adults published by *USA
Today*, "We are stressed: 52 percent of us reported being kept
awake with stress in the past month ... Nineteen percent have
been diagnosed with depression, more than any prior generation
... We are stressed about work (76 percent of those stressed),
money (73 percent) and relationships (59 percent)" (*Washington
Post*, February 18, 2013). Similarly, among some young adults,
there is frustration towards previous generations and the policies they pursued that have contributed to Millennials' dire
economic straits: "The economic tragedy of the Millennial generation was written before many of us had even learned to read –
Baby Boomer parents and grandparents who, at once, genuinely
love and care for us, but have also created or perpetuated institutions, policies, and economic realities that have now hobbled
us" (*Business Insider*, January 8, 2015). Clearly, the economy is
one of many problems that have faced those born after 1980 and
one of many other items of concern for this age group (the war
on terror, the state of education, and crime are others). Also, the
"economy" is a broad label and might include a whole host of
issues related to the economy including wages, unemployment,
national debt, and government spending. Still, the economic
well-being of young adults is a theme that resonates throughout this generation's history and is a worthy focal point for our
attention.

Looking at youth engagement differently

The goal of this portion of the text is to offer an example of an alternative approach to studying and appreciating youth political participation – one that considers the issues or problems motivating political action and the organized entities through which this political action takes place. As Brady points out (1999), there is more than one way to gather information about one's participation in politics. As detailed in Chapters 3 and 4, the most popular way for researchers to collect this information is the *political actions approach*, which asks individuals to document and describe their political activities. An alternative approach is the *problems approach*, which "recognizes that political actions to influence politics are almost always rooted in citizens' problems, needs, and concerns" (Brady 1999, 743). Typically, when this approach is followed, survey researchers will identify a selection of public issues and ask respondents to indicate if these issues have incited them to engage in political action (1999, 788–789).

Considering the context in which one takes political action also is a prominent research approach in political science. As Brady explains, "The institutions approach recognizes that political activity intended to influence politics must be rooted in the respondents' daily activities – in the basic relationships or organizations of culture, such as family, work, religion, and voluntary groups" (1999, 743). Attention to groups has deep roots in the study of politics. For Verba, Schlozman and Brady, membership and participation in civic associations such as families, professional networks, church-related organizations, and other public interest groups play a foundational role in political activity. The authors' "civic voluntarism" model holds that politics is rooted or embedded in civic associations and political participation is influenced by membership in these associations: "involvement in non-political spheres of American voluntary activity can enrich the stockpile of resources relevant to political action" (Verba *et al.* 1995, 8).

Theda Skocpol's research provides an excellent example of studying political participation from the institutional approach. In *Diminished Democracy*, Skocpol charts the transformation of civic associations that, at one time, "were large and translocal networks"

(2003, 23) into ones dominated by "professionally managed advocacy groups without chapters or members" (2003, 7). This transformation has been deleterious to democracy according to Skocpol. Calling upon Alexis de Tocqueville, she argues that the ideals of American thought hold that "vigorous democratic government and politics nourish and complement a participatory civil society" (2003, 11). Historically, she contends, the health of democracy has been part and parcel of the health of the civic domain: "American civic voluntarism always flourishes as a vital part of muscular representative democratic governance – and never was in any sense a substitute for it" (2003, 73) and "America's traditional voluntary membership federations fostered active citizenship and made a difference in politics and governance," resulting in a system in which "ordinary people could participate, gain skills, and forge recurrent ties to one another" (2003, 124). For Skocpol, then, to lose one is to lose another.

For Robert Putnam, relationships (both formal and informal) hold the same importance in American democracy as they do for Skocpol. The notion of "social capital," the social networks and connections that foster a generalized sense of reciprocity and trust, serves as the soil out of which civic virtue grows, according to Putnam, and that ultimately manifests in healthy and robust civic and political engagement (2000, ch. 1). To carry the metaphor further, without relationships and associations, civic virtue can't take root and an overall sense of civic connectedness diminishes. For both Putnam and Skocpol, then, it is the quality and quantity of institutions and organizations to which one must look when considering engagement rather than simply the quality and quantity of activities. To have a complete picture of youth engagement, there is value in considering the role associations and groups play in their political participation.

Designing an alternative method of study

In addition to an alternative approach to studying youth political participation – one focused on groups' reactions to a common problem – this text also offers an alternative research model to the survey research so commonly used. Inductive in nature, qualitative

methodologies are focused upon "understanding how people inter-
pret their experiences, how they construct their worlds, and what
meaning they attribute to their experiences" (Merriam 2009, 5).
As Merriam explains, qualitative research designs often are used
"because there is a lack of theory or an existing theory fails to
adequately explain a phenomenon" (2009, 15). Given the stark
contrasts in, among things, the demographics and conceptions
of citizenship of Millennials compared to previous generations,
this text argues that this is the state of affairs in our scholarly
understanding of youth engagement (as evidenced by the ongoing academic wrangling about conceptualizations of engagement
and the health of youth participation). For these reasons, future
studies might benefit by integrating qualitative methodologies into
research designs in order to identify appropriate themes or categories and even tentative hypotheses for future work – a few of the
possible outcomes of an inductive methodological approach (2000,
15–16).

To round out this text then, an example is offered of how qualitative data might inform our future study of youth engagement – a
selection of case studies of efforts by young people to respond to
the economic crisis facing their generation. This sort of design will
provide a glimpse, from their point of view, of why the issue of the
economy spurred young people into political action and the manner
in which they addressed the problem via their organization. In his
thorough examination of the study of political participation, Brady
concludes that one area in most need of scholarly attention in political science is what makes individuals participate:

> Most models of participation emphasize factors affecting the supply
> of participation … Little attention is given to those factors, typically
> the political and social context of an individual, that create a demand
> for political participation. These factors include the issues that moti-
> vate participation, the social networks and local context that support
> or impede it, and the recruitment mechanisms that draw people into
> participation. (Brady 1999, 798)

Close study of groups' efforts offers an opportunity, then, to
address this gap in the discipline's current understanding. With
case studies, researchers are focused upon "insight, discovery, and

interpretation rather than hypothesis testing" (Merriam 2009, 42). "Particularistic" in nature, case studies result in a "rich, 'thick' description of the phenomenon under study" (2009, 43) and possess a "heuristic" quality – they "illuminate the reader's understanding of the phenomenon under study" (2009, 44). For our purposes, looking at youth political participation not only from the point of view of groups responding to a pressing problem but via an inductive methodology offers both an alternative and potentially advantageous research perspective.

The issue of the financial straits facing young people featured prominently in the analysis of news articles addressing the topic of the Millennial Generation that was featured in Chapter 1. Through careful study of the database of articles (over 350 articles from four national newspapers), a handful of youth-led efforts were identified and three initiatives undertaken by young people to address the economic condition of the generation ultimately were selected to serve as the focal point of the case study research:

- San Bernardino Generation Now
- The Can Kicks Back
- Young Invincibles.

Consistent with qualitative research, case studies specifically, these groups were selected in a purposive manner, not randomly. Although these groups share some common features, they also differ starkly when it comes to such things as organizational structure and strategy. This variety is in line with a "maximum variation" sampling strategy – one that offers variation in group types and, thereby, allows the researcher to look at a phenomenon in diverse contexts (Merriam 2009, 81).

In order to gain a rich understanding of these groups and their efforts, my study of these groups includes content analysis of their websites, Facebook pages, and other social media platforms, as well as in-person observations and interviews.[3] To be sure, qualitative methodologies have their limitations. Generalizability of results certainly is limited when dealing with just a handful of subjects who are not chosen randomly. Considerations regarding reliability and validity also arise when the investigator plays a central role in interpreting data, as is the case in qualitative designs. There are strategies that can be undertaken in order to address these short-comings. For example, the case study analysis offered here has involved soliciting feedback from those interviewed in order to identify and address any biases. Merriam describes this process of improving internal validity as "member checks" or "respondent validation" (2009, 217).

The potential benefits of this portion of the text extend beyond research and theory and into practical politics and democracy. Although the Millennial Generation is large in size and scope, its connection to the political process, voting in particular, is uncertain. By highlighting and examining prominent youth-led efforts to address a problem dominating young people, this effort offers a model to young adults (and the public at large) of ways in which Millennials are engaging in politics and democracy.

San Bernardino Generation Now, The Can Kicks Back, Young Invincibles: origins and missions

Ultimately, this case study research will point the way towards future research questions and designs we might consider when studying the Millennial Generation's involvement with the political process.

In order to appreciate the work of San Bernardino Generation Now (SBGN), The Can Kicks Back (TCKB), and Young Invincibles (YI), it is important to begin at the beginning – the origins of these groups, their respective missions, and how these missions have been manifested in their structures. From the highly developed national focus of YI to the ultra-local SBGN to the hybrid and ultimately fading structure of TCKB, these groups offer diverse approaches to a common problem – the economic prospects of America's young adults.

The national office of Young Invincibles is located on the fourth floor of an office building on K Street in Washington, DC – a neighborhood often identified as the epicenter of political power. As the *Washington Post*'s Jeffrey Birnbaum writes, K Street is commonly considered "the lobbyists' boulevard" (June 22, 2005) and houses numerous think tanks and organized interests. Despite the implications associated with the address, the office of YI is low-key in decor and quietly bustling with young staff members and interns. It is here that interviews with the group's executive director Jen

Mishory and Rory O'Sullivan, the deputy director of YI, took place. Like the group's founders Ari Matusiak and Aaron Smith, Mishory and O'Sullivan are graduates of Georgetown University's law school. Although the university itself is located in the Georgetown area of Washington, DC, Georgetown Law is situated steps away from Union Station and Capitol Hill. In many ways, their physical proximity to the nation's center of legislative power fostered the formation of the group.

The origin of the group coincided with the health care reforms that were being proposed by the Obama administration and were under consideration by Congress. As Mishory and O'Sullivan explained, there was a lot going on in Washington the summer before the last year of law school – health care was dominating the news and a number of assumptions were being made about young adults in the coverage. In response, the founding members of YI created a logo and put up a rudimentary website to serve as an "online hub to start talking about what young people actually think about health care and how these proposals will actually impact young people," according to Mishory. The name of the organization, "Young Invincibles," is a health care-related term that refers to young adults. According to Mishory, selecting it as a name for the group was meant to be "tongue in cheek."

The underlying goal in the formation of the group was to secure a "seat at the table" for young people when it came to crafting health care reform. In the view of YI's founders, when it came to health care policymaking, Millennials either were not being represented or were being misrepresented in the debate. YI's operating assumption at its formation was that Millennials wanted health care coverage – the cost of the coverage was the issue for them. With the founding members situated together at Georgetown Law, they reached out to their peers and began to talk to them about health care and how it affects them. At the same time, they began to research the health care system and its effects on youth – looking specifically at the financial challenges related to health care that could be great and could impact Millennials uniquely. Armed with this information and a growing network of peers joining their effort, Young Invincibles began to tell the health care story more broadly to policymakers and

Figure 5.1 Young Invincibles logo

the media at large. In a short time, the website was gaining press attention and YI began to grow.

Although the origins of Young Invincibles can be found in health care, it was not long before the interests of the organization spread beyond health care to include other economic issues. According to Mishory, nearly right away, the group's leaders realized how intertwined economic issues were with health care and that the economic concerns of young adults were missing from policy debates. Currently, the three core concerns of Young Invincibles are health care, jobs, and education, and YI's mission, as summed up by Mishory, is to "amplify voices of young Americans and expand economic opportunity for our generation."

The setting for the interview with the other Washington-based group under study offered a contrast. The interview with The Can Kicks Back's executive director Ryan Schoenike took place in a coffee shop in the Foggy Bottom neighborhood of Washington, DC, near the campus of George Washington University. The organization no longer maintains an office space in Washington or anywhere else and, as revealed during the course of our interview, TCKB is in the process of winding down. This book's study of TCKB allows for a consideration not only of the group's birth and ascendency but also the factors leading to its decline.

In comparison to Young Invincibles, the genesis of The Can Kicks Back seems to have had a slightly more personal element. As Schoenike explained, the group originated at a time when he found himself, at the age of 26 or 27, laid off due to the recession and watching with a friend the *Frontline* documentary "One Trillion and Counting" about the Obama administration's fiscal plan. With a degree in economics and a smattering of involvement in fiscal issues prior to this, Schoenike found himself wondering how the Obama administration would be able to meet their policy promises and control spending at the same time. Much like the founding members of YI, Ryan and co-founders Brandon Aitchison, Nick Triano, Michael Eisenstadt, and Jake Parent found that the youth perspective was missing in the debates over the nation's fiscal policy and wondered, as Schoenike stated, "where are other young people represented – where's our viewpoint"?

Also like YI, the founders of TCKB began by launching a website entitled "We Can't Pay That Tab." The purpose of the original website was "to create a conversation between policymakers and young Americans." Early on, though, it was clear that the group needed to find a way to secure resources if they were going to advance their efforts. This was an ongoing concern throughout TCKB's history and one upon which the group's existence really hinged. At the outset, motivated by the growing sense that legislative movement was imminent, the initial fundraising plan, as Schoenike explained to me, was to form a Super PAC. The founders of TCKB had seen other Super PACs, such as those founded by Carl Rove, as an effective vehicle to raise money and advance a cause.

It didn't take long for them to realize, though, that this was not going to be a successful way for the group to secure funds. Instead, they formed a relationship with an organization with a similar outlook that had a need TCKB could fill. The Committee for a Responsible Budget was a think tank focused broadly upon fiscal issues who had pulled together an effort called "Fix the Debt." The

Committee had an interest in reaching out to young people and the founding members of TCKB – Schoenike, Aitchison, Triano, Eisenstadt, and Parent – already had put together a plan for reaching out to young adults and connecting them with the nation's fiscal concerns. With the Committee for a Responsible Budget serving as its fiscal agent, TCKB could put that plan into action.

The name "The Can Kicks Back" was on the group's earliest founding plan and, as Schoenike explained, was meant to convey the message that "we're the generation kicking back." On a side note, the group's name also was conducive to its marketing campaign – the logo of the can was an effective emblem for both virtual and in-person messaging. As previous generations had, Millennials were not going to put off addressing the nation's fiscal problems or continue to kick the can down the road. Instead, TCKB believed that "young people needed a voice" and, according to Schoenike, it was young adults who would be most affected by the nation's fiscal situation and were the one age group most likely to do anything about it. Around the time of the group's founding, Senator Alan Simpson and Erksine Bowles had traveled the country as co-chairs of the bipartisan National Commission on Fiscal Responsibility and Reform formed by President Obama to alert the nation about the country's fiscal crisis and to promote their fiscal plan.[4] As Schoenike explained, it was unlikely that Baby Boomers were going to do anything to address the situation and older citizens, the World War II generation, might be worried about losing their benefits.

The founders of The Can Kicks Back believed that Millennials were the one age group that no organization had reached out to or had sought to connect with on fiscal issues, that it was young adults who could make a difference, and that TCKB (an organization founded and maintained by Millennials) was the group to communicate with and engage fellow Millennials. Pointing to the generation's size, their share of their workforce, their levels of education, their spending power, and their electoral power, Millennials were in a unique position to effect change. Moreover, there was a compelling reason for young adults to join the effort: "As a generation we've seen both the best and the worst. We watched as a world of infinite possibilities has shrunk with economic recession. We've struggled through political and social changes, yet we're still trying

Figure 5.2 The Can Kicks Back mascot

to remain optimistic that we can each have our own little piece of the American Dream" (www.thecankicksback.org/principles).[5] By mounting an aggressive grass-roots plan, the goal of the group was to activate the Millennial Generation or, more specifically, to "build a grassroots army to leverage action in Congress," according to Ryan Schoenike. This goal is reflected in their mission statement: "To educate, organize and mobilize young Americans in order to promote a sustainable, generationally balanced federal budget."

The third group under study is situated far from the nation's capital in both location and outlook. Of the three groups studied, San Bernardino Generation Now's origins seem to have the most direct link to personal experiences. Unlike YI and TCKB, this organization didn't form as a response to the effects of the nation's fiscal policy on young adults but something much closer to home – the bankruptcy of their hometown. In order to understand SBGN, it's important to understand the city in which it's rooted – the group's origins, outlook, and even logo are closely intertwined with the city of San Bernardino.

San Bernardino is located in what's referred to as the "inland empire" of Southern California. East of Los Angeles and at least 90 miles from the nearest beach, the inland empire consists of such cities as Pomona, Riverside, and Ontario. It's a region of California known for its agriculture, its industry, and even its ski resorts. The city is situated at the foot of the San Bernardino Mountains on the northern edge of the inland empire. According to the city's website, San Bernardino was founded as an outpost early in the nineteenth century by Spanish missionaries as they sought conversions among the tribes of Native Americans. The early years of the city were imprinted by these missionaries and their influence is reflected in the missions they built throughout the area. These missions later served as rancheros and haciendas as the area came to be an important trading post on the "Spanish Trail." In the 1850s, San Bernardino experienced an influx of Mormons who, during their time in the area, built a number of schools, roads, and a strong government – the city was officially incorporated in 1854. Around the time of the turn of the century, gold mining and railroad industries dominated the city.[6]

Nearly 100 years later, the *Los Angeles Times* labeled San Bernardino a "Broken City" (June 14, 2015). As the *Times* reported, by 2010, the city that the National Civic League had once designated an "All American City" found itself the second-poorest city in the nation – forced to declare bankruptcy in 2012. Severely affected by the recession, by the time it declared bankruptcy, San Bernardino's unemployment rate stood at 15 percent and the mortgage foreclosure rate was four times the national average at 8.8 percent (*Wall Street Journal*, November 4, 2013). Much of the city's decline was attributed to poor leadership and political corruption within its city council, ranging from charges of stalking, perjury, and identity theft. With a population of just over two million, San Bernardino has a sizable number of young people – the city's median age is 32 years and 54 percent of the population is 34 years or younger. Of the city's two million residents, 49 percent are Hispanic or Latino (of any race).[7]

The city's landmark is an arrowhead imprinted in the neighboring mountains that is visible nearly 30 miles away – 1,375 feet long and 449 feet wide, the arrowhead has been visible for centuries (before the arrival of Spanish missionaries).[8] It's a symbol that represents not only the city but also San Bernardino Generation Now itself – the group's logo features a raised fist against an outline of the iconic arrowhead. The city is a presence in both the group's image and its reality. As key members of SBGN explained, it was the city's bankruptcy and their unhappiness towards the city's elected officials that prompted the group's formation.

SBGN does not maintain an office space and none of its members earn a salary for their involvement with the organization. The interviews with a selection of the group's leaders and supporters were held at an office borrowed from another nonprofit organization located in San Bernardino. We met late in the evening – all of the participants in the discussion either work or go to school during the day. To be sure, the financial and political crisis facing the city was the impetus for the group's formation, but it was clear from both our discussion and the actions of SBGN that community organizing heavily influenced the group's founding and continues to shape the organization today.

Regarding its origins, key founders of San Bernardino Generation Now had been members of the Inland Congregations United for Change (ICUC). Rooted in the congregations, schools, and neighborhoods of Riverside and San Bernardino, ICUC "brings

Figure 5.3 San Bernardino Generation Now logo

people together to strengthen families and improve communities." Motivated by "ordinary people building their power to make extraordinary change," ICUC's issues of concern include access to health insurance; public safety, parks and recreation opportunities; and public works projects.[9]

It was with ICUC that some of the founding members gained an education in community organizing, and they brought this vision to SBGN. Much as ICUC envisioned change as coming from members of the community, the founding members of SBGN – Matthew Aguayo, Jennifer Elizarraraz, Christian Flores, Simon Hall, Michael Segura, and Richard Tejada – drew from their existing networks and groups of peers in the formation of the group. This core group already had close relationships via school, church, and neighborhoods, and they all brought others into the SBGN circle. According to notes SBGN provided to me, each founding member came to the group with their own set of values, skill set, and vision of where they "wanted to see San Bernardino go."

Certainly, this diversity of skills and vision was evident among the SBGN members who participated in interviews – a few studied political science in college, one is studying mathematics at Cal State San Bernardino, while another is in a graduate program in linguistics. Moreover, each came into the group with particular passions or interests and found not only that their involvement has allowed them to further these interests but that, by pursuing their passions, they've been able to further the mission of SBGN. For example, Fabian Torres is the group's de facto photographer – the group's Facebook page is filled with photo album after photo album of the group's activities and Torres's photographs. As he explained, his involvement with the group has offered an opportunity to further his interest and has helped him build the confidence to speak out to public officials about the homeless – an issue that concerns him. Torres's work also has provided the public with a picture of SBGN – highlighting not only their efforts but the city that they seek to revitalize. Marven Norman is a bicycle enthusiast and is passionate about improving bike safety throughout the area. He brought that passion to SBGN and played a role in the group's get-out-the-vote bike rides because "we're for anything that gets people out to bike," according to Norman. Michael Segura, a key leader of SBGN, is another good example of someone who came into the group with a particular skill and has integrated it into the group's work. Michael Segura is an artist whose forte is graphic design. A review of SBGN's brief history shows a notable emphasis on using painting not only to beautify San Bernardino but to bring together residents who share the same passion. An excellent example of this was the Seccombe Lake Park Mural Project that took place in the spring of 2015 and brought together a number of local muralists (both experienced and apprentices) to paint murals throughout the park – a park that at one time was lush and green but has deteriorated in recent years. As Segura explained, this event drew together not only different segments of the community but members of rival gangs who, through painting, focused their energies on serving San Bernardino.

At their formation, then, the group worked collectively to consolidate their ideas and their respective visions for San Bernardino into their current mission, "to empower and unite our communities through education and economic development. By encouraging the youth to be civically engaged, we will develop them into community leaders who will create a new cultural identity for our city." In line with their roots in community organizing, the message the group seeks to impart involves inspiration, revitalization, and empowerment. Specifically, they aim to spread

> The message of HOPE and UNITY. To bring hope to the apathetic and unity to those who divide themselves because of stature or race. We also hope to create a culture of accountability where the community is driven to take action and responsibility for their impact to their community. We would like people to see San Bernardino in a new light and empower themselves through a united voice.

If Young Invincibles and The Can Kicks Back were motivated to ensure youth a seat at the table or a voice in the political process, it seems that SBGN was motivated to help community members find their political voice and recognize the value of having a seat at the table. As members of SBGN explained in notes they prepared, they all came of age during the decline of their city, and it came to be the norm to see poverty all around them. For the founders of the group, the bankruptcy was "an eye opener" and a realization that elected officials had failed to represent them and their interests: "We realized those in power had failed us, and our frustration grew as we were not able to vote because of our age. We did not choose who were elected at the time, and there is where we began to understand the need for good policy making."

Building a structure to advance the mission

Although they vary, Young Invincibles, The Can Kicks Back, and San Bernardino Generation Now are mission-driven organizations that, to varying degrees, center on the economic circumstances of young people. The following chapters describe at length the ways in which these groups have pursued these missions and address more specifically the research questions enumerated earlier. In order to pursue their organizational goals, though, there needs to be some sort of structure in place – whether it's hierarchical and broadly dispersed or tight-knit and rather loose in structure. In many ways, the manner in which these groups organize themselves reflects their resources (financial and otherwise). The groups' structures also are reflective of their missions and shed some light on their strategies as well as the effects of their efforts.

Like San Bernardino Generation Now, Young Invincibles began as a volunteer organization driven by a dedicated team of friends. As Jen Mishory and Rory O'Sullivan explained, it was not long after graduation that the group began to open offices and build a staff. Without a 501(c)(3) status, YI needed a fiscal agent at the outset. 501(c)(3) organizations are tax-exempt charitable organizations and, as such, contributions to them may be deducted from a contributor's income tax. The Young Invincibles found a fiscal agent in the Center for Community Change. A Washington-based organization, the Center for Community Change's mission is "to build the power and capacity of low-income people, especially low-income people of color, to change their communities and public policies for the better" and its issues of concern include "jobs and wages, immigration, retirement security, affordable housing, racial justice and barriers to employment for formerly incarcerated individuals."[10] Like SBGN, the Center for Community Change reflects the community-organizing model, and it was to this sort of model that YI was tethered until fairly recently – at the time of our interview, YI had nearly

attained its own 501(c)(3) status. As Mishory explained, it was won-
derful to work with the Center for Community Change, but it was
time for YI to be on their own.

Young Invincibles is largely foundation funded, and its list of
funders includes such national (even worldwide) foundations as
the Annie E. Casey Foundation, the Kresge Foundation, and the
Bill and Melinda Gates Foundation.[11] According to Mishory, foundations have seen the value of funding a nonpartisan organization
such as YI that is focused on the issues central to the organization.
Moreover, YI is fairly unique in its focus on the economic effects
of health care on Millennials. As Mishory and O'Sullivan stated,
there are more organizations focused on youth and education and,
although there are other organizations focused upon the economy,
few are youth-specific.

Young Invincibles has had the resources, then, to develop an
organizational structure with a national reach that is staffed by paid
employees. In addition to YI's national office in Washington, DC,
the group has regional offices in Los Angeles, Chicago, New York,
and Houston, all of which have staff members on site. The group
does not have chapters or campus-based offices. In total, YI has 45
full-time staff members as well as five YI scholars, who receive a
paid fellowship, and a selection of interns – all of whom are paid.
Young Invincibles' reach is broadened by its partnerships – partnerships that include national organizations such as the March of
Dimes, local organizations such as Forward Montana, and a number of organizations that appeal to particular demographic groups
such as the AARP, Voto Latino, and the NAACP Youth and College
Division.[12] Through these collaborations, YI is able to reach out
to various segments of the population at various levels and engage
them personally.

The Can Kicks Back also sought to have a broad national reach
and the staff to support such a reach but found themselves consistently hamstrung by funding constraints. Thanks to their partnership with Fix the Debt, TCKB received the seed funding they
needed to get the group off the ground. There were other benefits
to being connected to the group – Fix the Debt had a large and
supportive staff, significant resources, and a number of contacts that
were accessible to TCKB, and provided the group with office space

in Washington, DC. As TCKB's executive director Ryan Schoenike indicated, "In the end we probably wouldn't have gotten off the ground without their support." At their height, key leaders Nick Troiano and Ryan Schoenike were working full-time for TCKB and had eight staff members with interns here and there.

There also are constraints involved with such a partnership. Although TCKB received its seed money from Fix the Debt, TCKB was tasked with raising the funds to support their activities, from recruiting, to crafting and disseminating messages, to taking action. Raising such funds was a challenge and, according to Schoenike, it held them up and limited what they could do. Specifically, they found it challenging to raise money when their focus was on young people and they wanted to remain nonpartisan. As Schoenike explained, "if we had decided to toe the line for one party or another, there would have been a lot of money available." In the founding members' minds, the nation's fiscal problems shouldn't be a partisan issue. Moreover, TCKB's founders didn't believe that's what Millennials wanted – they were independent politically and that was reflected in their membership, which was a mix of liberals and conservatives.

The additional challenge TCKB discovered when it came to their relationship with Fix the Debt was the limitations it put on their tone and tactics. For all intents and purposes, TCKB and Fix the Debt were separate groups – TCKB basically was contracted to do the grass-roots work for Fix the Debt, according to Schoenike. From the outset, TCKB tried to be aggressive in their messaging and even take actions Fix the Debt couldn't take. Rather than rely simply on data and facts and figures to communicate, TCKB utilized cultural memes, edgy and often irreverent humor, and funny videos to engage Millennials and get the message out. What they found, though, was that they couldn't always be as aggressive as they wanted; their connection to Fix the Debt placed limits on TCKB – the actions of one group reflected on the other.

The group's financial limitations undermined their organizational strategies. In an effort to build a youth-centered and broadly dispersed network, TCKB focused on building chapters at the outset. Nick Troiano, one of the group's founders, had a good deal of campaign experience and a background in politics and had done a good deal of work on college campuses. As Schoenike explained, reaching out to college students also made good strategic sense in that it's much easier to engage in politics when you're in college – the greater challenge is to engage those out of college and in their early twenties and thirties. As they were building, TCKB reached out to politically active campuses to spread their message and build chapters in order to build the college and young professional network they sought.

Fairly quickly, TCKB had nearly 100 chapters in 38 states. As Schoenike explained, it helped that the group had an attractive website that delivered dense information in a fun way, an appealing mascot, and was focused on an issue that was hot at the time. What they quickly learned, though, was how much effort it took to maintain these chapters. Given the setting, contacts at these chapters change on an annual and sometimes semester basis. Moreover, these chapters need a purpose and the consistent guidance necessary to pursue action. Such an organizational structure required an active local presence – a presence TCKB couldn't afford.

In order to avoid just these sorts of distractions, San Bernardino Generation Now maintains a much smaller, more nimble, and practically organic structure. As Michael Segura indicated, he conceives of SBGN more as a movement than an organization – this certainly reflects the founders' roots in community organizing. The efforts of the group and the manner in which they pursue these efforts stem from the needs of the city. At the same time, there seems to be a sense among the group that such an approach risks limiting the group's effectiveness and longevity.

As the group was founding and asserting an identity independent of the ICUC, there was some discussion among the members about either incorporating into their own nonprofit organization or having the ICUC, a 501(c)(3) organization, serve as SBGN's fiscal agent – the route Young Invincibles and The Can Kicks Back took. From the outset, the group was uncomfortable with the limits involved with being a nonprofit organization – 501(c)(3) organizations, tax-exempt charitable organizations, must remain nonpartisan and may not be aligned with or endorse particular parties or candidates. As Michael Segura expressed, they chose not to incorporate or attach themselves to a nonprofit in order to maintain the freedom to engage in their communities in a number of ways – including politics.

Consequently (and purposely), the SBGN effort, for all intents and purposes, is kept alive by the passion and dedication of a small group of friends who volunteer their time to the group – a core group of ten members. It is this core group that plans and executes the actions of SBGN and ensures that they're meeting their mission – the group members vote on their actions with a simple majority required for approval. Members of the core group are expected to serve on at least one SBGN Committee (Community Relations, Media, Operations), be present at monthly SBGN Mixers, donate a minimum of $5 monthly to the SBGN fund and/or participate in an SBGN fundraiser during each month, and be a presence and contribute to the core group's monthly meetings.

It's clear that this core group, working collaboratively, is bound together both by friendship and a common passion for the city and its revitalization. SBGN's structure reflects this. At the same time, although SBGN's structure and mode of operation is true to its grass-roots mission, it also can be frustrating and even limit their actions, as the group made clear in notes they provided:

> Our structure at the moment is very loose, we have experimented with different types of structure and we are still in the works of finding the correct one. It's difficult because there are many voices and ideologies that we try to accommodate to, also we are primarily a social group composed of friends working together to improve the city, therefore we see each other as grassroots to the core.

If it were a nonprofit organization, SBGN could pursue grant money, perhaps open an office space and hire some staff. These organizational trappings aren't within the group's aspirations, though – instead, they believe such an approach risks both their mission and their success. With grant money, there's the danger, as Michael Segura indicated, of funders diverting the group from its mission and core values. Even more, in another portion of our interview on the subject of funding, Segura asserted that "Money complicates things and it takes the passion out of life." In line with

this sentiment, Richard Tejada postulated that the constant search
for funding that nonprofits must undertake in order to cover over-
head costs undermines the key ingredient of SBGN – passion for
the mission of revitalizing their city:

> A big part of it is the fact that everyone contributing to the group is
> there because they want to be there – not because there's a paycheck.
> All these guys are definitely here because they're passionate, there's
> no monetary gain. From a personal point of view, that's part of the
> problem with a lot of the nonprofits – when a majority of their fund-
> ing goes to administration, then that might be one of the reasons why
> they're ineffective. I can't say that for all nonprofits – in some situa-
> tions, that's the case.

Needless to say, as Miriam Nieto explained, a group fueled by
young volunteers who work, are in school, and who need to pay their
own bills faces challenges. All of the group's funding for events and
activities comes from donations and membership dues and limits
their capacity. As she summed up, Nieto worries that their limitations compromise their ability to be as successful as they and members of their community wish:

> At least for me, it's also very scary. There's so many organizations and
> so many people that are very powerful that are reaching out to us. We
> don't have the capacity to be able to meet all of these requirements –
> to be able to fulfill all these requests that they're making of us … so
> I think that we have this kind of status where people trust us but at
> the same time, if we can't meet those requirements, it kind of feels
> like a letdown and it's not just a letdown to this organization but it's a
> letdown to the entire city.

Still, despite the very small structure and limited funding, the group
is able to list a number of successes. As Fabian Torres stated, "We're
not the normative group that follows certain guidelines – we're just
very sporadic, but somehow it works." As Nieto put it, quoting the
moderator of one of their recent workshops, "Nobody really under-
stands how you're doing it, but you're doing it."

The ability to endure, though, is what occupies much of their
attention now – specifically, building the sort of structure that will

ensure longevity. As Jorge Heredia made clear, "The reality of it is that the group right now is dependent on us being here and being passionate about what we're doing." In order to bring in new people and train them, "it's crucial that we have that structure," according to Nieto. Just what is the right structure, though, is the question the group seems to be wrestling with. It seems that, whatever structure the group ultimately settles on, it will be rooted in San Bernardino's youth population. Currently, the group is building a chapter at the local college that may serve as a source of future SBGN leaders. Their greatest hope seems to lie in the extensive work they do in high schools. From the time some of the founders were involved with ICUC to today, the group has visited high schools to spread their message.

There also is interest from national civic education organizations in incorporating SBGN into the curriculum – fostering a sense of civic engagement in the area's youth so they can continue the group's work. Much like the city struggling to revitalize that it represents, SBGN is a work in progress whose future is uncertain.

Although they differ fairly dramatically in origins and structure, there are a few elements that unite SBGN, TCKB, and YI. Obviously, they all are motivated to one degree or another by the economic conditions facing their generation. There also is a resonance in their missions. The Can Kicks Back seeks to "*educate*, *organize* and *mobilize* young Americans in order to promote a sustainable, generationally balanced federal budget"; SBGN aims to "to *empower* and *unite* our communities … By encouraging the youth to be civically engaged, we will *develop* them into community leaders"; Young Invincibles' goal is to "*amplify* voices of young Americans and *expand* economic opportunity for our generation" (italics added). How have these groups gone about educating, organizing, mobilizing, empowering, uniting, and amplifying the voices of young adults and how do these methods fit with competing conceptualizations of engagement? More importantly, why have these groups followed these strategies and targeted their efforts in the way they have in pursuit of their missions? These are the questions taken up in the next chapter.

Think It Out

- The Can Kicks Back and Young Invincibles were motivated to form because they felt young adults needed a "seat at the table" when it came to policymaking. To what extent do you believe legislators consider the interests of young adults when crafting and passing legislation? What explains their degree of attentiveness (or lack thereof)?

Act It Out

- As a group, conduct a brainstorming session on the issues that matter to young adults. Create a word cloud to visually depict which issues are most important to young adults. Conduct some research to determine if there are any groups that represent young adults on this issue.
- Using this brainstorming session as a foundation, simulate the creation of a new group to address an issue facing young adults:
  - create a mission statement and name;
  - outline a structure for your organization and a plan for recruiting supporters;
  - devise a fundraising strategy to support the new group.

Notes

1 "Cluster of Concerns Vie for Top U.S. Problem in 2014," Gallup: www.gallup.com/poll/180398/cluster-concerns-vie-top-problem-2014.aspx.
2 Harvard University, Institute of Politics, Public Opinion Project: www.iop.harvard.edu/harvard-public-opinion-project-0.
3 This research protocol was reviewed and approved the Institutional Review Board of Rutgers University, Protocol #15–507M.
4 For more information on the National Commission on Fiscal Responsibility and Reform: www.fiscalcommission.gov/about.
5 Not long after the completion of data analysis and during the writing process, the group's website was taken down. The URLs cited throughout the text indicate where this information was found at the time of data analysis.

6 City of San Bernardino, California: www.ci.san-bernardino.ca.us/about/history/history_of_san_bernardino_(short_version).asp.

7 US Census Bureau: American Fact Finder: http://factfinder.census.gov/faces/tableservices/jsf/pages/productview.xhtml?src=bkmk.

8 City of San Bernardino, California: www.ci.san-bernardino.ca.us/about/history/history_of_san_bernardino_(short_version).asp.

9 Inland Congregations United for Change: www.icucpico.com.

10 Center for Community Change: www.communitychange.org/real-people/mission.

11 http://younginvincibles.org/about/our-partners.

12 Ibid.

## 6

Citizen now: responding politically

The fundamentals of the groups under study – San Bernardino Generation Now, The Can Kicks Back, and the Young Invincibles – have been established. Their origins, the missions of each group, and the structures that each has built (or continues to build) in order to meet their goals have been laid out. This chapter addresses the fundamental research questions of this book, including how the issue of the economy motivated the actions of the groups under study, the segments of the youth population responsive to this issue, the groups' preferred strategies and the targeting of their efforts, and ultimately the effects and results of these efforts.

Primarily through survey research, much of the existing scholarship has focused on defining and quantifying the engagement of today's young adults in relation to previous generations, measuring the effects of social, historical, and attitudinal factors on such behavior and ultimately declaring youth either "disengaged," "better engaged," or somewhere in between. What has been given less consideration are the targets of youth action, the context out of which these actions arise, and the effects or impacts of these efforts. A clear and complete appreciation of how youth are engaging the world of politics, why they are taking the actions they're taking, and what they're accomplishing is where we've fallen short.

Using these three groups as case studies, these topics are addressed from the point of view of the objects of our study – young adults. This close study of groups' responses to the economy also provides current examples of the sort of "engagement toolkit" young adults use to address an issue facing their generation and, thereby, contributes to our ongoing consideration of how young adults conceive of engagement – traditionally with a bulls-eye focus on politics or something broader that encompasses a wider range of methods with a more tenuous connection to politics specifically.

By utilizing a qualitative methodology that is inductive in nature, the aim here is to offer descriptive accounts of each case study that address the research questions proposed as well as identify some themes that unite all of the case studies. The accounts are based on interviews and observations of each group and the content available on each group's website as well as their social media platforms.[1] Such an approach often is appropriate when scholars' theoretical frameworks don't seem to be doing an adequate job of explaining, predicting, and understanding a phenomenon – youth political participation in this case. The work done in qualitative studies might provide a path for future study and future theory-building. The concluding chapter offers a set of research questions and designs that spring from these case studies. Offering rich accounts of these groups' actions in response to the economic consequences facing youth, their strategic approach and their reasons for following such an approach, and ultimately the effects of their work is the first step, though.

Taking action

As we consider the actions that these groups take in the pursuit of their missions, it's worth reviewing those key elements political scientists commonly have identified as intrinsic to political action – that participation needs to involve action rather than just expressing an interest in politics or possessing a sense of efficacy; that activities must be voluntary and undertaken by average, ordinary citizens and not elites; that action must be political in nature and directed at governmental policy or activity; and the participation must be geared towards influencing an outcome or result. As detailed in Chapters 3 and 4, although conceptions of engagement have expanded for some to include such methods as digital activism and even volunteering, these methods may not always satisfy the definition of "political." One clear finding resulting from the study of these groups is that, in advancing their cause, SBGN, TCKB, and YI pursue (or used to pursue in the case of TCKB) a variety of activities and utilize different platforms and venues to pursue these activities. Both within and between case studies, though, it's undeniable that political action in its truest form holds a prominent position in their strategic thinking and in their actions.

Raising awareness

All three groups under study, SBGN, TCKB, and YI, have an educational element to them – SBGN and TCKB even include education in their mission statements. Moreover, providing information is one incentive used by all three of these groups as a means of attracting supporters. Even the group leaders interviewed considered acquiring information to be one of the key gains of membership. As Jorge Heredia of SBGN stated, "I give credit to Generation Now for really informing me – making me get involved with knowing what's going on here in the city."

As Brady (1999) points out, gathering and possessing political information or connecting with organizations that provide information about an issue doesn't necessarily constitute political activity. Instead, they are passive measures of concern for politics or ways of learning about politics but don't involve activity or an effort to influence (1999, 739). Although they don't meet the threshold of political action, acquiring political information or receiving messages regarding politics certainly have been considered indirect political efforts. For example, Zukin *et al.* (2006) argue that cognitive engagement (learning about politics) is a necessary but not a sufficient indicator of citizenship and that political activity sometimes spurs understanding. Levine (2007) agrees and even holds that, in many instances, use of political methods is a function of knowledge. For San Bernardino Generation Now, The Can Kicks Back, and Young Invincibles, informing supporters about the effects of their city's economic health, or the nation's fiscal policy, or the economic consequences of health care on them as young adults is one of their prime functions, and they use both real-life and virtual platforms to get this message across (see Table 6.1 for a listing of each group's various media platforms and activity on each platform).

At the outset, raising awareness for Young Invincibles meant helping young adults see the connection between the costs

Table 6.1 Social media presence

Social media platforms	San Bernardino Generation Now	The Can Kicks Back	Young Invincibles
Website	Yes but not broadly advertised	Yes	Yes
Blog on website?	N/A	Yes	Yes
Facebook	Yes	Yes	Yes
# of likes	2,772	12,343	16,356
# of posts (March 1–August 27)	297	1	299
Average # of posts per week	50	1/6	50
Twitter	Yes	Yes	Yes
# of tweets in all	100	2,199	18.2k
# of followers	206	4,050	10.7k
YouTube	Yes	Yes	Yes
# of subscribers	87	182	N/A
# of views – total	13,328	280,032	203,944
# of videos	139	48	79
Most popular video	www.youtube.com/watch?v=le43db1OLYg	www.youtube.com/watch?v=kjLuj0EhsQg	www.youtube.com/watch?v=wpRNAkG-Nx0
Tumblr	Yes but not used often	No	Yes
Instagram	Yes	No	Yes
# of posts	335		437
# of followers	550		628

associated with health care and their everyday lives. As they were getting started, the founding members began by researching the effects of health care on youth with specific attention to the financial challenges related to health care that could be great and could impact Millennials uniquely. Armed with this information, YI began to tell their story to their target audience (18–35-year-olds) – beginning with their peers and young adults in their respective family circles. Fresh out of law school, YI's founding members were young professionals, which opened up various professional networks and allowed them to spread their message about the costs of health care to those segments of the youth population. As YI broadened their issue areas to include jobs and education, their messaging included information on those topics also. Coalitions were also a critical route for raising awareness for YI at the beginning and collaborations with youth-focused groups continues to be a method for educating young adults.

Interviews with YI's executive and deputy directors explored whether the nature of the subject matter – health care policies, student loan debt, and the job market – made messaging difficult. Was it difficult for their target audience to have a visceral connection to the issues YI was discussing? Quite the contrary, according to Mishory, who argued that these are "pocketbook issues" that matter to young people and motivate them considerably – especially the subject of student loan debt when, as Mishory puts it, they're "seeing it coming out of their paycheck every month." From the executive director's point of view, the topics YI tackles are "very resonant in people's day to day lives" and, therefore, facilitate messaging.

How do they get their message out today? Conducting research and mounting public education campaigns to disseminate this research and raise awareness remain important components of YI's strategic approach and serve as routes for involving young adults in the group. Much of this material is housed and disseminated via their website, and the result is a significant amount of content. For each issue area – jobs, health care, and education – there are numerous reports, fact sheets, infographics, and blog entries that address each topic broadly as well as the various facets of each subject area. For example, under the heading "Education," there are fact sheets that address various topics involved with student loan debt, including "Understanding Student Loan Interest Rates," "Understanding Your Financial Aid Award Letter," and "Facts about College Affordability."

Much of this content is delivered via infographics that not only are visually appealing but pinpoint the relevant key issues surrounding education, health care, and jobs. At the same time, much of the content YI delivers comes in the form of reports – detailed research

MILLENNIAL PARENTS:
THE MOST IMPOVERISHED PARENTS IN A QUARTER CENTURY

4.3 MILLION young parents are living below the poverty line.

Despite pursuing higher education more than any generation before, Millennial parents lack the time and the money to have a satisfactory quality of life.

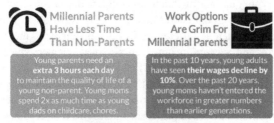

Millennial Parents Have Less Time Than Non-Parents

Young parents need an **extra 3 hours each day** to maintain the quality of life of a young non-parent. Young moms spend 2x as much time as young dads on childcare, chores.

Work Options Are Grim For Millennial Parents

In the past 10 years, young adults have seen **their wages decline by 10%**. Over the past 20 years, young moms haven't entered the workforce in greater numbers than earlier generations.

Millennial Parents Have More Expenses Than Non-Parents

Single Millennial college grads with children have debt levels **40% higher than non-parents**. In 2014, childcare and education accounts for 18% of the cost of raising a child.

For more info on young U.S. parents, visit:
YoungInvincibles.org

YOUNG **INVINCIBLES**
together, invincible

Figure 6.1 Young Invincibles infographic

conducted by the YI team. Recent reports include "Closing the Race Gap: Alleviating Young African American Unemployment Through Education" and "The Future of Millennial Jobs." Finally, through their blog (nearly always up to date), YI keeps their site and the topics of concern fresh and topical. YI's "Millennial Memos" cover such topics as "keeping tabs on higher education debates" in the context of the Republican primaries and Starbucks' new jobs program.

In numerous ways, YI offers interactive opportunities on their website and social media platforms as well as tools to personalize the messages being delivered. Each Monday, for instance, YI hosts hour-long question and answer sessions with various policy experts on such topics as "Creating Job Opportunities for Young Adults," "How Affordable Housing Impacts Millennials," and "LGBTQ Couples: Getting Married, Getting Covered." On their website, YI's "It's Not Always Sunny in Young America" tool allows visitors, by typing in their birthdate, to compare the various economic, social, and educational conditions of their generation to those of their parents, such as differences in rates of unemployment, cost of college, and average income.[2] To personalize their educational message, YI offers the "Student Debt in Perspective" tool where visitors, by typing in the amount of student loan debt they hold, can contextualize that debt and make comparisons to the generation preceding theirs. For example, according to this tool, a young adult today who types in $20,000 in student debt soon learns that, with that amount of money, she could make 0.5 average down payments on a new home, buy 540.7 toaster ovens, or even 10,050.3 rubber

Figure 6.2 Young Invincibles Millennial Monday advertisement

duckies! This same visitor also would learn that the debt she holds actually is $5,000 less than the average person's student loan debt but twice as much as the average rate in 1990.[3]

These public education efforts go a little further or are more specific than simply raising awareness about how these issues intersect with the lives of young adults, though. Instead, the leaders of YI view consumer education as a key element of their approach – making people aware of what coverage is available to them. To be sure, they use digital venues to accomplish this goal – their website, earned media, social media, and even some digital advertising. The emphasis on virtual outreach complements rather than replaces in-person communication, though. Thanks to their regional organizational structure, the YI is also able to hold workshops and health fair events at which they not only disseminate their research but even engage in direct service to community members by signing them up for health care coverage (more on that come).

YI's efforts when it comes to raising awareness certainly reflect not only what we know about young adults today but also the study of young adults. In the nature and delivery of YI's message, we hear echoes of comparisons between generations that the content analysis of news coverage presented in Chapter 1 uncovered, as well as use of the generational lens that scholars frequently use. On a more practical level, opportunities for interaction rather than simply swallowing information force-fed to them also is reflective of Millennials' consumer tendencies (both of news and goods). Young Invincibles' strategy when it comes to raising awareness also says a lot about what a group can do when it has resources. The group's broad physical reach (with five different regional offices) allows them to engage in national in-person outreach efforts – something that groups with one (or no) office can't pull off. Moreover, the amount of content generated and disseminated by the group is most likely reflective of their large, paid staff – again, an unlikely feat for organizations with either a small staff or a team of volunteers.

Educating young adults about the effects of the nation's fiscal policy on their everyday lives was a core function of The Can Kicks Back as well. Building the "grassroots army" that executive director Ryan Schoenike referenced really was dependent upon an informed body of young adults. As noted on the TCKB website,

"Our experience has shown us that young people will get involved once they learn about this issue and are given a way to make an impact."[4] TCKB's efforts in raising awareness, although dependent certainly on the hard work of the group's key figures, highlight both the advantages and disadvantages of a successful social media campaign as well as a structure in which chapters on college campuses are at the core.

From Schoenike's perspective, the content TCKB was trying to get across was dense – how fiscal responsibility relates to employment opportunities, long-term growth in the nation's infrastructure, and global competitiveness.[5] The hallmark of the TCKB, according to Schoenike, was presenting this content in edgy and even irreverent ways (with the help of a fun mascot). As he stated, rather than simply posting facts and figures when delivering this content, their method effectively was, "you're screwed, here's a funny video" – a reminder that, as they were building, the group was reaching out to college students and building chapters throughout the country. Like YI, much of this content was housed on their website – a sleek and vibrant platform – and disseminated via their various social media outlets. This sort of approach promised to be successful given that audience. As noted in the previous chapter, a sign of the group's decline, TCKB's website was taken down not long after data analysis for this book was completed (although their Facebook and Twitter accounts remained active).

Again like YI, TCKB offered visitors to their site a good deal of substantive content on such topics as how "federal support for research and development is being crowded out by decreasing tax revenues and unsustainable entitlements" and how investments in infrastructure have been hampered by "growing interest on the debt, entitlements, and tax loopholes."[6] Although their site included detailed reports such as "Swindled: How the Millennial Generation Will Pay the Price of Washington's Paralysis" and "Restoring Balance: Millennial Perspectives on America's Spending and Investment Challenges," TCKB's messages mostly were delivered through attractive yet substantive infographics and highlighted how these fiscal problems will affect TCKB's target audience specifically.

The message regarding infrastructure, for example, read, "Without investment in our infrastructure today, our economy of

Figure 6.3 The Can Kicks Back infographic

tomorrow will not succeed. We'll leave future generations unpre-pared to deal with the challenges of the 21st Century economy." Rather than juxtaposing the status of today's youth with that of pre-vious generations, TCKB's content seemed to compare the promise of the Millennial Generation with the realities young adults face today. If there's anyone to blame, it seems that TCKB points the finger at Congress. For example, the infographic "Building the Millennial Dream," which depicts a cartoon figure of a young man sitting at his desk and dreaming of his girlfriend, reads:

> Mike Millennial is in search of a job that will allow him to pay his stu-dent loans, buy a car, own a home, and eventually marry his girlfriend Jessica. He wants to remain optimistic but he's grown frustrated with Congress's inability to agree on what needs to be done to spur eco-nomic growth. Creating sustained economic growth will require a combination of fiscal reform and strategic investment.[7]

When it came to spreading the word nationally, TCKB also relied on their college campuses and key supporters on these campuses. As Schoenike explained, the group viewed recruiting as a funnel – starting broadly in the hopes that they'd identify leaders in key areas and on key college campuses. Once these leaders were identified, the goal then was to give these supporters "actionable" items to do such as holding an event on a campus or in a community, writing op-eds

Millennial Dream

VS.

MILLENNIAL REALITY

Figure 6.4 The Can Kicks Back, Millennial Dream vs. Reality

or letters to the editor for their local newspapers. To get these chapters up to speed and effectively spreading the group's message, TCKB created a kit that included detailed background information on the group's key issues and logos to download and even offered strategic advice and support. As Schoenike explained, providing consistent support to these fledgling chapters around the country from their office in Washington was a labor-intensive process.

The Can Kicks Back's hard work in building awareness and spreading their message paled in comparison, though, to the boost they received via an unlikely route – the "Gangnam Style" video. In 2012 and 2013, South Korean musician Psy was everywhere – his song "Gangnam Style" was all over the radio and the video for the song was a YouTube sensation. At the time of this writing, Psy's video had been viewed over 2.3 billion times.[8] Capitalizing on the song's success, TCKB used the tools of social media to their advantage and, with the help of TCKB Advisory Board member Senator Alan Simpson, launched the "Three-a-Week" recruitment challenge in a YouTube video. In the video, Senator Alan Simpson sends a message to young people on why they should take to social media to fix the nation's fiscal crisis. His message, though, is punctuated with clips of Simpson dancing "Gangnam Style" with TCKB's mascot:

> Stop instagramming your breakfast, and tweeting your first-world problems, and getting on YouTube so you can see "Gangnam Style",

and start using those precious social media skills and go out and sign people up on this baby – three people a week and let it grow. And don't forget – take part or get taken apart and boy these old coots will clean out the treasury before you get there.[9]

As Schoenike explained, the video was Nick Troiano's idea. The group posted the video on Reddit on December 4, 2012, and it went viral. Political commentator David Frum saw the video and was one of the first high-profile figures to tweet it out. The Simpson "Gangnam Style" video had 100,000 views in the first 24 hours and all the cable channels picked it up. CNN's Anderson Cooper covered the video on his "RidicuList" segment as well as every other cable channel. Thanks to the video, the group picked up 5,000 new supporters.

The viral success of the "Gangnam Style" video changed everything for TCKB. The group was still fairly new when the video exploded and, according to Schoenike, they weren't ready for it. If TCKB's leadership had been better prepared and had a sense of how successful the effort was going to be, they could have really capitalized on the attention and captured even more supporters. Here lies the challenge: supporters need "actionable" items to do, and groups need the resources to provide and support these "actionable" items – resources that were hard to come by for TCKB. Ironically, this event in the life of TCKB highlights the drawbacks or at least the limited utility of social media tools, according to Schoenike. Without a doubt, the video garnered the group a lot of attention and a lot of supporters. If these supporters don't have consistent support (and quickly), there's the risk of losing them. It didn't take long for TCKB's college chapters to lose steam and fold. To rebuild them every semester takes time and money – resources the group didn't have. Moreover, social media tools are no substitute for personal attention. Schoenike explained that it's a "false conception that you can just open up a Facebook page and start a Twitter account and you're going to create change." Especially when the group's message is dense or difficult to understand, spreading the word is no easy feat.

The prominence of in-person outreach as a strategy is best exemplified by San Bernardino Generation Now. Rooted in community

Take the "Three-A-Week" Challenge!

TheCanKicksBack

Subscribe 184   193,739

+ Add to   < Share   ••• More   👍 501 👎 67

Figure 6.5 Senator Alan Simpson, The Can Kicks Back

organizing, raising awareness is an essential element of the group –
in order to increase their sense of power and effect change, a threshold of understanding must be met among all age groups of the
community and even among the key leaders of the organization.
As their mission statement reads, "SBGN strives to empower and
unite our communities through education and economic development." Unlike YI and TCKB, the focal point for raising awareness
for SBGN is not a website. At the time of this writing, the group
has a newly designed website but hasn't released it broadly. Instead,
the group's Facebook page serves as its primary digital platform. In
reality, though, their page is just an electronic extension or proxy for
the real focal point of their campaign to raise awareness – personal
contact.

San Bernardino's bankruptcy seems to have taken many by surprise and a firm understanding of the city's conditions and the roots
of its condition was lacking. Although a few key founders possessed
a good sense of how the city had found itself in economic tur-
moil and the role of their elected officials in getting them into the

situation, for some founding members, gaining more information regarding the city's status was the motivation for joining up. "That's what drew me to the group," said Richard Tejada, "these guys were much more informed than I was."

For SBGN, raising awareness has many facets and, although promoted via Facebook, are delivered through various in-person venues. For example, the group holds monthly workshops for supporters and the public at large at which they bring in experts to discuss topics ranging from the history of the city or its economic status to the principles of "value-based leadership." Like YI and TCKB, there's a sense with SBGN that the engagement of supporters is based on a clear understanding of the issues facing them. As the advertisement for the workshop "History of San Bernardino: Where It's Been & Where It's Headed" read in encouraging attendance, "Get some insight onto the true economic, social & political challenges affecting San Bernardino. Learn where and how you can get involved to help improve our city." Another goal, though, is to position the city's residents to be effective and principled leaders for their community.

Interestingly, raising awareness also has to do with educating followers about what the city of San Bernardino has to offer its residents. For example, the group frequently holds a "Food Flood" for which, on a specific date, the group identifies a particular restaurant, advertises its location, encourages residents to come together to support the local restaurant, and uses the occasion as a community building event. For example, on a Thursday evening in March 2015, SBGN called a Food Flood at the "Taste of Thai" restaurant and advertised the event this way in their Facebook post:

> Join SBGN as we flood a local business to eat some of their delicious food. We ask that you bring at least $10 to spend and help one of our local restaurants in the area. Come mingle with the group and talk about how we envision a better San Bernardino for our entire community.

Similarly, SBGN holds "Business Floods" to identify local businesses such as the "San Bernardino Raceway" or the bowling alley "Del Rosa Lanes." Again, local business are highlighted and these events are offered as an opportunity not only for community members to get together but as affordable and fun ways to support the city. As Miriam Nieto explained, this approach is a purposeful method to engage members of the community and begin the process of revitalizing the city:

> I do like the idea of going out into the community and talking to them and engaging them and saying – this is what's available in your city – especially in San Bernardino cause there's not much to do in San Bernardino, so if we have a lot of bored people in a city, there's going to be a lot of chaos in the city … so we need to … engage them.

SBGN's mixers, although ostensibly social and effective at building community, also have an educational element. Frequently, the groups will hold get-togethers in a local business that allow different segments of the community to meet one another, learn what the others do, and even build contacts. For example, in March 2015, the group held an arts mixer for "open minded artists, community leaders, elected officials and people who have a general interest in supporting the arts to come mingle and network for current and future collaboration." With music, food, and drinks, the mixer was advertised as an "educational and fun setting to meet and network." On a larger scale, SBGN's "CommUnity Fest" performs a similar function. Described as "a celebration & coming together of the people of San Bernardino city to inspire unity, creativity & encouragement for positive changes," the festival is another vehicle the group utilizes to raise awareness of what the city has to offer as well as to bring the city's residents together.

The final facet and possibly the most dominant component of SBGN's outreach efforts is voter education. Interestingly, if one were to learn about San Bernardino Generation Now solely through their Facebook page, it would be reasonable to assume that politics or voter education is just one of many areas of interest for this group – equally as important as park clean-ups and mixers. When one digs deeper and speaks to the group's organizers, though, it's clear that politics permeates much of their work from Food Floods to CommUnity Fest – more on this later in the chapter. On the topic of raising awareness, though, one key reason people are drawn to SBGN is not only to learn more about their city and its challenges, but to learn more about those who seek to lead their city. This process of learning more, much like some of the interactive

Figure 6.6 San Bernardino Generation Now arts mixer advertisement

digital efforts of the other groups under study, allows the participants themselves to be a part of the process and serves, then, as a
vehicle for empowerment.

San Bernardino Generation Now formed in the wake of the
city's bankruptcy, which involved accusations and charges against
city council members that included perjury and identity theft. As
Michael Segura stated, the bankruptcy "hit home for a lot of us,"
and they were "unhappy with past and current elected officials"
given that some of the city's problems stemmed from laws passed
before the founding members were even born.

In the wake of the bankruptcy, the next election took on a heightened level of importance and a host of new candidates emerged to run for mayor – nine candidates whom few knew. As Segura put it, "we had a lot of homework to do." The group set about interviewing the candidates. As Richard Tejada explained, "At the beginning, a lot of them didn't want to meet with us for interviews." "They didn't know who we were back then," interjected Segura. "By the end of the mayoral race, they were talking about us," says Tejada, "and trying to be our friend," according to Segura.

On the surface, these interviews of candidates were a means of gaining essential information for potential voters. These interviews, as well as those the group plans to conduct in the future, offer another opportunity for SBGN supporters to be personally involved in the process – rather than being offered the information, they are a part of their own voter education. This personal involvement makes it more meaningful to those involved – it's different when you meet candidates themselves, according to Segura. These opportunities to interact with public officials and candidates for office extend beyond the interviews conducted by the core members. At the group's second Annual CommUnity Fest, for example, they sponsored a "Civic Lounge Mixer" described as "a harmonious and quality environment within Community Fest of San Bernardino City set up for the purpose of community leader networking and voter engagement dedicated to showcasing leaders on a more intimate level."

In addition to learning more about the city of San Bernardino and even its elected officials and candidates for office is the opportunity to be involved in the learning process. The hope, for SBGN's core group, is that this personal involvement will enhance community members' sense of confidence in their ability to be active citizens. As Miriam Nieto explained,

> I would like to see a community that's well-educated and confident enough to feel like they can speak out about certain issues and speak out against certain city officials that they don't feel are correct ... We're so insecure and we feel like we're so uneducated that we can't talk about politics because we don't know what we're talking about, & I think that culture needs to change in San Bernardino and we need

to feel strongly about it and say "yes, we don't like what you're doing and we're going to speak out".

In many ways, it was this lack of awareness as well as a lack of political confidence, or internal efficacy as political scientists call it, that allowed the city to slip into bankruptcy. The driving members of SBGN hope that improved awareness and better voter education will drive the city's revitalization and prevent a similar situation from happening again.

Serving the community

In a few instances already noted, the groups under study pursue strategies that involve what was referred to earlier in the text as "civic engagement" – going out directly into communities to address public problems. It's a component of Millennial engagement that has received a good deal of attention from both media and scholars – Millennials have been viewed as more community-oriented than past generations, with even some speculation that it's their preferred mode of engagement over political action. It's worth taking a moment to explore how these groups weave community service into their overall strategies. As this analysis shows, especially with SBGN, the community work is nearly indistinguishable from their political efforts.

In interviews, Young Invincible's executive and deputy directors indicated that, although their primary strategy is political, their group also has a consumer education arm. Part and parcel of this component of their strategy is direct service – not only making supporters and residents at large aware of the status of current health care law and the effects of these laws on them, but actually signing people up for health care. One of the benefits, then, of being a supporter of YI is access to a counselor and access to services.

With their regional structure, the group is able to situate staff locally, in communities around the country. For example, out of their California office, YI organized a "National Youth Enrollment Day: East LA Health Fair" in January 2015. Billed as the "the biggest annual day of Millennial enrollment outreach across the country," residents of East Los Angeles were encouraged to celebrate the day by joining YI "for a community health fair, featuring on site enrollment counselors, free health screenings and more!" Once again, this sort of direct outreach is facilitated by the group's organizational structure and the resources to support such a structure. It also serves as a complement to the group's overall mission – directly intersecting with the issue areas and related policies that are the focal point of Young Invincibles.

Similar to their Food Floods and Business Floods, San Bernardino Generation Now seems to use their community service efforts as an opportunity to make residents more aware of sites around their city and to make them a part of revitalizing them. Again, these events are advertised via the group's Facebook page and offer an opportunity not only to do something good for the community but also to come together with residents from the city. Many of these efforts center on cleaning up and restoring Seccombe Lake Park. Seccombe Lake Park is one of the city's 26 parks and, 44 acres in size, holds two baseball fields, volleyball courts, playgrounds, a central gazebo area, and a lake with fishing.[10] Like many of the public spaces in San Bernardino, the park has fallen into disrepair. In describing the decline of many of the city's landmarks from its parks to its shopping malls, Fabian Torres remarked that he remembers when these areas, such as the mall, were thriving and has a "vague image of when it was nice" but sees it as it is now. Michael Segura interjected that they have seen "our parks go from green parks to dirt."

So much of SBGN's community service centers on cleaning up Seccombe Lake Park – of the 45 events listed on the group's Facebook page at the time of this writing, 21 involved a park clean-up at Seccombe Lake Park. Nearly every clean-up culminates in a fun activity such as a game of freeze tag or softball and all are offered as an opportunity for residents to play a direct role in revitalizing not only the park but the city too. As the group advertised for a clean-up October of 2014,

> Change doesn't happen overnight so we invite all of you to join us. There's strength in numbers. We can make a piece of our city much nicer if only for a moment – but we will be consistent and hopefully we can pass on our passion to make our home a better place to live.

At the time of this writing, SBGN had just completed a mural project done in tandem with their park clean-up. The effort reflects core group member Michael Segura's interest in art and brought

Figure 6.7 Seccombe Lake Mural project

together not only muralists and amateur painters but community members who supported the effort by donating money and supplies and playing a part in the beautification effort.[11]

These community service projects and the outreach efforts surrounding them certainly are not devoid of politics, though. Instead, Facebook posts advertising them include reminders that residents need to assume their power as citizens and hold their elected officials accountable. As one message for a clean-up in November 2014 read,

> We would love to see some events held at this park in the future – some music, dance, and art – but we must take ownership of it first. City officials, we hope, will soon get their budget in order and help towards this park's beautification. This park belongs to us, the community, and must therefore care for it as such. We appreciate everyone's help.

Figure 6.8 Seccombe Lake Mural project

Moreover, much like the efforts to highlight what's available to residents of the city – restaurants, family entertainment centers – these community service projects reflect the interconnection SBGN sees between the individual and the political process. For them, each core member of SBGN comes to the group with a particular interest or passion, whether it's bike safety, photography, or the arts. Pursuing that passion naturally prompts an intersection with the political process. As Jorge Heredia stated, "everything is politics … politics is a broad thing." Moreover, people's interests can prove to be a portal into the political process for those beyond SBGN's core group. By highlighting and supporting community members' interests, SBGN can use the opportunity to shine a light on how politics intersects. As Miriam Nieto explained, "Everything is politics but everyone's interests is a gateway into it ... we bring people in through our own passions and then say – hey, there's also these voting things that you'd probably be interested in."

Strategically, when it comes to both disseminating information and serving the community, SBGN's message (both implicit and explicit) is that the political process is interwoven in all aspects of one's personal and communal life, from enjoying a day with your family at the park to finding a restaurant for dinner to choosing a new mayor. In subtle contrast, when it comes to both disseminating information and serving the community, Young Invincibles and The Can Kicks Back work to raise awareness on how public policy – health care reforms, fiscal policies, jobs bills – affects the everyday lives of young adults. These effects can be quite personal and touch many aspects of a Millennial's life, from getting engaged to buying a home, and can have a long-term impact. Less organic an approach, perhaps, than SBGN, but close study of each group's effort in raising awareness and civic engagement suggests that the political process looms large in the strategies of all three groups.

Influencing politics

To meet classic definitions of political engagement, the participation in question needs to involve action rather than just raising awareness, must be political in nature and directed at governmental policy or activity, must be undertaken not just by elites but voluntarily by citizens, and actions must be geared towards influencing an outcome or result. A central argument in this text is that by essentially watering down our conception of engagement, we risk losing the essential nature of democratic engagement – we even risk failing to look for it. The potential result is that we overlook actions by young adults that reflect not only engagement but "political" engagement. This section provides a description of the ways in which The Can Kicks Back, Young Invincibles, and San Bernardino Generation Now pursue such strategies and their motivations for such actions. It's fair to say that, at least for these three groups, young adults today are engaged in the political process for a reason – for something beyond themselves.

Given the location of their national office, K Street in Washington, DC, it probably comes as no surprise that a good deal of Young

Invincibles' strategy when it comes to meeting the mission to "expand economic opportunity for our generation" involves advocacy. Given their physical location, such advocacy comes in the form of communicating directly with legislators – providing them information and support as they make policy decisions. Thanks, though, to their organizational structure, another component of their strategy entails directly involving supporters in setting policy agendas. This two-pronged approach to the group's political activities offers a route not only to influence legislative outcomes but also to build the skills of their supporters so they can be effective political actors.

To a great extent, YI is driven by the notion that young adults deserve a "seat at the table" when it comes to making policy – specifically in the areas of health care, jobs, and education. As deputy director Rory O'Sullivan argued, "it's a big belief in our organization that we also have a stake when some of those big policy decisions get made." Consequently, the group works to influence the legislative process. A reminder that, at its outset, YI's founders believed that the Millennial viewpoint was missing or inaccurately represented in the health care debate – YI's goal was to make sure that youth voice was heard.

The effort to influence the legislative process takes place both directly and indirectly. As O'Sullivan explained, YI frequently conducts surveys and focus groups at the local level and then delivers this information to legislators. Delivering this information is often buttressed with "technical assistance" or, as O'Sullivan explained, imparting to officials, "this is how you would get this done and in a way that would benefit our generation and meet their needs." These messages are often delivered directly and in person via "Lobby Days" on Capitol Hill – visible efforts to express the group's stance within earshot of elected officials. For example, in November 2014, the group held a Hill Day to promote job opportunities for young adults. Those physically present met with members of Congress to express their opinion. Those who couldn't attend in person were encouraged to show their support virtually. As the event was advertised on YI's Facebook page, supporters were urged to:

> Join Young Invincibles on Capitol Hill as we meet with Members of Congress to make sure they understand our generation's economic

concerns, and the importance of job creation ... Even if you can't make it to DC, you can still take action by tweeting your Representative, and using the #YoungAmerica hashtag. We'll post regular updates here on how you can advocate to get young Americans back to work. Don't forget to invite your friends on Facebook, and help us spread the word!

It's worth noting that YI's regional presence affords them the opportunity to engage in advocacy campaigns for state and local policies as well. The group's Facebook page, for instance, advertised a "California Student Impact Legislative Visit Day" in Sacramento, CA as well as the Florida Student Association's "Rally in Tally" for a College Tuition Equity event at the Florida State Capitol.

Advocacy efforts such as these seem quite traditional really – walking the halls of legislative offices, providing information to elected officials, advocating your group's policy positions, and urging members to support the group's agenda. The "Millennial" angle of course is the virtual component – urging supporters to advocate on their own and spread the word via social media.

From a strategic standpoint, this approach is of more interest to Young Invincibles than influencing electoral outcomes. As YI's executive director indicated, the group is not necessarily interested in supporting or electing particular candidates but focused upon "how do our issues become an important part of the priorities of whoever is going to be elected." Again, the group's goal is to get Millennials a seat at the policymaking table. Moreover, when it comes to strategy, the group is keenly interested in involving themselves in policies and activities in which they can make a difference. As they explained, there are a number of good groups working to register young adults to vote and encouraging their political participation. What makes their organization unique is their youth focus regarding health care. The group offers a unique package, according to Jen Mishory, with a policy arm focused upon pushing for policy solutions not only for college-age students but also for 18–34-year-olds. "We're really an issue organization," stated Mishory, and, according to O'Sullivan, are careful to act in such a way that their participation will make an impact: "We've positioned ourselves where we think we can have the most value-added." For YI, that's the legislative rather than the electoral arena. To be sure, the YI example reflects political activity in its most traditional form – strategic and geared towards political change.

The role of supporters of the group ensures that the political action being undertaken is not done solely by those situated in Washington. Moreover, the involvement of supporters at the state and local levels affords these young adults political learning opportunities that will facilitate political involvement throughout their lives. As Mishory and O'Sullivan explained, in addition to gaining information about health care and economic issues and access to these services, a benefit of being a part of Young Invincibles is the opportunity to participate in advocacy campaigns. YI supporters receive training from the group's communication team and are supported as they write letters to elected officials, visit these officials in their offices, and even testify before relevant committees. Involvement in the group's action, then, offers real opportunities for skill-building and leadership development. It seems, too, in speaking to the group's leadership, that offering this support to the young adults involved in YI is of real importance to the organization. As Rory O'Sullivan explained,

> having those different tools in our toolbox allows us to make sure that when that young person testifies on health care, education that they're able to do so in a sophisticated way because we've trained them with that background information that they need to substantively contribute to the debate.

When it comes to political strategy, The Can Kicks Back's approach was similar to YI's. According to TCKB's Ryan Schoenike, it was the group's founding belief that "younger people needed a voice." Like YI, the group's approach in ensuring that their voices were heard was legislative advocacy. In order for such advocacy to work, though, there must be a vast and active base of supporters to amplify the effects of in-person advocacy – a "grassroots army." Ultimately, legislators will only hear a group's message if they believe that supporters have real leverage and that they'll use it. As Schoenike explained, the goal is to "make members fear you – that's the tactic here in DC, that's what the AARP does … and the ability to mobilize them." As referenced frequently, the difficulty lies in not only building that base of supporters but also keeping them active. As it was winding down, TCKB had constructed an alternative advocacy model that might achieve this end. The reality, though, is that, once funds dry up, a group structured as TCKB was can do very little.

From the outset, TCKB purposefully engaged in legislative advocacy at the federal level. This approach made sense – the policy goals of the organization were federal in nature and the group had a small staff and lacked the resources to build a strong structure at the state and local level. Again, the mission of the organization centered on promoting "a sustainable, generationally balanced federal budget," and TCKB's role was to make policy recommendations that would advance that mission. Early on, the key leaders of the group worked with Larry Kotlikof, an economist from Boston University, to devise policy solutions to address the gap between federal spending revenue that would reflect "generational equity." These ideas informed TCKB's policy recommendations – ideas the group took to Capitol Hill.

Probably the centerpiece of the group's advocacy work was the role they played in introducing the INFORM Act. The introduction of the legislation stemmed from a "Hill Day" when the leaders of dozens of TCKB chapters descended on Washington in February 2013 to meet with congressional leaders and spread the group's message of generational equity. A YouTube video of the event features Representatives Adam Kinzinger (Republican, Illinois), Aaron Schock (Republican, Illinois), Cathy McMorris Rodgers (Republican, Washington), and House Budget Committee Chairman Paul Ryan (Republican, Wisconsin), who states in the video, "we know without a shred of doubt we are giving the next generation a lower standard of living because of this debt."

This Hill Day not only offered an opportunity to spread the message of generational equity and fiscal reform, but also planted the notion that young adults will hold elected officials accountable when it comes to these issues. As one chapter leader stated in the video, "it's important for them to know that our generation is up for grabs, we're going to reward those that deal with this in a responsible, balanced way and in a more bipartisan way more importantly." Striking a similar tone, another TCKB supporter, standing on the steps of the Capitol Building, states, "my generation isn't going to be giving a trophy to the party that holds onto their ideology the longest. I believe that my generation is going to hold their politicians accountable based on their ability to actually govern and that requires some principled compromise."[12] Senator John Thune, a Republican from South Dakota, took an interest in the group's policy recommendations, brought in co-sponsors Senator Tim Kaine (Democrat from Virginia), Representatives Jim Cooper (Democrat from Tennessee) and Aaron Schock, and introduced the INFORM Act in July 2013. The Act was endorsed by 1,000 economists and even 16 Nobel laureates. With the introduction of the legislation, TCKB launched the "Generational Equity" tour – a 6,000-mile tour traveling through 20 states that involved dozens of college chapters and hundreds of students. Along the way, the group collected hundreds of tin cans containing messages from young adults nationwide. In a rally to promote the INFORM Act, these cans were delivered to Congressional offices. Ultimately, though, the legislation didn't pass. Although representatives from TCKB were an active presence – holding 80 meetings on the Hill, meeting with Congress members' staff, providing information to elected officials on why they should support the INFORM Act – the bill wasn't a priority for members of Congress, and besides, as Schoenike pointed out, it's really hard to pass a bill.

It was at this point that the group transformed and shifted tactics – partly due to a change in approach and partly due to the limitations of its organization. By the end of 2013, there was little public discussion of fiscal reform, TCKB's fiscal sponsor Fix the Debt was winding down, and the two groups parted ways. At the same time, the group's founders began to go out on their own – Nick Troiano left TCKB to run for office. Due to limited funding, the group had to operate in 2–3-month windows – they let their chapters fold and shifted to an outreach campaign that encouraged supporters to become "Digital Advocates" by downloading their media kit and supporting the group's social media campaigns.

The group's driving members also came to realize where they'd gone wrong strategically – the focus on building chapters didn't bring the millions of consistently active supporters that an organization needs to make a difference. They also realized the limitations of both in-person and virtual legislative advocacy. As Schoenike explained, everyone does a "Hill Day," and these in-person meetings with members of Congress don't necessary result in members shifting their positions. Social media campaigns and a well-designed website don't guarantee success either. "Likes don't translate into action," according to Schoenike. Just because a supporter "likes" a group's efforts, it doesn't mean that they'll follow up or that a member will be moved to support a piece of legislation, for that matter.

The key for a group to be successful, TCKB surmised, was to find a way to activate nonvoters. As Schoenike explained, this approach is more likely to make legislators responsive: "if I can show you that I can activate those nonvoters, then you're really going to listen to me." Specifically, if a group can demonstrate that they can mobilize young people to vote on fiscal issues and not just social issues, they're more likely to make an impact. This was something that people didn't really think could be done and, in Schoenike's mind, really hadn't been tried:

> That's not true – in our experience, actually going out and talking to people, that they're really concerned about this issue, you're just not talking to them in the right way and you're actually not making an effort … just like politicians pander to older people about social security and Medicare, they pander to younger people on social issues.

So TCKB set about devising and testing the messages that would successfully move fiscal concerns to one of the top three voting issues for Millennials. In targeted ad buys (online ads, banner ads, and videos) in districts with a high percentage of Millennials in two non-competitive districts in California and New York, the group tested these ads one month prior to the 2014 midterm election, measuring response rates to gather data on the demographics with which these fiscal policy messages resonate. According to Schoenike, the test was successful – the ads performed better than most ads by candidates and parties and, in his mind, confirmed his theory that "younger people will vote and they'll vote on fiscal and economic issues if properly engaged."

Using this as a base model, the group hoped to build out nationally – to create a well-developed messaging system in time for the 2016 elections and utilize it in districts where the message might make a difference. The ultimate goal of this effort was that the group would find, via exit polls, that young adults voted on these fiscal issues, allowing TCKB to go to elected officials and say, "this is what Millennials in your district look like, this is what they vote on, and here's how we know they did it." It's this sort of micro-targeting that will get legislators to introduce your legislation and vote for it.

Although it may have been to all intents and purposes a last-ditch effort, Schoenike believes that with this model, TCKB did something no other group has done or is doing. At this point, though, there's nowhere for this effort to go – the group has "knocked up and down pretty much every door we know of," but fiscal reform has waned as a funding priority and it's an issue that neither the media nor members of Congress are talking about. For a group with a far-reaching mission and approach, changing course realistically can't be done.

In contrast, San Bernardino Generation Now's local focus and looser structure allow the group to be nimble when it comes to influencing the political process. As of yet, legislative advocacy has not figured prominently in the group's strategy. When it comes to elections, their focus has been on registering voters and getting them to the polls. For them, creating a culture of political and civic engagement among residents of their city is their primary goal with voter education efforts at the forefront of this strategy. Still, SBGN is leaving its options open – options that include not only legislative advocacy but even running for elected office.

When it comes to influencing legislation or policy, SBGN's most significant efforts have revolved around amending San Bernardino's charter. A good portion of the discussion with core members of the group centered on long-standing problems with the charter that have fostered conflict between the city and unions – restrictions on the city's ability to engage in collective bargaining with police and firefighter unions as other cities do. Although the group's political efforts are usually confined to voter registration, the core members stated that they've "delved into speaking about certain measures that we know would affect our community directly." Measure Q, an effort to amend this portion of the charter, was one such issue for SBGN – the group launched a social media and arts campaign to engage the city around Measure Q.

Although the measure failed, this policy failure doesn't seem to have deterred the group's willingness to use their platforms to educate residents not only about voting and candidates but also about the effects of public policies on individual residents. Involving the group in such efforts is not without risk, however. As Miriam Nieto recognized, "it's really touchy" – speaking out regarding legislation can affect relationships the group has built. For example, Nieto noted that speaking out about policies or singling out groups can affect donations – in past years, the fire department had given to SBGN's community events but didn't the year SBGN spoke out about Measure Q.

Still, the focal point of the group's political efforts are electoral. As of yet, SBGN has not endorsed candidates running for office, but instead, as discussed earlier in this chapter, focus their attention on voter education campaigns. Although they are encouraged as individuals to support the candidates of their choice, SBGN's core group members' sense of responsibility for building a sense of engagement seems to override the desire to elect one candidate over another:

> People don't understand the power of their vote and the power of their voice. We would like to increase voting in our area, but more importantly build the culture of civic engagement and get our community educated on politics and the policies affecting our families and our generation.

In focusing attention on voter registration and voter turnout, not only is the goal a sense of engagement among members of the community, but also better representation. As Jorge Heredia explained, "Just improving the voter turnout, our hope is that the result would be more representative of what the community needs and wants." Refraining from endorsements, though, poses a challenge, as Heredia indicated, "there's a fine balance – do you tell the community who to vote for or do you allow them to figure it out for themselves?" "That's voter education," interjected Michael Segura, "giving them the right information where it's nonbiased but at the same time, it's truth."

Again, much of this work is done in the high schools. In going about this work, Segura is mindful of the potential effects of their efforts on the electorate as a whole: "If you could turn out all the senior classes who are about to turn 18 to vote, that's 2000 in about a year from all the high schools combined." Additionally, the group hopes that not only will young adults be infused with a sense of engagement but that they'll carry that sense home to their families. As Segura explained, "the younger you can get them educated, the easier – to build the culture – if they're engaged, they're going to engage their families." Even in high schools, there seems to be an emphasis in SBGN's voter education on representation – in this case, generational representation. As Segura stated, "getting out the idea to young people that our vote really does matter and that together we can outvote the older generation that's been running the city for ages – that would be ideal."

In elections, SBGN seems to have built a reputation as a group that can turn out young voters. Given the low turnout rates and the small margins of victory, such a reputation matters. As Jorge Heredia stated, "At the very least, they're paying attention to us." Fabian Torres emphasized, "we have a strong presence."

Finally, running for elected office themselves certainly is within the realm of possibility for this core group of SBGN – the group's "all for one, one for all" attitude extends to supporting each other if one of them decides to run for office. Fabian Torres, for example, indicated that he has thought about it and would consider running once he completes graduate school – he's in a master's program now and will possibly pursue a doctorate. The others expressed interest in running for office one day – once they had gained more knowledge. Currently, two of the core group members sit on local committees – Segura was appointed to serve on the local government's fine arts commission and Heredia sits on the service council. For Segura, the experience has been revealing. As he stated, it's "opened my eyes to how bad our city has been run through commissions – there's not enough people who know what they're doing. Our leadership in the city is lacking." Instead of fostering a desire to run for office himself, though, it's spurred him to generate candidates of quality through SBGN: "I want to make sure we're training our candidates ... to fill those roles and be effective leaders for the whole of the community."

Although SBGN isn't as involved in legislative advocacy as YI and TCKB and don't pursue those traditional methods of influencing the governmental process, it's fair to say that SBGN's efforts qualify as both political and traditional. Between mounting voter education campaigns, organizing voter registration and get-out-the-vote drives, sitting on local governmental commissions, and considering running for elected office, the group's strategic approach reflects classic modes of effecting political change – with specific desired outcomes anticipated as a result of their actions.

Defining success

Each group's definition of success varies and the outcomes they seek seem to reflect their missions and their structure. Although some of their goals are more amorphous than others, each group's definition of success provides more support for this book's finding that the work of these groups is a contemporary example of our classic conceptions of political participation – conceptions that we risk overlooking as we continually expand our definitions of engagement.

For Young Invincibles, their desired outcomes stem from their three-pronged strategy of research and public education, direct service, and advocacy. Defining success depends on the nature of the group's effort, then. When it comes to educating the public about their three core issues – health care, jobs, and education – the group looks to who's been educated and how well they're taking that information to change their lives. Clearly, this outcome is difficult to measure but remains an indicator of success. An effort that's more conducive to measurement is the direct service arm of YI – how many health fairs did the organization hold, how many people attended, and how many people did the organization sign up for health care coverage? When it comes to legislative advocacy, success for the group's leaders is whether or not there have been any desired changes in public policy – either incremental or large. For example, the group's executive and deputy directors pointed to the expansion of California's Pell Grant B as an example of a policy success.

Achieving such measurable success seems to be a priority for the group, and they have the structure to support it. For example, YI's initiative "Student Impact Project" is a national effort with the aim "to equip students with the tools and resources to organize and advocate for state policies that support college access, affordability, and success." Included in this initiative is even "Legislation to Watch" – targets of legislative advocacy at the state and local levels around the country. Like much of their advocacy work, YI's efforts, whether at the federal or state and local levels, seem to be focused upon devoting their resources to efforts not only in line with their mission but where they can make a positive difference.

As they look ahead to the future, the group hopes to build out their networks so they can take on significant state campaigns and play a role in setting policy agendas in states as they continue to play a role in national policy discussions. Moreover, they hope to bring more young adults into their network. Specifically, they hope to reach a diverse range of young adults who aren't necessarily well-organized and who are harder to reach – non-college youth and those enrolled in community colleges. As they go about this effort, Jen Mishory states that she's "very hopeful" about the future of the Millennial Generation and their involvement in the political process. She's found that there are many young adults who have wanted to get involved but haven't had groups offering them these sorts of opportunities. She finds that there's a level of excitement and, as the group strives to build a "culture of civic engagement," that "people are hungry for it, they're excited about it."

Clearly, exploring the topic of "success" is bittersweet for a group such as The Can Kicks Back as they wind down. Still, it's clear that the group aimed to make a tangible political difference and believes that their generation possesses the power to make a difference. Although they had just released a new report at the time of this research and continue to keep their Twitter account active, in Ryan Schoenike's mind, it's not enough just to make speeches or maintain a website. As he stated, "If we're going to do this, we need to be impactful."

With the base model they created towards the end, he believes the group took an important step in making a difference. Their plan, after successfully testing their Millennial-focused fiscal messaging campaign, would have been to take this model and hone it – if they had the funding. The goal was to find competitive districts, learn more about the young people in these districts, learn ways to activate them politically, and identify local leaders to direct the effort. The initial focus would have been on national races in 2016 and, at the same time, plant the seeds necessary to engage in state work after 2016.

Without funding and with the group's leaders heading in different directions professionally, the group is left to consider not only how it could have done things differently but also its accomplishments. Over a fairly brief period of time, it launched 100 college chapters throughout 38 states, played a central role in crafting and introducing legislation that addressed the burden the fiscal gap places on younger generations, and completed a "Generational Equity" tour to raise awareness among young adults nationwide.

Two factors that probably worked in the group's favor initially ended up being intrinsic to its ultimate decline – social media and the national mood. TCKB came about at a time when lawmakers and the media were interested in fiscal reform. Moreover, the group's edgy messaging and viral social media success with the "Gangnam" video catapulted it into the public sphere. The group needed the resources and the structure to maintain itself when these factors diminished – TCKB possessed neither. For Schoenike, keeping the organization alive was personally draining and even disheartening. In the end, he learned a great deal about the political process and remains hopeful that his generation can make a difference: "younger people certainly have power." In his mind, "any group that can vote in large numbers" at least possesses the potential to "create the change they're seeking."

Much like YI, San Bernardino Generation Now's definition of success is a function of the multiple roles the group plays, from building a culture of civic engagement to providing information to residents, to registering and turning out voters. Unlike the other groups, though, defining successful outcomes also stems from what brought core group members to SBGN initially. For example, Fabian Torres looks at the change he's captured via his photos – photos of parks before and after clean-up are a gauge of success for him. As Torres explained, "that's my way of seeing change." Miriam Nieto looks at their events – how many people attended, how well did they do at spreading the word, how many volunteers participated, how many donations were made, is the community engaging in these activities? For Michael Segura, "seeing the art culture grow in the whole IE [Inland Empire]" is a sign of success – the mural projects in the parks in particular. To be sure, a tangible sign that the group is making an impact politically is the fact that members of the core group find themselves serving in positions in city government – Richard Tejada in the mayor's office, Michael Segura on the arts commission, Jorge Heredia on the service council.

Yet, there are other intangible measures the group considers when evaluating its success. "Having the trust in the group ... faith in us to be able to do this much in the community" is a sign of success, according to Nieto. She added, "It's so easy to lose faith, especially in a bankrupt city." Reflective of their organic nature, Heredia made it clear that just like their group, their desired outcomes are a work in progress:

> I think we're still trying to figure it out – we're definitely still trying to figure it out. Our goal is pretty simple – we just want to see our city improve. How we're going to do it and how it's going to be achieved, we're still figuring it out.

Given the city's bankruptcy (both in literal and figurative terms), any signs that residents are more engaged, holding their leaders more accountable, are more connected to each other, to their city, and to the political process are worthy of celebration. As Michael Segura stated in reference to the coming together of rival gangs for park clean-ups and mural projects, "Little successes, give me hope for our future."

Think It Out

- When considering the three case studies, what aspects of each seem uniquely "Millennial" or representative of the generation? Do these features enhance or dampen the likelihood of their success?

Act It Out

- Continuing the simulation in the previous chapter, devise an action plan to further the mission of your youth-focused and youth-led group:
  - Will the group's actions be educative, civic, or political in nature (or a combination)?
  - Will your group's efforts include legislative advocacy or influencing elections?
  - Who will be targets of your group's efforts and what strategies will the group pursue?
  - What are the desired outcomes or how will your organization measure success?

Notes

1 Only the communication generated by the group itself was included in the qualitative database when it came to analyzing the content on the groups' social media platforms – not comments from the public at large.
2 Young Invincibles, "It's Not Always Sunny in Young America": http://generation.younginvincibles.org.
3 Young Invincibles, "Student Debt in Perspective": http://debt.young-invincibles.org.
4 The Can Kicks Back: www.thecankicksback.org/our_story.
5 The Can Kicks Back: www.thecankicksback.org/principles.
6 The Can Kicks Back: www.thecankicksback.org/innovation, www.thecankicksback.org/infrastructure.
7 The Can Kicks Back: www.thecankicksback.org/growth.
8 Psy's "Gangnam Style": www.youtube.com/watch?v=9bZkp7q19f0.
9 The Can Kicks Back's "Three-a-Week Challenge": www.youtube.com/watch?v=kjLuj0EhsQg.
10 San Bernardino Parks and Recreation: www.ci.san-bernardino.ca.us/cityhall/parks/parks/default.asp.
11 Video regarding mural project: www.youcaring.com/help-a-neighbor/seccombe-lake-park-mural-project/323875.
12 www.youtube.com/watch?v=XX9LD_o2cVo.

Conclusion

Providing readers with a solid understanding of the Millennial Generation and their participation in the political process has been the central aim of this book. This effort has involved a description of the realities of the generation's demographics as well as a systematic assessment of how the age group is perceived, a depiction of the nature and extent of young adults' involvement in the political process, a synthesis and critique of the academic literature addressing engagement and youth political participation, and an example of how we might study youth engagement from a different approach and with a different methodology.

Although their explanatory and predictive power is limited, case studies offer a promising route for reframing theoretical considerations and reordering methodological priorities. This chapter reviews the relevant "takeaways" from the case studies of San Bernardino Generation Now, The Can Kicks Back, and Young Invincibles – what they suggest about youth engagement today and what possibilities they open up for future research. Out of these case studies and the body of literature reviewed in this text, a number of research questions and designs emerge. These research questions and designs are enumerated in this last chapter and, along with current research, are considered in a normative context – what are the ideals of American citizenship and how does the changing definition of engagement and, as a by-product, youth political participation coincide or conflict with what the Founders had in mind? Finally, if much of this text has been focused upon mapping how we study youth engagement, the book will conclude more practically and consider what we as educators, as policymakers, and as citizens (young and not so young) can do to encourage political participation among "citizen now."

Lessons learned

It bears emphasizing that San Bernardino Generation Now, The Can Kicks Back, and Young Invincibles aren't necessarily representative of all youth, nor are they representative of all groups. To be sure, other groups of young adults concerned about the economy and wanting to effect change have pursued different avenues. For example, some young adults have directed their efforts towards enhancing opportunities for entrepreneurship among young adults in response to the poor economy. "Buy Young," for instance, is an initiative that urges consumers to buy products and support companies that are owned by Millennials (*New York Times*, August 17, 2011). The efforts selected for this study, although all had the economy's effects on young adults as a core concern, offered a varied take on how Millennials have come together and engaged in public life to advance their respective missions.

What's to be gained by this qualitative approach? Qualitative studies allow researchers to consider how subjects (young adults in this case) understand or appreciate their experiences, how they "construct their worlds" (or go about their work), and the meaning they ascribe to their work (Merriam 2009, 23). These case studies offered the opportunity to explore, from the groups' point of view, considerations that haven't received much attention – the context in which youth actions arise, the targets of these actions, and the effects or impacts of these efforts not only for each case individually but also across cases. Out of this exercise, a few themes emerged, including:

- both the limitations and the promise of organizations in reaching and representing young adults in the world of politics
- the opportunities groups offer for providing supporters with the skills of citizenship (given the right conditions)
- an "old school" sense of political action buttressed by a contemporary sensibility and a cutting-edge toolkit

- the attention paid by such groups to making an impact on issues
  of concern in terms of both their actions and their targeting

The nation's Founders practically assured the prevalence of
organized interests in American politics. They viewed the presence of "factions" as inevitable in a free society and constructed
a governmental system that would protect them. Although they
feared the "mischiefs" associated with them, the Founders
believed that factions were an expression of freedom deserving of
protection: "Liberty is to faction what air is to fire, an aliment
without which it instantly expires. But it would be less folly to
abolish liberty, ... than it would be to wish the annihilation of
air" (Madison, 1787, *Federalist Paper 10*). Due in large part to the
Founders' efforts, interest groups have been a fixture throughout
American history.

Defined by Truman as "any group that is based on one or more
shared attitudes and makes certain claims upon other groups or
organizations in the society" (1951, 33), the interest group world
grew steadily over the nation's history but exploded in size during
the 1960s and 1970s thanks in large part to the sizable number of citizen groups that emerged (Schlozman and Tierney 1986, 75; Walker
1983). In line with Putnam's concerns surrounding the decline of
"social capital" and the resulting effects on engagement, Theda
Skocpol offers an account of the history of the world of organized
interests that emphasizes the democratic benefits associated with
groups in the early years of the nation and the steady diminishment
of these benefits in recent years. She argues that voluntary organizations once served as meaningful associations for citizens and a
portal into public life – a life that represented a co-mingling of the
civic or communal and the political. These organizations, rooted in
"members," served as a way for citizens not only to advance their
issues of concern but to learn the skills of citizenship. Citing Alexis
de Tocqueville, she writes,

> Voluntary associations have always rivaled voting as pathways
> Americans follow into community and public affairs. Organized vol-
> untary groups mediate between government and society, empower
> participating citizens, and embody relationships between leaders
> and supporters. Associations are, moreover, sites where citizens

learn – and practice – the "knowledge of how to combine" so vital to democracy. (Skocpol 1999, 462)

In contrast, according to Skocpol, the relationship between organizations and members today lacks the meaning it once did: "national public life is now dominated by professionally managed advocacy groups without chapters or members. And at the state and local levels 'voluntary groups' are, more often than not, nonprofit institutions through which paid employees deliver services and coordinate occasional volunteer projects" (2003, 7). Moreover, she asserts that contemporary thinking regards groups as entities separate and distinct, even antithetical, to political life: "America's most visible and loquacious politicians, academics, and pundits have proclaimed that voluntary groups flourish best apart from active national government – and disconnected from politics" (2003, 8). The result, Skocpol argues, is a "top-heavy civic world" that "encourages 'doing for' rather than 'doing with'" (1999, 502). When we consider the link between members and the groups under study here and how well these groups represent those who support their cause, much of Skocpol's argument rings true. These three groups also offer some noteworthy counterpoints – counter-examples that suggest their promise at empowering supporters to be active citizens.

National in scope, originated and headquartered in Washington, DC, The Can Kicks Back and Young Invincibles hold some resemblance to the groups Skocpol describes – "advocates without members" (1999, 461). In fact, Jen Mishory emphasized the fact that YI was not a membership group. Instead, it has regional offices with paid staff who advocate at the state and local level. The group's community events, at which YI not only disseminates information but signs people up for health care, certainly resemble Skocpol's notion of "doing for" rather than "doing with." That being said, each group originated to provide young adults a "seat at the table" or to ensure that the voice of Millennials was being heard in the halls of government. In numerous ways, they not only advocate for young adults but offer avenues for meaningful participation in the goings on of the group and opportunities to build political skills.

Many of YI's regional offices have "young advocates" – local leaders who organize and advocate for policies at the state and local level. The group's "Student Impact Project" is a campaign for college affordability designed to *organize* students and student groups, *advocate* for college affordability in state legislatures, and *change* or "convince lawmakers to invest in higher education for our generation and the future."[1] Through this project and through the work of their "young advocates," young adults are trained and have the opportunity to participate in campaigns by testifying, writing to representatives, and helping with visits to representatives. As Mishory pointed out, these opportunities allow for skill-building and leadership development. True, these are opportunities constructed by the group itself and the group's resources facilitate the necessary oversight. Still, these are real opportunities for learning the skills of political action. This facet of the group also highlights the reality that, although YI engages in educational and civic actions, political action is prominent.

When at full capacity, The Can Kicks Back offered the same sort of opportunities for skill-building to those students active in the group's college chapters and young professionals who had launched their own chapters. As we know, not all young adults are enrolled in college or even in established professions, so certainly in this way, the group was somewhat limited in its representation. As explained earlier, these chapter-level supporters were provided "actionable" things to do, such as hold an event or write an op-ed, and were provided support from the organization – again, actions that are political in nature. Although somewhat dependent upon those administering or managing the group, these experiences did represent real political learning moments for those involved. As resources became more constrained and such personal support diminished, these learning experiences diminished and the group's resulting strategy offered few meaningful opportunities for supporters.

The interactive nature of each of these groups, facilitated by social media platforms, blogs, and Twitter events, provides another avenue by which supporters can be involved in the workings of the group – or at least make their opinions known. Of course, a comment on a group's Facebook post or a blog entry don't mirror the nature of engagement between members and leaders in the sort of associations Skocpol holds up as exemplary. Still, they undermine to some extent the notion that membership or support in these efforts lacks meaning. As discussed in the first chapter, one distinct feature of the Millennial Generation is a desire to have a choice or a say in what's offered to them. Moreover, a resistance to institutions and authority pervades the generation. The interactive efforts of both YI and TCKB reflect that reality – the extent to which their interaction makes a difference to leaders is another question.

Although San Bernardino Generation Now would not necessarily fit within the scope of Skocpol's theoretical framework, it also is worth highlighting its promise not only in representing supporters' interests but in equipping them with the tools of political engagement. SBGN's mission is rooted both in representing the needs of their city's people and in empowering residents to hold their elected leadership accountable. Much of this process of skill-building comes in the form of raising awareness but it also comes via voter registration and get-out-the-vote efforts – effectively offering residents of San Bernardino an entry card into the political process. As explained in the previous chapter, politics is interwoven in all of the group's work – even in less obvious ways such as park clean-ups and "Food Floods." SBGN's highly responsive and organic nature, rooted in the city it represents, is reflected in a loose structure, though that threatens to limit its longevity and maybe even its effectiveness.

All three groups, then, show some promise at both representing young adults and equipping them with the tools of political action. That organized interests can play such a role is not novel in the discipline of political science, although it has been overlooked in the study of youth political participation. As cited earlier, there has been some research on the rise and implications of youth activism and youth movements in recent years, but less on the prominence of more organized interests. Of course, into which category SBGN falls – organization or movement – is open for debate. Recent research by Strachan and Senter (2013) offers support for the idea that campus organizations, Greek organizations in particular, do an effective job at cultivating members' civic identities as well as their political skills and sense of political preparedness. This finding dovetails with research highlighted in the CIRCLE and Carnegie Corporation report *Guardian of Democracy*, which demonstrated that participation in extracurricular activities is a key component in high-quality civic education programs and offers a route for political learning for schoolchildren. It's reasonable to assume that groups geared towards young adults and their interests, the economy in this case, would offer democratic benefits that resemble, if not perfectly, those celebrated by Skocpol and others.

Again, recognizing the limitations of case studies in terms of generalizability, the collection of activities these groups pursued and the targeting of these activities demonstrate that politics, or influencing the make-up or actions of government, was a driving force for the groups under study. It's clear that our scholarly appreciation of engagement has broadened to include a number of activities – some of which are purely political and some simply border on political. To be sure, Young Invincibles, The Can Kicks Back, and San Bernardino Generation Now include these modes of action in their "engagement toolkit" and reflect a Millennial mindset when going about their work. The study of these groups, though, suggests that these tools and this approach are meant only to supplement or enhance traditional or "old school" methods of influencing the make-up and actions of government and not replace them. For YI, SBGN, and TCKB, these tools and this approach are only useful if they produce a political impact or effect tangible change.

It should be remembered that, for those scholars who promote a "bulls-eye" view, engagement is measured by what one puts into one's political activity and the effects of that activity on political institutions. Verba and Nie (1972) hold that different types of political behavior influence the political system in different ways and that the preferred governmental outcome often dictates the appropriate method of political participation. Outcome is just as important as the target and method of political action for Verba and Nie – meaningful engagement involves effectively conveying policy preferences, via an appropriate choice of political activity, to those public officials responsible for seeing to these preferences and then achieving a "concurrence" or agreement with public officials that affects their actions. Similarly, Verba et al. (1995) hold that the information conveyed in political activities and the pressure they exert on public officials distinguishes them. These acts can be further distinguished by the extent to which they can be multiplied, or the "volume of the activity," in an effort to put pressure on public officials and influence their actions. Given this research, then, it's reasonable to conclude that the attention paid to results by these groups as well as their targeting and methods of choice are a reflection of political engagement in its traditional sense.

YI and TCKB share a clear-cut and easily identifiable goal – to influence the policymaking process. Although influencing legislative outcomes wasn't their sole purpose, both measured their groups' success according to their policy victories. The tools they utilized to achieve this purpose were extensive and ranged from the "tried and true" swarming of Capitol Hill and lobbying legislators face to face to raising awareness about policy via a funny video on YouTube or a forum conducted on Twitter. In the end, though, each group was driven to facilitate the sort of "concurrence" envisioned by Verba and Nie – a situation in which there is synergy between the group's stance and legislators' views. As suggested earlier, a good deal of research has been conducted regarding the role and influence of organized interests in politics. Much of a group's power in the legislative process comes from the information they offer to legislators and the value of this information. As Wright explains, "interest groups achieve influence in the legislative process not by applying electoral or financial pressure, but by developing expertise about politics and policy and by strategically sharing this expertise with legislators through normal lobbying activities" (1996, 8).

The study of these groups presented here suggests that, by providing legislators valuable information on how health care reform or fiscal policies affect young adults, Young Invincibles and The Can Kicks Back perform this classic function in American politics. As Rory O'Sullivan of YI explained, the value of their group comes in systematically gathering data at the local level, delivering this information to legislators, and offering them the guidance or "technical assistance" to accomplish policy goals that will benefit the legislators' young constituents. Certainly TCKB's late initiative to hone a message-delivery system that would boost the importance of fiscal issues in voters' minds tells the same story – finding a way to gather information valuable to legislators that will ultimately affect their actions. Here, then, the goal of the groups is clear and nearly exclusively legislative, this goal determines the targets of their actions, and the source of their influence comes in delivering information to policymakers via both classic and novel methods.

Similarly, San Bernardino Generation Now's targets reflect their objectives – given the motivation to empower their city's residents, the residents themselves are the targets of much of the group's activities. As documented, it is voter education, registration, and mobilization that dominate the group's work. Again, SBGN uses contemporary methods of communication to facilitate its efforts, but in the end, much of this approach is carried out via traditional and even low-tech actions from park clean-ups, to community festivals, to classroom visits. Much more limited in scope than YI and TCKB and with perhaps less tangible outcomes, like the others, however, SBGN offers an example of youth engagement in its most traditional sense – political.

Research roadmap

In no small part, these case studies were motivated not only by the research conducted on the political participation of today's young adults but also by the work that hasn't been done. Study of these groups suggests research possibilities at the group level but also at the individual level. This section outlines these research questions as well as some methodological approaches for addressing them. Taken together, the small-scale qualitative work presented in this book in conjunction with the total body of literature on Millennials and political engagement suggest a research agenda that might offer a fuller picture of today's youth as citizens.

Again, there is a long and quite broad strain of political science literature that addresses the topic of organized interests including how groups attract and maintain members, the actions they take and their effects, and the democratic implications associated with organized interests. Our understanding of young adults would benefit from exploring the connection between youth political participation and groups and, certainly for reasons Brady argued, there's value in approaching the topic of youth engagement from the institutional level. Moreover, the role of such bodies takes on greater relevance precisely for the reasons Putnam and Skocpol have stated – as far as we know, contemporary generations haven't benefited from the sorts of associations that older generations did. At the very least, though, we know that such youth-led and youth-focused groups exist. For example, in this research, at least another eight groups organized around the economic status of young adults were identified, including "Generation Opportunity," "Our Time," and "Generation Progress." Furthermore, given the scarcity of civics instruction in contemporary classrooms compared to that of previous generations, involvement in such groups might offer Millennials sorely needed lessons in citizenship not always provided in schools – another reason for including more of such research in a research agenda.

Further developing this area of research in the study of youth political participation might include some of the following work:

- Given the potential research questions associated with youth-led and youth-focused groups, an important first step would be to conduct a census of such groups in order to learn more about them in a systematic manner. One possible and well-trodden method would be to reference the *Encyclopedia of Associations* to document the number and type of such organizations currently in operation. To make the task more manageable, researchers might take the approach used in this text and identify sub-sections of this body of organized interests – perhaps those organized around specific issues of concern such as education or the environment. Loosely structured groups such as San Bernardino Generation Now most likely would fall through the cracks using such a tactic and supplementary searches (most likely qualitative in nature) would be required.

- Once constructed, such a database would allow for more systematic research – either qualitative studies involving case studies, interviews, and content analysis or quantitative research – a survey of groups' leaders and even supporters. Such systematic study derived from a representative sample of youth-led and youth-focused organizations would allow for a consideration of a host of research questions including:

  ○ How do such groups recruit and maintain members or supporters? Like TCKB, do groups reach out primarily to college

    students and young professionals or does their mission and
structure allow for a broader reach?

- ○ What methods do groups use to recruit and maintain members and, relatedly, what incentives entice young adults to these groups? Traditionally, some combination of material, solidary, and purposive incentives has been viewed as the foundation of recruitment (Wilson 1973). Is this still the case – especially given the role of the Internet and social media in building networks? This area in particular would be conducive to experimental research.

- ○ Content analysis of social media platforms might allow researchers to consider the nature and impact of groups' messaging and the quality of the dialogue between supporters and those constructing group strategy. Are interactive tools such as blogs and "Twitter town halls" legitimate methods for engaging members or simply "window dressing" for groups with a strong online presence?

- ○ Looking at a representative sample of youth-led and youth-focused groups, how are they structured? With a Washington-based office, on college campuses, with local or regional offices, or some combination of these structures? What are the implications of their structure when it comes to recruiting and maintaining members as well as the actions the group is able to undertake?

- ○ What is the mission of these organizations? More specifically, how closely aligned to the traditional political goal of influencing the make-up and actions of government are these missions? Part and parcel of this question, how do groups go about their work? Like SBGN, does the work of the group involve primarily raising awareness and providing a sense of power or are these groups engaged in advocacy?

- ○ How are they impacting the national agenda and/or legislation? On these questions, interest group literature is most instructive. For example, scholars might consider the extent to which groups interact with legislators (at all levels) as legislation is being crafted – to what extent are groups involved in the formulation of bills? Are groups a presence at committee hearings? Do groups try to influence floor deliberations? To what extent do groups interact with the courts or agencies (Wright 1996, ch. 3)? Once a bill has made it to a vote, how do groups access and influence the votes of legislators? If the group has a political action committee (PAC), what is the strategy behind their contributions (Wright 1996, ch. 5)? In the end, systematically evaluating groups' actions and legislative outcomes offers insight into the influence (or lack thereof) of youth-led and youth-oriented groups.

○ Interwoven in all of these questions is the topic of representation. This concern was highlighted in the earlier discussion of Skocpol's work and permeates the literature on organized interests. Concerns surrounding the representativeness of groups perhaps is crystallized best by Schattschneider in *The Semisovereign People* (1960), who warns that, unless the world of interest groups or "scopes of conflict" are expanded appropriately, there is a risk that elite interests will dominate: "The flaw in the pluralist heaven is that the heavenly chorus sings with a strong upper-class accent." The small study presented in this text has highlighted how this might be a justifiable concern. In the interest of efficiency, groups reach out to pockets of young adults on college campuses, thus risking overlooking those not enrolled in college. Unless hyper-local like SBGN, it's only those groups with appropriate resources who are able to reach vulnerable populations at the local level. In those instances, the Skocpol question arises as to whether such groups, then, are "doing for" or "doing with."

The case studies presented in this text as well the synthesis and critique of the body of literature presented earlier suggest unexplored areas of research that extend beyond the topic of youth-led groups. These potential research areas address those facets that have been least explored, including the context in which youth action arises, how such action is directed, and the effects of youth political action. Further study into these areas might include some of the following research:

• Now that the oldest Millennials are reaching 40, it's a good time to carefully consider the effects of their history on the generation. How have such factors as a poor economy, the terrorist attacks on 9/11, ballooning education costs, the Obama presidency, the ongoing "war on terror," and the rise of social media affected their political outlook and behavior? Even in the formation of YI, TCKB, and SBGN, we see the impact of these factors. The groundwork for such a historical approach can be found in Putnam (2000), Zukin *et al.* (2006), and Howe and Strauss (2000). As we phase into the next generation, the history of Millennials' young adulthood is set and can be considered more seriously in our study of young adults.

- Another contextual issue worthy of further study is the connection between the ethnic diversity of the generation and the effects on young adults' political participation. As indicated in Chapter 2, different subsets of the youth population engage in politics in different ways and to different degrees. In addition to some of ethnographic research cited earlier, Fox *et al.*'s youth participatory action research and youth organizing approach offer a model for studying how low-income, immigrant youth come together to organize and engage in activism to address injustices they face (2010). In their study of digital activism, Cohen *et al.* speculate that Latino youth, although not strong voters, are more engaged in local and civic participation (2012, 26). The work of SBGN supports this suggestion to an extent – a locally focused effort with a strong Latino presence among the group's leadership working in a city that's approximately 50 percent Latino. The community-level work of SBGN certainly is not devoid of politics – in fact, politics permeates all that they do. Moreover, although rooted in activism, it certainly suggests more organized political action. More systematic research certainly is in order, then, to discern the factors influencing the political attitudes and behavior of the various ethnic groups composing the Millennial Generation.

- A running theme through this text is that much of our attention, when studying younger adults, has been to compare their actions to older adults, and we've gone about this by using a fairly common set of methods and instruments. Our understanding would benefit from a careful consideration of the choice and targets of actions as a function of what's most appropriate for the individual undertaking that action. It may be, in fact, that young adults choose different tools of participation today for good reasons. Levine argues, for example, that

> There is very little theoretical or empirical work that asks whether a person in a particular situation, having particular political objectives, would be wise to vote, to form an organization, to protest, to petition, to make a documentary film, or to act in various other ways. (2007, 56–57)

As a result, according to Levine, we assume that young people should engage in politics in the ways their parents and grandparents did. Zukin *et al.*'s work makes a similar argument but extends it to the aggregate – the proper balance of types of engagement (civic or political) adjusts according to conditions, and it's not so much that young adults today are disengaged but engaged differently (2006). Herein lies the value of looking at engagement from the viewpoint of young adults themselves. The case studies presented here asked in what sort of context did the group leaders and supporters situate their actions and who were the targets of their actions? The research showed that, although their tools might be different from previous generations, the context and the targets were traditionally political.

- In offering their multi-faceted conception of engagement, Zukin *et al.* assert that they're "not sure if the glass is half-empty or half-full. In some measure it depends whether one is pouring or drinking. We will let our readers judge for themselves" (2006, preface). As argued earlier in the book, one key deficit in theoretical frameworks that offer a broad conception of engagement is the extent to which key elements of politics are overlooked – the impact or effects of these efforts in particular. Measuring effectiveness is no easy task of course, but this oversight offers a wealth of research opportunities that allow scholars to approach the topic from various angles:
  - One possible approach for demonstrating the connection between youth action and political impact is to study the alignment between legislators' behavior and the young adults they serve. For example, earlier in this book, those states with the lowest median age were identified – states with large pockets of young adults. Researchers might consider the extent to which legislators (either at the state or federal level) are

responsive to the concerns of the young adults in their state (in the variety of ways young adults express their concerns). This might be done through content analysis of legislators' floor speeches, committee behavior, or even the messaging coming out of his or her office. The relationship between young constituents and their representatives might be explored by looking at the correlation between voting behavior and the interests of young constituents. As reported in Chapter 2, data from the US Census make clear that Millennials traditionally "under-vote" or are voting at rates lower than their share of the eligible electorate compared to older Americans who "over-vote" or vote at rates higher than their share of the electorate (File 2014, 7). Does this reality translate into policymaking that favors the "over-voters" at the expense of the "under-voters"? This hypothesis would need to be disproven in order to embrace the sort of argument Dalton and others are proposing.

Matching the reality with the ideal

There are a number of reasons why participation may appear high to some and low to others. One obvious reason is that definitions vary. Insofar as one expands one's definition of participation to include such psychological states as political interest or such activity as media attention or political discussion, one finds more activity. The more narrowly one limits the scope of what one considers participation, the smaller the amount one will find (Verba and Nie 1972, 29).

Dalton bases his criticism of the "duty-bound" model of citizenship and his endorsement of the "engaged" model on the supposition that one's evaluation of the health of a democratic system is a function of one's definition of participation. Likewise, it's upon this idea that different conceptualizations of engagement have been enumerated in this text and placed along a continuum ranging from "disengaged" to "engaged differently" to "better engaged." A final question to consider, then, is a normative one – "how is it supposed to be?" Which depiction of engagement or conceptualization of citizenship is most in line with the ideals of American democracy?

Those who endorse a depiction more closely in line with a traditional or more "bulls-eye" view are more consistent with the nation's roots in classical liberalism, but the vitality of this argument is diminished not only with young adults' changing views regarding civic duty and responsibility but also with the intricacies of an electoral system that are challenging to navigate – for young adults in particular. On the other hand, the argument that a broader conceptualization is more democratic doesn't take into account America's ideological roots. Consequently, broad depictions of participation place a burden on citizens that they weren't meant to bear. Moreover, it's a burden borne more easily by some than others – threatening how well some are represented compared to others.

As indicated in Chapter 4, Dalton's model and his notion of "social citizenship" or concern for "social responsibility" resembles European social democratic traditions – even Rousseau's notions of "general will" and social contract. The sort of government Rousseau proposes in *The Social Contract* – one that resembles a sort of direct democracy with concern for the general welfare as its centerpiece – was one that even he saw as impractical or unlikely (Book 3, ch. 4). Moreover, Dalton's discussion of social citizenship reflects the notion of positive rights or the assertion that government bears the responsibility of acting or providing certain services to its citizens (such as health care or a particular standard of living).[2]

Clearly, American history is peppered with examples of citizens asserting and gaining protection for such positive or social rights, as well as examples of direct democracy initiatives. It bears emphasizing, though, that the nation's roots are more in line with the notion of the social contract embodied in classical liberalism. This Lockean view holds that the role of government is to protect man's self-interest. Because man is rational, he determined that it made good sense to emerge out of the state of nature and engage in a contract with those selected to serve in government – in exchange for obeying the laws devised and enforced by government, government would protect man's self-interest and those natural rights he possesses by virtue of being human – his natural rights. Here then, the role and purpose of government is limited – a tone clearly set in the Declaration of Independence:

> We hold these Truths to be self-evident, that all men are created equal, that all are endowed by their Creator with certain inalienable Rights, that among these are Life, Liberty, and the Pursuit of Happiness. That to secure these Rights, Governments are instituted among Men, deriving their just powers from the consent of the Governed, that whenever any Form of Government becomes destructive of these Ends, it is the Right of the People to alter or to abolish it, and to institute new Government …

In contrast to the idea that positive rights are provided by the government, classical liberalism is more aligned with the notion of negative rights or the right to be left alone. As Jefferson makes clear in his first inaugural address in 1891, mechanisms such as the vote are in place to ensure that government doesn't infringe upon man's natural rights: "A jealous care of the right of election by the people, a mild and sage corrective of abuses, which are lopped by the sword of revolution, where peaceable remedies are unprovided" (1985, 54).

An argument can be made that the more "bulls-eye" view of participation that involves traditionally political behavior such as regular voting and expressing opinions to legislators is an extension of the ideals of classical liberalism. It involves using the blunt tools of popular sovereignty to either check or direct the actions of government. Regular participation in these activities in order to consistently check the government requires a shared understanding or sense of responsibility, though – a sense that doesn't exist among younger generations as it did in previous generations.

In their *2006 Civic and Political Health of the Nation* research, researchers at CIRCLE asked respondents, "Which statement do you agree with more?: It is my RESPONSIBILITY to get involved to make things better for society OR It is my CHOICE to get involved to make things better for society?" Of all youth respondents, 53 percent indicated that they viewed such involvement as a choice rather than a responsibility, compared to 40 percent who viewed such activity as a duty or responsibility.

What about community engagement that is more obviously political in nature? In the same 2006 survey, respondents were asked,

"Which of the following reasons BEST describes why you would choose to vote in elections: Because voting is my responsibility as a citizen; Because my vote, along with others, can affect the outcome of the election; Because my vote is the expression of my choice." A plurality of respondents (34 percent) indicated that the vote is his or her expression of their choice, followed by 30 percent who indicated it was a responsibility, and 27 percent who suggested that they vote to affect the outcome of an election.[3]

This diminished sense of duty impacts participation in traditional political activities. Zukin *et al*.'s multivariate analysis demonstrated that the contrasting sense of duty between older and younger generations played an important role in explaining differences in voting behavior between the age groups (2006, 121–154). On top of that, the realities of the electoral system – from the variety in electoral law between states to requirements to update one's registration with every address change – fall hardest on young adults who are newest to the electoral system and most transient. In these ways, although the "bulls-eye" depiction might be most in line with the nation's ideological roots, the sensibilities of young adults along with the practicalities of the political process diminish its vibrancy.

On the other hand, Dalton's model places an enlarged sense of responsibility on young citizens – one that wasn't necessarily expected in a system built on checking the power of the government or negative rights. Dalton recognizes a few of the downsides of engaged citizenship, including "disaffection for political parties and elections" that "leads many otherwise engaged citizens to sit home on Election Day" (2009, 166). Additionally, he admits that "feelings of distrust and alienation can limit the activities that are essential for democracy to function as a social contract between citizens and their government" (2009, 167).

Additionally, the expectation that citizens are "involved in a wider repertoire of activities that give them direct voice in the decisions affecting their lives" (Dalton 2009, 29) places a burden on young adults that the nation's representative democratic system does not support (either in theory or reality). Moreover, it's fair to say that this is not the sort of engagement for which they are prepared. Such an active sense of citizenship requires young adults to meet a fairly high threshold of attentiveness and political sophistication.

For instance, with viral campaigns, its not always clear what actions are necessary or required beyond changing one's Facebook profile picture or retweeting a message. Lessons learned via The Can Kicks Back campaign are instructive here – there are limits to what can be accomplished virtually. In the end, supporters need to be given concrete tasks. Given these additional civic burdens, it's unlikely that those with lower levels of education (civic education in particular) and resources will be equipped to meet such an enlarged standard of citizenship and, as a result, risk being unequally represented.

Engaging "Citizen Now": a practical roadmap

Any effort to prepare and encourage young adults to be active citizens, whether it's by educators, policymakers, campaigns, or youth themselves, necessitates an understanding of what we know about the Millennial Generation compared with what we think we know. As stated at the outset, this is especially challenging given the contradictions and the contrasts pervading the generation. As the content analysis presented in the first chapter showed, it's a common perception that this is an age group to be reckoned with – that Millennials are making a difference economically, culturally, and technologically. The perceived impact of this age group on politics is, at best, uncertain, and at worst negligible. These perceptions are not so far from reality. We know that the body of citizens who came of age at the turn of the millennium is brimming with promise – in sheer numbers, ethnic diversity, educational attainment, optimism, and technological savvy. We also know that this generation is not making the most of this potential for power in the world of politics. In contrast to older citizens, young adults are chronic "under-voters" – they vote at a lower rate than their share of the eligible electorate. Any excitement surrounding young adults' political interest and engagement in 2008 has been met with an unpleasant contemporary reality – record low voter turnout (19.9 percent) and registration rates (46.7 percent) in 2014.[4] These contrasts and contradictions run through our study of young adults as well. Depending on a scholar's' position on the "disengaged"–"engaged" continuum, young adults have been either maligned or heralded, with varying degrees of evidence to support the characterization.

As we transition from the Millennial Generation to the one that follows it (whether we call it Generation Wii, Generation Z, or something else), it's time to move beyond knee-jerk character- izations of young adults encapsulated in either these perceptions or these realities. It's unproductive to continue to characterize this age group as "narcissistic" or "anti-civic" or to continue to chastise them for not having a sense of civic duty, especially when we're not offering them the sort of civic education they need to be engaged cit- izens or providing an electoral system that facilitates participation. Moreover, those who would label young adults as "disengaged" also need to recognize that new tools such as social media platforms and apps might be effective methods for accomplishing political goals that once were achieved via face-to-face meetings with legislators or letters to the editor. At the same time, it's not enough to herald the Millennial Generation as the next Greatest Generation and extol the citizenship norms of today's young when we haven't demon- strated that this enlarged approach to engagement has a political effect or addresses their needs. It's not enough to celebrate these norms of engaged citizenship when those young adults possessing these norms are unsure how to actualize them.

Thankfully, there is an alternative to these convenient and some- what predictable responses – evidence-based methods for equipping and encouraging youth political participation. There are practical efforts that educators, candidates and their campaigns, policymak- ers, and young adults themselves might undertake to ensure that "citizen now" is making an impact not only in the worlds of enter- tainment, business, and technology but in politics as well.

Parents and schools

As Verba *et al.* demonstrated, there are three youth experiences that affect later civic participation: education, "political stimu- lation in the home," and involvement in high school activities (1995). The role of parents as "agents of political socialization" has been explored extensively in the academic literature (includ- ing Andolina *et al.* 2003; Jennings and Niemi 1968, 1974; Jennings *et al.* 2009; Langton 1969) – when parents model active citizenship through news consumption, political discussion, and regular voting, it rubs off on their children. Moreover, there's a growing body of literature that shows that schools are a critical institution for instilling civic knowledge, skills, and attitudes (*Civic Mission of Schools* 2003, *Guardian of Democracy* 2011) and that civic education is an effective method for addressing youth civic engagement (Niemi and Junn 1998; Verba *et al.* 1995). Given discussions throughout this book, there clearly is a need to prepare students to engage in both traditional forms of engagement and an "enlarged" version of democratic participation and to engage in such a way that change is likely to result (even if not immediately). A growing toolkit of civic education practices has emerged from this research that, if offered, will enhance the chances of future political participation, including:

- offering classroom instruction in government, democracy, and history;
- discussing current events in the classroom (even of controversial topics);
- service-learning that is linked to their curriculum;
- extracurricular activities (either in school or in their communities);
- active school government;
- simulations that highlight the procedures of democratic government.[5]

This education in citizenship doesn't have to end once students graduate from high school, nor should it. The Association of American Colleges and Universities' report, *A Crucible Moment: College Learning and Democracy's Future* (National Task Force on Civic Learning and Democratic Engagement 2012) calls on college educators of all disciplines to include civic learning and democratic engagement as a core part of each student's education. As this report and the American Political Science Association's *Teaching Civic Engagement: From Student to Active Citizen* (McCartney *et al.* 2013) show, there are a number of opportunities for including political learning in classroom instruction taking place on college campuses. Some of these instructional techniques, such as involving students in voter registration drives, are electoral in nature but other facets of citizenship certainly can be addressed. Not only can these efforts be done in a nonpartisan way, but they will enhance the likelihood of students' political participation in years to come.

Campaigns and candidates

Mobilization by candidates and campaigns positively affects voter turnout – even among younger voters (Rosenstone and Hansen 1993, Zukin *et al.* 2006). When campaigns reach out to young voters, educate them about the issues surrounding the campaign, and ask for their vote, opportunities for electoral participation emerge for that voter and the costs associated with voting, such as gathering information about candidates, are reduced. Campaign resources (both time and money) are precious, though, and by necessity, mobilization efforts by campaigns are strategic. As Rosenstone and Hansen write, "citizen participation is a resource that political leaders use selectively in their fights for political advantage. For maximum effect, they target their efforts on particular people, and they time them for particular occasions" (1993, 30).

More often than not, young adults don't figure into these campaign strategies. As Zukin *et al.* found, young adults are less likely to be contacted by parties and campaigns than older adults (2006, 131). This reality is a function of both young adults' inexperience and their unreliability as voters. As Rosenstone and Hansen write, "Resources parties devote to people who are unlikely to turn out or unlikely to support them are wasted" (1993, 163). Typically, then, in presidential years, political parties are more likely to contact the most experienced voters (age 65 or older) than the least experienced voters (18-year-olds) (Rosenstone and Hansen 1993, 168). Recent declines in turnout don't help matters and only add to this pervading sense that campaigns can't count on the youth vote.

Although this mindset is understandable, the research shows that, when approached, young adults are likely to respond (Zukin *et al.* 2006). Certainly the Obama candidacy in 2008 is a practical example of this finding – a campaign that not only reached out to young adults but made good use of Millennials' tools of communication. Recent research by CIRCLE even asserts that, had the Romney campaign's mobilization strategy included young adults, the election might have gone in his favor – specifically, if he'd mobilized young adults in Ohio, Florida, Virginia, and Pennsylvania.[6] Again, elections are not the only form of political engagement and not always the most important form. Given both the chronic undervoting of young adults in comparison to older adults and the promise of youth mobilization, though, it seems to be a chance worth taking for candidates and their campaigns.

Policymakers

At the time of this writing, a handful of states are taking steps to simplify the voter registration process. In Oregon, Governor Kate Brown signed into law legislation that made voter registration automatic for those eligible (*Reuters*, March 16, 2015). Similarly, California's Governor Jerry Brown signed a bill passed by the state legislature requiring drivers who are eligible to vote to be registered automatically when they get a new license (*Los Angeles Times*, October 10, 2015). At the same time, following a trend set by other state legislatures in recent years, Kansas recently passed legislation requiring proof of citizenship in order to register to vote (*New York Times*, October 15, 2015). According to the National Conference of State Legislatures, 36 states have passed laws that require voters to show some form of identification at the polls. Due to judicial actions, 32 of such laws are in force (laws in Arkansas, Missouri, and Pennsylvania have been struck down and North Carolina's law has yet to go into effect).[7]

The patchwork system of voter registration and Election Day regulations is a product of federalism of course – each state is responsible for conducting its own elections. The reality is that, for young adults, this patchwork can serve as a barrier or, at a minimum, an additional hurdle. At least, that's the perception. As one high school senior trying to register to vote in Kansas complained, "I think it's ridiculous and restrictive ... A lot of people are working multiple jobs, so they don't have time to get this stuff done. Some of them don't have access to their birth certificate" (*New York Times*, October 15, 2015).

When it comes to the effects of voter identification and Election Day laws on youth voter turnout, evidence that they dampen youth voting has yet to be established conclusively. Still, America's voter registration system always has been cited as a key factor in the nation's low voter turnout rates relative to comparable democracies (Wolfinger and Rosenstone 1980) and such measures as mailing sample ballots listing poll locations and offering extended poll hours have been shown to enhance turnout (for all voters – not specifically youth) (Wolfinger *et al.* 2004). We also know that states with such measures as Election Day voter registration have higher rates of voter turnout. Although reducing the likelihood of voter fraud is the oft-cited rationale used by policymakers in favor of voter identification laws or in opposition to measures that streamline the process such as registering online, it stands to reason that enhancing voter participation also is an imperative of policymakers. Voters are justified in expecting policymakers to take steps to ease the process by which constituents are able to express their preferences via the ballot box.

In an era when nearly everything can be done online, including such sensitive transactions as paying bills and completing financial aid forms, students are frequently surprised by how confusing and outdated the voter registration process seems. Although many states are taking strides to ease and modernize the process, these changes haven't touched all states or all voters. Herein lies a good example of the need for those who embrace a "bulls-eye" version of democracy – one focused on traditional methods of politics such as voting – to make use of cutting-edge technological opportunities to facilitate such old-school goals as voting. Rather than criticize young adults for not showing up on Election Day, at least meet them halfway by administering an election process that they recognize and can participate in with some facility.

Young adults

Ultimately, it's up to young adults themselves – that demographically unique generation brimming with democratic promise – to engage in politics and democracy. In the arts, culture, technology, and world of business, Millennials' preferences have been heard and felt. If their preferences are going to be reflected at the ballot box and in the halls of power, it's going to require young adults making sure they're heard and their interests are addressed. To do this, "citizen now" must not only be responsive to efforts to engage them but cultivate a sense of accountability and even generate, to borrow an expression used by San Bernardino Generation Now, a "culture of engagement" that will ensure that they're fulfilling their potential as citizens.

Recognizing that the burden of being an involved citizen is a shared burden, there are ways in which young adults can capitalize on opportunities to participate:

- When teachers, professors, and college campuses offer opportunities for students to register to vote, be involved in a campaign, host a legislator, or participate in an advocacy effort at the state capital, it's up to young adults to take advantage of them. When these opportunities aren't made available to them, it's up to students and young adults to demand them of their schools and institutions of higher education. Often, students have the law on their side. For example, federal law has designated September 17 as "Constitution Day" and all colleges and universities that receive federal funds are required to host programs that celebrate it. Here lies a perfect opportunity for young adults on college campuses to hold educators accountable and bring civic and political learning activities to students.

- In the midst of a campaign, whether it's for the mayor or the state legislature or the president, it's ultimately up to young adults to pay attention. There are approximately 80 million young people in the United States – approximately 49 million were eligible to vote in 2016. It's up to those millions to pay attention to campaigns at all levels and follow them for more than the spectacle. Instead, young adults following a campaign might listen carefully to discern whether candidates are talking to them. In debates and speeches and on their website and social media accounts, are candidates talking about issues that matter to young adults specifically, such as student loan debt or college affordability? When candidates discuss the economy or health care or immigration, are they discussing policies that will impact this sizable portion of the population as they head into the job market, try to pay off student loans, and build a future?

• Likewise, it's up to young adults to pay attention to the actions of their local officials, state legislators, and representatives in Washington and to respond. When state legislators are considering education and financial aid funding, are they talking to the young adults who feel these decisions most directly or to their parents and grandparents who might be affected financially? When a social media campaign such as "#Bring Back Our Girls" or "#Black Lives Matter" piques their interest or lights a spark, it's ultimately up to young adults to investigate and find out how else, beyond changing their profile picture, they can effect change on this issue.

An implicit theme in this text is that politics matters to young adults and young adults matter to politics. Certainly, these themes reflect core tenets of democratic thought – consent of the governed, rule of law, popular sovereignty. It's the case studies offered in this text, though, that bring these themes to life. As these models demonstrated, it was the actions of officeholders at the federal, state, and local levels that resulted in policies that affected young adults' lives, whether it was access to health care, fiscal policies, or transgressions that led to a city's bankruptcy, and it was these political outcomes that stirred a reaction by young adults. Youth-led and youth-focused reactions to these political outcomes, either through legislative advocacy or electoral engagement, also offer examples of how young adults might assert themselves as citizens. Although their missions, structures, and tools varied, these efforts serve as models of how young adults might engage the process to ensure they are represented.

There's another lesson to be learned from these case studies. Although it may return in some way, shape, or form, it's clear that young adults today don't possess the same sense of citizenship or civic duty as past generations. Much discussion has taken place in this book and beyond on why this is the case and whether this is a cause for alarm or a cause for concern. When studying these three very committed groups, though – Young Invincibles, The Can

Kicks Back, San Bernardino Generation Now – civic duty didn't seem to be the force motivating their actions. In interviews, none of the representatives of these groups cited a sense of duty as inspiration. Instead, their words and deeds conveyed a deeper sense of accountability – acceptance of responsibility for one's actions (or inaction). For example, YI and TCKB believed that policymakers were not taking into account the interests of young adults and that Millennials needed a seat at the table. Moreover, by providing them valuable information and state- and local-level data, the groups sought to hold legislators accountable for their actions and the effects of their actions on young constituents. Similarly, SBGN was motivated by the city's collective failure to hold elected officials accountable for their actions – actions that bankrupted their city. Now, the group seeks to hold not only officials accountable but themselves as citizens by cultivating a "culture of engagement."

The actions of the groups highlighted in this book reflect a sense of recognition among the young adults involved of the effects of political actions on them as a generation as well as the influence their actions can have on the political process. This may be a more productive route for engaging young adults in politics and democracy – demonstrating how the actions taken by those serving you in the city council, state legislature, Congress, and the White House have a direct effect on our daily lives and the clearcut, tangible tools available to influence not only who is in office but what they do when they're there. Out of this recognition of the effects of politics and the accountability embedded in the relationship between the public servant and the public he or she serves can spring a "culture of engagement." In this way, the promise of "citizen now" might be realized and reflect the vision enunciated by the 26th Amendment's proponent, Senator Randolph, when he stated, "I believe that our young people possess a great social conscience, are perplexed by the injustices which exist in the world and are anxious to rectify these ills." Whether at the ballot box or throughout the legislative process, "a culture of engagement" rooted in an understanding that politics matters to young adults and young adults matter to politics might translate Millennials' social conscience into action – political action – that will rectify the ills of their time.

Think It Out

- Consider the notion of "consent of the governed" and the writings on the subject that influenced the ideological origins of the nation (i.e., Thomas Paine's *Common Sense*). What sort of participation among citizens does consent of the governed require in the view of the Founders?
- Write your own "6 word essay" that captures the essence of "citizen now."

Act It Out

- During the next political campaign (at any level of government), keep a log of the manner and extent to which candidates are speaking to young adults. During debates, on their websites, in their interviews and speeches, are they talking about youth-specific issues (such as college affordability)? When they discuss issues relevant to all age groups such as health care, from whose perspective are they speaking about these issues (from the perspective of a young adult or an older citizen)?
- Keep a log of your average day in which you track the occasions when your daily life intersects with the world of politics (such as following traffic laws or visiting a public building). Then determine the local, state, or federal public offices or officials that influence these tasks (i.e., state legislatures set state speed limits or national monuments are overseen by federal agencies and funded by federal tax dollars appropriated by the US Congress).

Notes

1 Regarding Young Invincibles' "Student Impact Project": www.studentimpactproject.org.
2 In contrast to the notion of negative rights that involves limiting government interference with the freedom of individuals, positive rights requires action from the government or involves an expectation that the government will provide certain goods and services.

3 *2006 Civic and Political Health of the Nation Report*, Center for Information and Research on Civic Learning and Engagement: www. civicyouth.org/2006-civic-and-political-health-of-the-nation.
4 Center for Information and Research on Civic Learning and Engagement: www.civicyouth.org/2014-youth-turnout-and-youth-registration-rates-lowest-ever-recorded-changes-essential-in-2016.
5 *The Civic Mission of Schools* and *Guardian of Democracy* offer these broad recommendations as well as a number of more detailed conclusions: www.civicmissionofschools.org.
6 Center for Information and Research on Civic Learning and Engagement: www.civicyouth.org/data-indicate-gop-candidates-should-make-concerted-effort-to-talk-to-involve-young-republican-voters-in-campaigns.
7 National Conference of State Legislatures: www.ncsl.org/research/elections-and-campaigns/voter-id.aspx.

Appendix A: Top news events, 1983–2012

Year	#1 news story	#2 news story	#3 news story
1983	Soviet Union condemned for shooting down South Korean airline	United States assigns finding cause of AIDS as top priority	Andropov consolidates his power as US–USSR relations flounder
1984	Suicide terrorist destruction of marine barracks in Beirut	US invades Grenada	Walter Mondale selects a woman, Geraldine Ferraro, as vice-presidential nominee
1985	Shiite Muslim extremists hold hostages taken from TWA airliner	President Reagan orders partial sanctions of South African government	Mikhail Gorbachev succeeds Chernenko as leader of USSR
1986	Space shuttle *Challenger* explodes	Major accident at Soviet nuclear power plant of Chernobyl	Marcos flees the Philippines, Aquino named new president
1987	Iran–Contra hearings	Oil tankers in Persian Gulf targets of Iranian and Iraqi missiles and warplanes	Spread of AIDS concern

(cont.)

Year	#1 news story	#2 news story	#3 news story
1988	George Bush elected as 41st President	Host of environmental concerns (drought, closed beaches, "Greenhouse Effect," ozone depletion, acid rain)	INF Treaty signed by President Reagan and Soviet leader Gorbachev
1989	Student demonstrations in China crushed	Exxon Valdez oil spill in Alaska's Prince William Sound	In Poland, rise to power of Solidarity and formation of new government under Lech Walesa
1990	Reunification of Germany	Saddam Hussein's forces overrun Kuwait – leads to UN-backed economic sanctions and US military intervention	Gorbachev attempts to move USSR from Communist authority rule to democracy and capitalism
1991	Demise of Communist Party and reorganization of Soviet Union	US-led coalition defeats Iraqi forces in Persian Gulf, liberates Kuwait but leaves Saddam Hussein in power	Unstable economy due to savings and loan failures, recession, unemployment, health care costs, budget deficits
1992	Bill Clinton elected as the 42nd president	Economy heads list of issues in 1992 presidential campaign	Rioting and racial tension in South Central Los Angeles after officers acquitted
1993	Bill Clinton inaugurated as the 42nd president	Clinton proposes to Congress plan to provide health insurance to all Americans	Clinton wins passage of a bill to reduce federal budget deficits by $496 billion over 5 years

1994	Republicans win resounding victory on Election Day 1994	Middle East peace process continues	Haiti's President Jean-Bertrand Aristide restored to power with aid of US troops
1995	Federal Building in Oklahoma City target of car bomb, killing 169 people	O.J. Simpson tried for murders of wife Nicole Simpson and friend Ronald Goldman and acquitted	First Republican-controlled Congress in 40 years convened
1996	Bill Clinton re-elected President of the US	TWA flight 800 traveling from NYC to Paris explodes and crashes	Boris Yeltsin re-elected president of Russia
1997	Billions mourn death of Princess Diana	Hong Kong restored to Chinese rule	Timothy McVeigh convicted and sentenced to death
1998	US House votes to authorize House committee to consider impeachment of President Bill Clinton	Republicans fail to make any gains in Congress	Catholic and Protestant groups in Northern Ireland sign major peace accord
1999	Bill Clinton second president in US history to be impeached by House and tried in the Senate	NATO begins airstrikes against Yugoslavia	2 teenagers fatally shoot 12 students and a teacher at Columbine High School
2000	George Bush and Al Gore battle for electoral votes with neither gaining a majority	Scientists discern structure of genome	Yugoslav President Slobodan Milosevic concedes defeat

(*cont.*)

Year	#1 news story	#2 news story	#3 news story
2001	Hijackers commandeer 4 commercial airliners, crash 2 into the World Trade Center and 1 into the Pentagon	Violent clashes between Israeli and Palestinian forces	George W. Bush sworn in as 43rd President
2002	United States and allies continue war on terrorism	Congress passes mandate giving president broad powers to use military force	Violence between Israelis and Palestinians continues
2003	Saddam Hussein deposed in Iraq	Space shuttle *Columbia* disintegrates during re-entry	US economy continues to grow at a steady pace but number of job continues to decline
2004	US transfers authority to Iraqi government	George Bush in tight race against John Kerry	Fighting terrorism – 9/11 report issued
2005	War in Iraq continues	Hurricane Katrina hits United States	Pope John Paul II dies, Cardinal Ratzinger of Germany elected
2006	Sectarian violence in Iraq	US midterm congressional elections to decide if both Houses remain under Republican control	US and allies continue to fight global war against terrorism
2007	Bush outlines new war strategy featuring "surge" of some 30,000 troops	Housing market starts to crumble as foreclosure rates spike	Democratic majorities pass increase in minimum wage and new ethics rules

2008	Global economy in turmoil	Financial crisis raises fears of US recession	Obama triumphs in Democratic sweep
2009	Obama Presidency begins	Recession in US ends but jobless rate rises	US pull-out from Iraq takes place but build-up in Afghanistan
2010	Republicans take House of Representatives	Economic recovery stalls	US winds down conflict in Iraq but conflict surges in Afghanistan
2011	Arab Spring uprisings sweep North Africa and Middle East	Japanese earthquake and tsunami cause nuclear disaster	Commando raid in Pakistan kills Osama Bin Laden
2012	Barack Obama wins re-election	Supreme Court upholds "Obamacare"	Middle East news dominated by terrorism, turmoil, and transition

Note: Each year's edition lists the top ten news events for the previous year. In this table, the events listed as top ten news events for 1983, for example, appeared in the 1984 edition of the World Almanac and Book of Facts. The language used in this table to describe each event is paraphrased and/or very similar to the language utilized in the text but not necessarily identical.
Source: World Almanac and Book of Facts (1986–2013 editions).

Appendix B: Joint Resolution Proposing the 26th Amendment, January 21, 1971

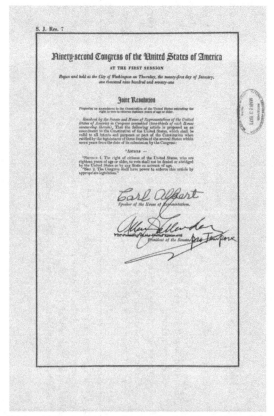

Source: Richard Nixon Library. Rights Status: Unrestricted. Permanent link: www.presidentialtimeline.org/#/object/1515.

Ninety-Second Congress of the United States of America

AT THE FIRST SESSION

Begun and held at the City of Washington on Thursday, the twenty-first day of January, one thousand nine hundred and seventy-one

JOINT RESOLUTION

Proposing an amendment to the Constitution of the United States extending the right to vote to citizens eighteen years of age or older.

Resolved by the Senate and House of Representatives of the United States of America in Congress assembled (two-thirds of each House concurring therein), That the following article is proposed as an amendment to the Constitution of the United States, which shall be valid to all intents and purposes as part of the Constitution when ratified by the legislatures of three-fourths of the several States within seven years from the date of its submission by the Congress:

"ARTICLE –

"SECTION 1. The right of citizens of the United States, who are eighteen years of age or older, to vote shall not be denied or abridged by the United States or by any State on account of age.

"SEC. 2. The Congress shall have power to enforce this article by appropriate legislation."

Appendix C: 26th Amendment, July 5, 1971

ADMINISTRATOR OF GENERAL SERVICES

UNITED STATES OF AMERICA

TO ALL TO WHOM THESE PRESENTS SHALL COME,

GREETING:

KNOW YE, That the Congress of the United States, at the first session,
Ninety-second Congress begun at the City of Washington on Thursday, the
twenty-first day of January, in the year one thousand nine hundred and seventy-
one, passed a Joint Resolution in the words and figures as follows: to wit--

JOINT RESOLUTION

Proposing an amendment to the Constitution of the United States
extending the right to vote to citizens eighteen years of age
or older.

Resolved by the Senate and House of Representatives of the United
States of America in Congress assembled (two-thirds of each House
concurring therein), That the following article is proposed as an
amendment to the Constitution of the United States, which shall be
valid to all intents and purposes as part of the Constitution when ratified by the legislatures of three-fourths of the several States within
seven years from the date of its submission by the Congress:

"ARTICLE --

"Section 1. The right of citizens of the United States, who are
eighteen years of age or older, to vote shall not be denied or
abridged by the United States or by any State on account of age.
"Sec. 2. The Congress shall have power to enforce this article
by appropriate legislation."

And, further, that it appears from official documents on file in the General Services Administration that the Amendment to the Constitution of the
United States proposed as aforesaid has been ratified by the Legislatures of
the States of Alabama, Alaska, Arizona, Arkansas, California, Colorado,

Source: Richard Nixon Library. Rights Status: Unrestricted. Permanent
link: www.presidentialtimeline.org/#/object/1516.

Connecticut, Delaware, Hawaii, Idaho, Illinois, Indiana, Iowa, Kansas,
Louisiana, Maine, Maryland, Massachusetts, Michigan, Minnesota, Missouri,
Montana, Nebraska, New Hampshire, New Jersey, New York, North Carolina,
Ohio, Oklahoma, Oregon, Pennsylvania, Rhode Island, South Carolina,
Tennessee, Texas, Vermont, Washington, West Virginia, and Wisconsin.

And, further, that the States whose Legislatures have so ratified the said
proposed Amendment constitute the requisite three-fourths of the whole number of States in the United States.

NOW, Therefore, be it known that I, Robert L. Kunzig, Administrator of
General Services, by virtue and in pursuance of Section 106b, Title 1 of the
United States Code, do hereby certify that the Amendment aforesaid has become
valid, to all intents and purposes, as a part of the Constitution of the United
States.

                              IN TESTIMONY WHEREOF,

                              I have hereunto set my hand
                              and caused the seal of the
                              General Services Adminis-
                              tration to be affixed.
                              DONE at the City of Washington
                              this 5th day of July in the
                              year of our Lord one thousand
                              nine hundred and seventy-one.

                              Robert L. Kunzig
                              ROBERT L. KUNZIG

The foregoing was signed in our presence
on this 5th day of July, 1971.

Richard King
Paul J. Larimer
Joseph H. Laird, Jr.
Julianne Jones

References

Acosta, Yesenia D., Luke J. Larsen, and Elizabeth M. Grieco. 2014. *Noncitizens under Age 35: 2010–2012 – American Community Survey Briefs*. US Census Bureau, February. Online: www.census.gov/prod/2014pubs/acsbr12-06.pdf.

Andolina, Molly, Krista Jenkins, Cliff Zukin, and Scott Keeter. 2003. "Habits from the Home, Lessons from School: Influences on Youth Civic Engagement." *PS: Political Science & Politics*, 36, 275–280.

Bauerlein, Mark. 2009. *The Dumbest Generation: How the Digital Age Stupefies Young Americans and Jeopardizes Our Future (Or, Don't Trust Anyone under 30)*. New York: Tarcher.

Bennett, W. Lance. 2003. *News: The Politics of Illusion*, 5th edn. New York: Longman.

Brady, Henry E. 1999. "Political Participation." In *Measures of Political Attitudes*, edited by John P. Robinson, Philip R. Shaver, and Lawrence S. Wrightsman, 737–801. New York: Academic Press.

Brokaw, Tom. 1998. *The Greatest Generation*. New York: Random House.

Brown, Meta, and Sydnee Caldwell. 2013. "Young Student Loan Borrowers Retreat from Housing and Auto Markets." Liberty Street Economics Blog. New York: Federal Reserve Bank of New York. Online: http://libertystreeteconomics.newyorkfed.org/2013/04/young-student-loan-borrowers-retreat-from-housing-and-auto-markets.html#.U0bfiPldV8E.

Carnegie Corporation of New York and Center for Information and Research on Civic Learning and Engagement. 2003. *The Civic Mission of Schools*. Online: www.civicmissionofschools.org.

Clay, Adreana. 2012. *The Hip-Hop Generation Fights Back: Youth, Activism, and Post-Civil Rights Politics*. New York: New York University Press.

Cohen, Cathy J., Joseph Kahne, Benjamin Bowyer, Ellen Middaugh, and John Rogowski. 2012. "Participatory Politics: New Media and Youth Political Action." Youth Participatory Politics Research Network, July 1. Online: http://ypp.dmlcentral.net/publications/107.

Colby, Anne, Thomas Ehrlich, Elizabeth Beaumont, and Jason Stephens. 2003. *Educating Citizens: Preparing America's Undergraduates for Lives of Moral and Civic Responsibility*. San Francisco, CA: Jossey-Bass.

Dalton, Russell J. 2009. *The Good Citizen: How a Younger Generation Is Reshaping American Politics*, rev. edn. Washington, DC: CQ Press, a Division of SAGE.

Delli Carpini, Michael X., and Scott Keeter. 1996. *What Americans Know about Politics and Why It Matters*. New Haven, CT: Yale University Press.

Etheridge, Marcus E. 1990. *The Political Research Experience: Readings and Analysis*. Armonk, NY: M.E. Sharpe, Inc.

File, Thom. 2013. "The Diversifying Electorate: Voting Rates by Race and Hispanic Origin in 2012 (and Other Recent Elections)." *Current Population Surveys Reports*, P20–569. Washington, DC: United States Census Bureau. Online: www.census.gov/prod/2013pubs/p20-568.pdf.
———. 2014. "Young-Adult Voting: An Analysis of Presidential Elections, 1964–2012." *Current Population Surveys Reports*, P20–572. Washington, DC: United States Census Bureau. Online: www.census.gov/prod/2014pubs/p20-573.pdf.

Fitzgerald, Mary. 2003. "Easier Voting Methods Boost Youth Turnout." Center for Information and Research on Learning and Civic Engagement, February. Online: www.civicyouth.org/PopUps/WorkingPapers/WP01Fitzgerald.pdf.

Fix, Michael, and Jeffrey S. Passel. 2003. *A New Citizenship Day*. Washington, DC: Urban Institute. Online: www.urban.org/publications/900671.html.

Fix, Michael, Jeffrey S. Passel, and Kenneth Sucher. 2003. *Trends in Naturalization*. Washington, DC: Urban Institute. Online: www.urban.org/UploadedPDF/310847_trends_in_naturalization.pdf.

Fox, Madeline, Kavitha Mediratta, Jessica Ruglis, Brett Stoudt, Seema Shah, and Michelle Fine. 2010. "Critical Youth Engagement: Participatory Action Research and Organizing." In *Handbook of Research on Civic Engagement in Youth*, edited by Lonnie R. Sherrod, Judith Torney-Purta, and Constance Flanagan, 621–649. Hoboken, NJ: John Wiley & Sons.

Frankfort-Nachmias, Chava, and David Nachmias. 1992. *Research Methods in the Social Sciences*, 4th edn. New York: St. Martin's Press.

Godsay, Surbhi, Kei Kawashima-Ginsberg, Abby Kiesa, and Peter Levine. 2012. *That's Not Democracy: How out of School Youth Engage in Civic Life and What Stands in Their Way*. Center for Information and Research on Learning and Civic Engagement and The Kettering Foundation, August. Online: www.civicyouth.org/wp-content/uploads/2012/08/CIRCLE_ ThatsNotDemocracy_WebFinal.pdf.

Graber, Doris A. 1997. *Mass Media and American Politics*, 5th edn. Washington, DC: Congressional Quarterly Press.

Green, Donald P., and Alan S. Gerber. 2008. *Get out the Vote: How to Increase Voter Turnout*. Washington, DC: Brookings Institution Press.

Guardian of Democracy: The Civic Mission of Schools. 2011. CIRCLE and Carnegie Corporation. Online: http://civicmission.s3.amazonaws.com/ 118/f0/5/171/1/Guardian-of-Democracy-report.pdf.

Haenfler, Ross. 2006. *Straight Edge: Clean-Living Youth, Hardcore Punk, and Social Change*. New Brunswick, NJ: Rutgers University Press.

Heckman, J.J., and P.A. La Fontaine. 2007. "The American High School Graduation Rate: Trends and Levels." IZA Discussion Paper No. 3216. Bonn, Germany: IZA.

Howden, Lindsay M., and Julie A. Meyer. 2011. *Age and Sex Composition 2010: 2010 Census Briefs*. US Census Bureau, May. Online: www.census. gov/prod/cen2010/briefs/c2010br-03.pdf.

Howe, Neil, and William Strauss. 2000. *Millennials Rising: The Next Great Generation*. New York: Vintage Books.

Jamieson, Kathleen Hall, and Paul Waldman. 2003. *The Press Effect: Politicians, Journalists, and the Stories That Shape the Political World*. Oxford: Oxford University Press.

Jefferson, Thomas. 1985 (1891). "First Inaugural: The Essential Principles of the American Government." In *American Philosophy*, edited by Barbara MacKinnon, 54. Albany, NY: State University of New York Press.

Jennings, M. Kent, and Richard G. Niemi. 1968. "The Transmission of Political Values from Parent to Child." *American Political Science Review*, 62, 169–184.

Jennings, M. Kent, and Richard G. Niemi. 1974. *The Political Character of Adolescence: The Influence of Families and Schools*. Princeton, NJ: Princeton University Press.

Jennings, M. Kent, Laura Stoker, and Jake Bowers. 2009. "Politics across Generations: Family Transmissions Reexamined." *The Journal of Politics*, 71, 782–799.

Junn, Jane, and Elizabeth Matto. 2008. "The Changing Face of the American Electoral Landscape." In *New Race Politics in America: Understanding Minority and Immigrant Politics*, edited by Jane Junn and Kerry L. Haynie, 1–16. Cambridge: Cambridge University Press.

Kahne, Joseph, and Ellen Middaugh. 2008. "Democracy for Some: The Civic Opportunity Gap in High School." Center for Information and

Research on Civic Learning and Engagement, February. Online: www. civicyouth.org/PopUps/WorkingPapers/WP59Kahne.pdf.

Kawashima-Ginsberg, Kei, Amanda Nover, and Emily Hoban Kirby. 2009. "State Election Law Reform and Youth Voter Turnout." Center for Information and Research on Civic Learning and Engagement, July. Online: www.civicyouth.org/PopUps/FactSheets/State_law_and_youth_turnout_Final.pdf.

Kiesa, Abby, and Karlo Barrios Marcelo. 2009. "Youth Demographics: Youth With No College Experience." CIRCLE Fact Sheet. Medford, MA: Center for Information and Research on Civic Learning and Engagement. Online: www.civicyouth.org/PopUps/FactSheets/FS08_YthDemo_CollExp.pdf.

Kirby, Emily Hoban, Peter Levine, and Karlo Barrios Marcelo. 2008a. "The Youth Vote in the 2008 Iowa Caucus." CIRCLE Fact Sheet, January. Medford, MA: Center for Information and Research on Civic Learning and Engagement. Online: www.civicyouth.org/PopUps/FactSheets/FS08_iowacaucus.pdf.

Kirby, Emily Hoban, Samantha Linkins, and Conner Glennon. 2008b. "State Voter Registration and Election Day Laws." Center for Information and Research on Civic Learning and Engagement, October. Online: http://civicyouth.org/PopUps/FS_08_State_Laws.pdf.

Langton, Kenneth P. 1969. *Political Socialization*. New York: Oxford University Press.

Levine, Peter. 2007. *The Future of Democracy: Developing the Next Generation of American Citizens*. Medford, MA: Tufts University Press.

McCartney, Allison Rios Millett, Elizabeth A. Bennion, and Dick Simpson, eds. 2013. *Teaching Civic Engagement: From Student to Active Citizen*. Washington, DC: American Political Science Association.

Macedo, Stephen, ed. 2005. *Democracy at Risk: How Political Choices Undermine Citizen Participation and What We Can Do About It*. Washington, DC: Brookings Institution Press.

Madison, James, Alexander Hamilton, and John Jay. 1961 (1787). *Federalist Papers*, edited by Clinton Rossiter. New York: Mentor Books.

Merriam, Sharan B. 2009. *Qualitative Research: A Guide to Design and Implementation*. San Francisco, CA: Jossey-Bass.

Milbrath, Lester W. 1965. *Political Participation: How and Why Do People Get Involved in Politics?* Chicago: Rand McNally.

National Task Force on Civic Learning and Democratic Engagement. 2012. *A Crucible Moment: College Learning and Democracy's Future*. Washington, DC: Association of American Colleges and Universities.

Niemi, Richard G., and Jane Junn. 1998. *Civic Education: What Makes Students Learn?* New Haven, CT: Yale University Press.

Pew Research Center. 2010. "Millennials: A Portrait of Generation Next, Confident. Connected. Open to Change," February. Online: www.pewresearch.org/millennials.

———. 2012. "Young, Underemployed and Optimistic," February 9. www.pewsocialtrends.org/2012/02/09/young-underemployed-and-optimistic.

———. 2014a. "The Rising Cost of Not Going to College," February. Online: www.pewsocialtrends.org/2014/02/11/the-rising-cost-of-not-going-to-college.

———. 2014b. "Young Adults, Student Debt, and Economic Well-Being," May. Online: www.pewsocialtrends.org/files/2014/05/ST_2014.05.14_student-debt_complete-report.pdf.

———. 2014c. "Millennials in Adulthood: Detached from Institutions, Networked with Friends," March 7. Online: www.pewsocialtrends.org/2014/03/07/millennials-in-adulthood.

Pew Research Center for The People and The Press. 2007. "How Young People View Their Lives, Futures and Politics: A Portrait of Generation Next," January 9. Online: www.people-press.org/2007/01/09/a-portrait-of-generation-next.

Pew Research Center, Internet & American Life Project. 2013. Online: www.pewinternet.org.

Putnam, Robert D. 2000. *Bowling Alone: The Collapse and Revival of American Community*. New York: Simon & Schuster.

Rimmerman, Craig A. 2005. *The New Citizenship: Unconventional Politics, Activism, and Service*, 3rd edn. Boulder, CO: Westview Press.

Rosenstone, Steven J., and John Mark Hansen. 1993. *Mobilization, Participation, and Democracy in America*. New York: Longman.

Rousseau, Jean-Jacques. 1968 (1762). *The Social Contract*, transl. by Maurice Cranston. London, England: Penguin Books.

Schattschneider, E.E. 1960. *The Semisovereign People*. New York: Holt, Rinehart, and Winston.

Schlozman, Kay Lehman. 2002. "Citizen Participation in America: What Do We Know? Why Do We Care?" In *Political Science: State of the Discipline*, edited by Ira Katznelson and Helen V. Milner, 433–461. New York: W.W. Norton & Company.

Schlozman, Kay Lehman, and John T. Tierney. 1986. *Organized Interests and American Democracy*. New York: Harper & Row.

Singer, Audrey. 2004. *The Rise of New Immigrant Gateways*. Washington, DC: Brookings Institution. Online: www.brookings.edu/~/media/research/files/reports/2004/2/demographics%20singer/20040301_gateways.pdf.

Skocpol, Theda. 1999. "Advocates Without Members: The Recent Transformation of American Civic Life." In *Civic Engagement in American Democracy*, edited by Theda Skocpol and Morris P. Fiorina, 461–509. Washington, DC: Brookings Institution Press and New York, NY: Russell Sage Foundation.

Skocpol, Theda. 2003. *Diminished Democracy: From Membership to Management in American Civic Life*. Norman, OK: University of Oklahoma Press.

Skocpol, Theda, and Morris P. Fiorina, eds. 1999. *Civic Engagement in American Democracy*. Washington, DC: Brookings Institution Press and New York, NY: Russell Sage Foundation.

Smith, Aaron. 2013. "Civic Engagement in the Digital Age." Pew Research Center, Internet & American Life Project, April 25. Online: www.pewinternet.org/2013/04/25/civic-engagement-in-the-digital-age.

Smith, Christian, Kari Christoffersen, Hilary Davidson, and Patricia Snell Herzog. 2011. *Lost in Transition: The Dark Side of Emerging Adulthood*. Oxford: Oxford University Press.

Smith, Elizabeth S. 1999. "The Effects of Investments in the Social Capital of Youth on Political and Civic Behavior in Young Adulthood: A Longitudinal Analysis." *Political Psychology*, 20 (3), 553–580.

Steuerle, Eugene, Signe-Mary McKernan, Caroline Ratcliffe, and Sisi Zhang. 2013. *Lost Generations? Wealth Building among Young Americans*. Washington, DC: The Urban Institute. Online: www.urban.org/publications/412766.html.

Strachan, J. Cherie, and Mary Scheuer Senter. 2013. "Student Organizations and Civic Education on Campus: The Greek System." In *Teaching Civic Engagement: From Student to Active Citizen*, edited by Allison Rios Millett McCartney, Elizabeth A. Bennion, and Dick Simpson, 385–402. Washington, DC: American Political Science Association.

Taft, Jessica K. 2011. *Rebel Girls: Youth Activism and Social Change across the Americas*. New York: New York University Press.

Taylor, Paul and the Pew Research Center. 2014. *The Next America: Boomers, Millennials, and the Looming Generational Showdown*. New York: Public Affairs.

Torney-Purta, Judith. "The School's Role in Developing Civic Engagement: A Study of Adolescents in Twenty-Eight Countries." *Applied Developmental Science*, 6 (4), 203–212.

Truman, David B. 1951. *The Governmental Process*. New York: Alfred A. Knopf.

Twenge, Jean M. 2006. *Generation Me: Why Today's Young Americans Are More Confident, Assertive, Entitled – and More Miserable Than Ever Before*. New York: Atria Paperback.

Verba, Sidney, and Norman H. Nie. 1972. *Participation in America: Political Democracy and Social Equality*. New York: Harper & Row.

Verba, Sidney, Kay Lehman Schlozman, and Henry E. Brady. 1995. *Voice and Equality: Civic Voluntarism in American Politics*. Cambridge, MA: Harvard University Press.

Walker, Jack L., 1983. "The Origins and Maintenance of Interest Groups in America." *American Political Science Review*, 77 (June), 390–406.

Wattenberg, Martin P. 2012. *Is Voting for Young People?*, 3rd edn. Boston: Pearson.

Wilson, James Q. 1973. *Political Organizations*. New York: Basic Books.

Winograd, Morley and Michael D. Hais. 2008. *Millennial Makeover: MySpace, YouTube, and the Future of American Politics*. New Brunswick, NJ: Rutgers University Press.

———. 2011. *Millennial Momentum: How a Generation Is Remaking America*. New Brunswick, NJ: Rutgers University Press.

———. 2014. "How Millennials Could Upend Wall Street and Corporate America." Governance Studies at Brookings, May. Online: www.brookings.edu/~/media/research/files/papers/2014/05/millennials%20wall%20st/brookings_winogradfinal.pdf.

Wolfinger, Raymond E., and Steven J. Rosenstone. 1980. *Who Votes?* New Haven, CT: Yale University Press.

Wolfinger, Raymond E., Benjamin Highton, and Megan Mullin. 2004. "How Postregistration Laws Affect the Turnout of Registrants." Center for Information and Research on Civic Learning and Engagement, June. Online: www.civicyouth.org/PopUps/WorkingPapers/WP15Wolfinger.pdf.

Wright, John R. 1996. *Interest Groups and Congress: Lobbying, Contributions, and Influence*. Boston, MA: Allyn & Bacon.

Zaff, Jonathan F., James Youniss, and Cynthia M. Gibson. 2009. "An Inequitable Invitation to Citizenship: Non-College-Bound Youth and Civic Engagement." PACE, October. Online: www.pacefunders.org/publications/NCBY.pdf.

Zukin, Cliff, Scott Keeter, Molly Andolina, Krista Jenkins, and Michael X. Delli Carpini. 2006. *A New Engagement?: Political Participation, Civic Life, and the Changing American Citizen*. Oxford: Oxford University Press.

Index

Note: literary works can be found under authors' names.